Movement

Thalia Verkade lives in Rotterdam. She has been a staff writer and foreign correspondent for the Dutch national newspapers *NRC Handelsblad* and *nrc.next*. For the ad-free slow journalism platform *De Correspondent* she has written extensively about the topics she loves most: language, transport, and technocracy.

Marco te Brömmelstroet is the chair of Urban Mobility Futures at the Amsterdam Institute for Social Science Research at the University of Amsterdam. His teaching centres on the relationship between land use developments and mobility behaviour. As founding academic director of the Urban Cycling Institute he strengthens the links between academia and how cycling relates to the urban and social environment. Cycling offers him a lens to radically reimagine the way in which society thinks about mobility, transport systems, and the street. His @Fietsprofessor ('Cycling Professor') Twitter account has over 70,000 followers.

Together, they won the prize for the best Dutch journalist book of the year for *Movement*.

Fiona Graham is a British literary translator, editor, and reviewer who has lived in Kenya, Germany, the Netherlands, Luxembourg, Nicaragua, and Belgium. Her recent translations include Elisabeth Åsbrink's *1947: when now begins*, an English PEN award-winner longlisted for the Warwick Women in Translation Prize and the JQ Wingate Prize, and Torill Kornfeldt's *The Unnatural Selection of Our Species*.

Movement

how to take back our streets
and transform our lives

**Thalia Verkade and
Marco te Brömmelstroet**

Translated by Fiona Graham

SCRIBE
Melbourne • London

Scribe Publications
2 John St, Clerkenwell, London, WC1N 2ES, United Kingdom
18–20 Edward St, Brunswick, Victoria 3056, Australia

Published by Scribe 2022
Reprinted 2022 (three times), 2023, 2025

Typeset in Portrait by the publishers

Printed and bound in the UK by CPI Group (UK) Ltd,
Croydon CR0 4YY

Scribe is committed to the sustainable use of natural resources and
the use of paper products made responsibly from those resources.

978 1 911344 97 1 (UK edition)
978 1 922310 79 8 (Australian edition)
978 1 922586 38 4 (ebook)

Catalogue records for this book are available from the National Library
of Australia and the British Library.

This publication has been made possible with financial support from
the Dutch Foundation for Literature.

**N ederlands
letterenfonds
dutch foundation
for literature**

scribepublications.co.uk
scribepublications.com.au

Contents

Prologue

This book is about our streets and why we take it for granted that they are designed first and foremost for movement from A to B, rather than incorporating other uses that could benefit our communities in different ways.

I'm Thalia, a journalist based in Rotterdam, in the Netherlands, and I had never asked myself this question before I started writing this book. For me, the street was just a place outside my front door that I walked, cycled, or drove through on my way to somewhere else. The road markings, lanes, boxes, and traffic lights were necessary to ensure people's safety; I didn't think much more about them. What I did think about, while waiting at a red light yet again, was why things couldn't be faster and more efficient.

Then I met Marco, the 'Cycling Professor', a specialist in urban mobility who'd led a very different life to me, and who, as a social scientist, asked different questions. Such as: why do we accept that public space is unsafe and we need road markings and a highway code to make it safe? And: have our streets become through roads precisely *because* people view them as the exclusive domain of fast-moving traffic and design them accordingly? And: is this why people increasingly behave like mechanical moving parts in a traffic system instead of living, thinking human beings?

It was this clash between our implicit world views that sparked this book, a three-year shared journey of discovery into the possibilities of our streets. We've investigated and questioned the choices and mechanisms underpinning how these public spaces are designed, and looked at how they could be different, and we'd like to invite you to come along for the ride.

Just one significant caveat: read this book and you may well find that you can never look at the street outside your front door in the same light again. We can't, and many people who've read our book in Dutch have told us they've had the same experience.

And now there's an English edition. This has made us reflect on the relevance of our story in an international context. Almost everywhere, streets are designed on the basis that those who can travel at the highest speed, in the chunkiest vehicles, take precedence. And that includes in the Netherlands. You may be surprised to learn this, as we have the reputation of being a cyclist's paradise, with 37,000 kilometres (nearly 23,000 miles) of cycle paths, many of them segregated. We've also developed bike traffic lights, rain sensors that reduce cyclists' waiting times at traffic lights in wet weather, bike-friendly speed bumps, round-abouts with priority for cyclists, bike parking garages, bike high-ways (segregated cycle paths for fast-moving commuters), and bike streets (streets where cyclists have priority over motorists for once). Sounds great, right?

Yet we in the Netherlands are also coming to understand the limitations of our solutions. Our infrastructure, designed for cyclists alongside motorists, has led to a situation in which everyone can now get from A to B with maximum speed and efficiency. Cyclists can ride at full tilt, just like motorists, each traffic category in its own segregated channel. But has this made our streets safer? Studies suggest not — in the Netherlands, a higher proportion of people are killed in traffic accidents than in the UK,[1, 2] and in 2019 every sixth victim was a cyclist killed in a collision with somebody driving a car, lorry, or van.[3] Aside from this, what about people who want to move at a leisurely pace? What about children playing outside their homes? What about the street as a place to meet neighbours; a place with shade, plants, water; a place of belonging? Assigning everyone their own fast-moving channel further reinforces the notion that streets exist to accommodate drivers or speedy cyclists, rather than as public space to be shared by us all. We've also lost sight of the fact that bicycles have the advantage of enabling people to get about while *also* allowing the street to serve other purposes. And we've forgotten that getting about doesn't have to be a chore — it can also be an activity with a value of its own.

So, in this updated edition of the book, we will still talk about the Netherlands — what we can learn from the 1970s activists who battled against the belief that the design of public space should revolve around the car and the commuter, and how we can carry that forward today to make our streets serve our communities in more ways than just one. And we will also look at what other countries are doing and could do to diversify how they use their streets and make them safer.

Many major cities worldwide — partly because of the COVID-19 pandemic — are seeing a growing awareness of the questions at the heart of this book: who do our streets belong to, what do we want to use them for, and who gets to decide? It goes without saying that they must meet the demands of sustainability, liveability, and safety. That's the bottom line. But as ultimate aims, these aren't exactly inspiring, are they? With enough will and civil courage, the problems posed by traffic can be transformed into a challenge extending far beyond the technical aspects. What's at stake is far greater: the broad social question of how we want to live together. Real change could come if we seize the opportunity to rethink what public space is for, who decides, and what we want to do with it.

This is *Movement*. Will you join us?

I

The Streets Belong to All of Us

Why has traffic taken over our public space?

Our next car would be an electric model. That was what we decided when I returned home with my partner from Moscow in 2015, after one and a half years as a foreign correspondent for a leading Dutch newspaper. We'd had to leave behind the world's coolest car.

During our first winter in Moscow we'd watched Russians driving Nivas — four-wheel-drive Ladas — over frozen lakes. What the Niva lacked in heated seats or automatic windscreen wipers, it made up for with a lever that engaged the differential lock, so you could extricate yourself from snow or sand half a metre deep. Or go for a spin over the ice.

'*Lada. Just what you need. And nothing you don't.*' Our dark-blue Lada Niva came new from an official dealer. We drove her all over the Moscow region, and once my stint as a correspondent was over, she took us through the mountains of the Caucasus.

We camped out in the wilderness and spent half a year at 2,000 metres' altitude in a Georgian village without a single shop, not even a bakery. We'd have been lost without our Niva.

And then something unexpected happened. We had to sell her though she hadn't even clocked up 30,000 kilometres (nearly 19,000 miles). We'd have liked to take her back to the Netherlands, but it turns out you can't drive a Niva in the EU, not even a brand new one. What comes out of the exhaust pipe is too dirty for European standards. Bang went our dream of travelling home with a detour via the Balkans.

Once we were home — how nice it was to be back in a democratic country and to be able to cycle everywhere — we saw the advantages of those EU emissions standards. We had a baby on the way. Our child wouldn't have to blow black mucus into a hanky every evening, as we'd done in Moscow.

In Russia, I had seen what an economy overdependent on mineral resources can do to people. Those who control Russia's oil control the country. There is a yawning gulf between rich and poor. Another issue that struck me was climate change. With a direct link to the future growing inside me, I began to feel more urgency. How liveable would our planet remain? What could we do for the next generation? Did we really want to perpetuate existing problems by buying another petrol-guzzler?

I began to follow Elon Musk on Twitter — the man behind Tesla electric cars. From California, he aimed to convert the whole world to e-mobility, with a rechargeable car in front of every home.

'Tesla. Accelerating the world's transition to sustainable energy.' In his many media appearances, Musk said his over-riding aim is not to make Tesla a world-beater, but to nudge all car manufacturers into producing electric vehicles. And he's been as good as his word: in 2020, there were 10 million electric cars on the roads and sales were up 40 per cent on the previous year.[1] Sounds impressive, but this is still less than 1 per cent of all the cars out there.

I found Musk's message inspiring. The more I learned about electric cars, the more I saw them as the way forward to a green and democratic future. And how great it would be to walk the talk, so that one day our son would be able to say his parents had been among the first people to drive an electric car! That's how we decided our next car would be an electric model.

But it wasn't to be a Tesla. When we took a test drive in a Model S, the acceleration gave me acid reflux. On the back seat, my partner had to tilt his head; though the car looks big from the outside, it's cramped inside.

Impressive though Musk's take on energy might be, his car wasn't right for us. We carried on researching. Soon a clear winner emerged. The Renault Kangoo, with its pleasingly boxy design. The Kangoo would be our electric Lada. Now all we had to do was wait for a second-hand one we could afford.

Solving the Congestion Conundrum

While we were looking for our next car, I began writing articles about electric vehicles. Then another problem in search of a solution appeared on my radar — traffic jams.

Driving an electric car is all well and good, but you still don't want to come to a standstill. I'd had my fill of traffic jams in Moscow: staying alert while waiting gradually sapped my will to live. What a waste of precious time. Traffic jams are a major irritant to all drivers, and the delays they cause are a drain on the economy.

I discovered there are high-tech solutions from the United States targeting this problem too. Google, Uber, and Tesla are working hard to make self-driving cars a reality. It won't be long before your car can coordinate a trip efficiently with other vehicles, allowing you to relax with a video or a book.

Hopeful though that sounded, it was still some way off. Wasn't there a simpler solution?

Of course there was. Hey, this was the Netherlands!

The solution was bicycles.

'Every day, about half a million cars get stuck in traffic during the morning rush hour. If ten per cent of those drivers cycled instead, traffic jams would be a thing of the past.' So said Saskia Kluit (director of the Dutch Cyclists' Union) and four *wethouders* (members of the local executive, elected by the local council) from major cities, in a message to the new Dutch government in May 2017.[2]

'Yes!' I thought. If people cycled to work just once a week, traffic jams would all but disappear. If many more people cycled, the climate crisis and our petrol addiction would be history, surely? We already had electric bikes, enabling riders to cover much longer distances without getting tired. The first speed pedelecs, which could do 45 km/h (nearly 30 mph), were on the roads.[3] We even had recumbent bikes that could hit 133 km/h (over 80 mph), a world record established by Dutch students.[4] That was over the motorway speed limit.

Just one thing: not all Dutch cities were yet linked by high-speed bicycle highways. Why was that? What was the problem?

I set out to write a series of pieces on 'cycling versus congestion' in the seven weeks I had left before my maternity leave for my second baby. I contacted the Dutch Cyclists' Union, sketched out my plan for my readers, and arranged to interview Marco te Brömmelstroet, an urban planning expert at the University of Amsterdam.

And here's where the story really starts.

Let's Just Get those Bike Highways Sorted

Marco te Brömmelstroet, alias 'the Cycling Professor'. A handy moniker for a man with a tricky surname — and an intriguing one, too. A title like 'Cycling Professor' guarantees you a place in newsrooms' address books, including mine.

On the way to the interview I study a newspaper article featuring him. It describes an intersection in Amsterdam with broken traffic lights, where cyclists happily make their way through the traffic without any need for technical guidance.⁵ Watching them, Te Brömmelstroet comments that cyclists often move around like a flock of birds. 'It's precisely *because* traffic in Amsterdam is so risky that it's actually safe,' he says. 'Amsterdam cyclists are always on the lookout. You need to use all your senses in this city.'

Te Brömmelstroet thinks cyclists behave rather like starlings. Although they focus mainly on themselves, they're very much aware of those ahead of, behind, and alongside them. And that organised chaos creates ever-changing patterns.

An apt comparison, I think, cyclists and starlings. I'm sure this Cycling Professor will have some nugget of wisdom to impart about bike highways too. We shake hands in a temporary building made entirely of glass next to Amsterdam's South Station, the office of a cycling organisation where he had a meeting before I arrived.

'I'm looking into what we need to be able to create a network of bike highways in this country,' I enthuse.

Te Brömmelstroet gazes at me in silence. Officially, the Cycling Professor is actually an associate professor. A year younger than me, he sports a brown T-shirt with a picture of a bicycle pump — a nice detail for my piece.

I rush on. 'Can I call you Marco?' He nods. And then I put my most burning question to him: 'I read in an American study that more commuters cycle to work if the local authorities provide bike highways and employers put in showers. Would that work in this country too, do you think?'

Marco continues to look at me for a moment before responding with a counter-question.

'Why do you want showers at work?'

'What?' I say.

'Why do you think cyclists have to get to work as fast as possible?'

What an odd question. And doesn't he look grumpy? You'd think he didn't want to be interviewed.

'Well ... the whole point of bike highways is to get a move on, isn't it?' I reply. 'But that means cyclists are going to get all swe ... er ... damp.'

'And what makes you say "bike highways", not "cycle paths"?' Marco asks.

I don't get where he's coming from. We want to be able to cycle to work as fast as possible, don't we? So we need bike highways. What's in a name anyway?

'Surely everyone wants to get from A to B as fast as possible?' I say.

'On the motorway, maybe,' Marco says. 'But in a cul-de-sac or on a campsite, a walking pace is the norm. And for many cyclists, speed isn't the top priority.'

'It is for me!' I say.

'Sure about that?' Marco asks.

I gaze out through the large windows at the bicycles parked by the front door and the tall office buildings: we are in the country's financial heart.

What am I supposed to make of this? You're busy, you have to get somewhere, so surely all you want is to be able to keep pedalling at a decent speed? Marco had asked to meet me at this particular spot, hadn't he, to save time? So why won't he give me a straight answer?

I start again. 'Governments can encourage changes in behaviour through facilities like showers and bike highways. And reduce traffic jams.'

'That's true,' says Marco. 'But what exactly are you doing when you build a bike highway? Encouraging people to get from one place to another as fast as possible. Maybe efficiency isn't the only reason people cycle to work. I'm involved in some research which shows that cyclists make detours and add on distance if that makes their route more pleasant. Don't you ever do that?'

I nod. Yes, OK, that's something I do every now and then. On the way back, if I'm not in a hurry. Once in a blue moon.

'And relaxed cycling seems to encourage creativity,' Marco continues. He cites behavioural biologist Frans de Waal, who came up with a theory about reconciliation between chimpanzees while out on his bike. 'And the graphic artist M.C. Escher, and Ben Feringa — the Nobel Prize–winning chemist — had some of their best ideas while they were cycling.' Dutch writer Jelle Brandt Corstius, too, says he writes on his bike.

I nod again. Now I catch his drift: getting from A to B isn't the only reason people cycle. Cycling is of value in itself. In an attempt to relieve the tension between us, I follow his line of thought and tell him about a holiday years ago when I set off from Rotterdam and cycled for weeks at the whim of the wind, ending up in Bremen. 'But that was a holiday,' I say.

Then I feel slightly bothered. Yes, I too enjoy cycling for its own sake. But I'm here as a journalist, to solve the traffic jam problem, and I have yet to write my story. The one about bike highways and showers. 'If more people could cycle to work,' I begin again, 'wouldn't that help us solve the problem of traffic jams?'

'Tell me, why do you think traffic jams are such a big problem?' Marco asks.

'Well, it's a pain getting stuck in traffic, isn't it? And on top of that, traffic jams cost us billions, don't they?'

'Do they?' he replies. 'How?'

'There are lots of people who don't get to work on time, and that reduces the number of hours they're productive for.'

'But how serious is that?' Marco asks with a twinkle in his blue eyes. 'Why does it matter so much if people arrive home or get to work a few minutes later because of a traffic jam? Don't you have to queue up at the supermarket from time to time?'

Again, I nod.

And then doubts assail me. How big a problem is it really, having to wait in a car, getting home later than you intended, compared with other problems?

Compared with mass extinction?

Inadequate healthcare?

Inequality?

War?

Why should traffic congestion merit seven weeks of investigative journalism?

On the train on the way home, my thoughts go off in all directions. I'm no techie — I studied Russian literature. But as a journalist I am used to searching for solutions to problems. And how can you solve a problem without ingenious technical fixes thought up by clever engineers?

I had thought that urban and regional planning was a technical discipline — which it is in most universities and institutes. But at the University of Amsterdam, in the Cycling Professor's department, it falls under the social sciences. That's why my conversation with Marco wasn't about the kind of bike highways you could speed along on a recumbent bike, e-bike, or speed pedelec, but about what people experience as they move about.

The first thing I do when I arrive home is take a shower. Then I run through readers' comments on my previous pieces on 'cycling versus congestion'. An older reader writes: 'Give me plenty of traffic jams. Nice and quiet for cyclists. I don't cycle because of road congestion. I know my own mind, thank you very much. I ride a bike because I want to, and because I've come to enjoy it, and because there are plenty of advantages to cycling.' This was a man who had cycled to and from work for 20 years, 52 kilometres (over 32 miles) a day. Yet he'd never done so for the express purpose of avoiding traffic hold-ups.

And there were other cyclists who were unconcerned about arriving at their destination as fast as possible. 'The provincial road is the most direct route, but I never go that way,' one had written. These people weren't in the least interested in solving the congestion problem. Another had commented: 'People going from A to B just need to stop believing they're in such a hurry.'

Once upon a time I would have labelled these people as curmudgeonly. But after my conversation with Marco, I hesitate. I keep thinking about the holiday I spent cycling with the wind behind me. Along with the journey through the Caucasus in our dark blue Niva, that had been the most carefree and adventurous trip of my life.

Could I afford to ignore that experience?

The Start of a New Journey

In the end, I simply type up my discussion with Marco. The result is a piece in which he argues that cyclists are liable to become motorists on two wheels the moment you start labelling cycle paths 'bike highways'. A piece in which he has nothing to say about showers at work, but talks instead about Frans de Waal's chimpanzees.

The story turns out to be the most-shared article in the 'cycling versus congestion' series.[6] It speaks to people.

In the weeks that follow, I let other cycling experts have their say and discover just how little I know about cycling, even though I do it nearly every day. The conversation with Marco lingers in my mind. I email him: 'I was so taken up with the future of mobility, but I know so little about how it works. I really want to pursue the subject.'

'Want to talk about it?' he writes back.

I do.

But first our second son is born, and for the next four months life slows down.

Then Marco and I arrange to meet again, this time in the canteen of Amsterdam University's Roeterseiland campus, where Urban and Regional Planning, the department where he works, is based.

'One of the things I want to understand', I say, 'is why I thought traffic jams were so important in the first place.'

Marco's response is enthusiastic. 'I wonder,' he says, 'how it affects us — the fact that we think it's so important. And the fact that we're always on the go. Why do we want things to be that way? And is that really what we want? Are there any alternatives, and what could change if we find the answers to these questions?'

Not long after our conversation, he sends me a private message on Twitter:

> **Cycling Professor** @fietsprofessor
> We're going to evaluate a new cycle path design at a crossroads in Amsterdam, together with some local civil servants. Want to come along?

> **Thalia Verkade** @tverka
> Yes please!

I'm expecting it to be rather dull. But this evaluation will radically change the way I look at our streets and roads.

Meet the 'Chip Cone'

At the intersection that takes you from Amsterdam's Jodenbreestraat towards the Meester Visserplein square, the cycle lane widens just before the traffic lights. Suppose you arrive when the lights are on red. There are already three cyclists next to each other at the line — there's just enough space for you to squeeze in alongside them because the lane is unexpectedly broad at this point. The cycle path on your left, for the cyclists who are about to cross from the other side of the road, is correspondingly narrow. They can ride two abreast at most, as in a normal cycle lane.

When the light turns green, cyclists from both sides cross the main road. The cycle lane you're in tapers, while the one to your left widens. The cyclists you were next to at the traffic lights a moment ago cross at different speeds, forming a long tail. Once you're on the other side, you can ride two abreast along the cycle path as usual.

Although the intersection looks quite odd with all the oblique lines running across it, most cyclists will cross unhesitatingly. This experiment has been nicknamed the 'chip cone'.

Cyclists' Crossing Point: The 'Chip Cone'

To improve the flow of cycle traffic where cycle paths cross roads,
a team of traffic engineers, spatial planners, and social scientists came up
with the idea of the 'chip cone'. The painted line dividing one cycle path
from the other runs diagonally across the road.

Red light
While cyclists wait at a red
light, they have more room
to stand next to each other

Green light
As soon as the light turns
green, the cyclists cycle at
different speeds towards a
narrower passing point

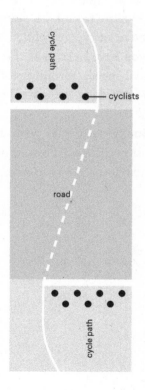
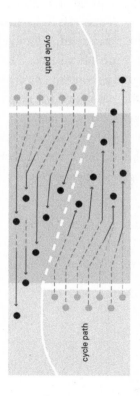

Source: Amsterdam municipal authority.

The chip cone is the subject of the evaluation I attend with Marco, who was involved in its design. He gives me some context: 'Eric Wiebes, the member of the local executive responsible for mobility issues, commissioned some research into possible ways to avoid bike tailbacks, but the condition was that any solutions had to let motor traffic flow unimpeded. The chip cone lets more cyclists wait at the red light than before. And that means more of them can cross at the same time once the light goes green.'

The evaluation is in an industrially styled municipal building that serves as a meeting point and flexible working space. Everyone seems to know everyone else, and people are in celebratory mood; the chip cone has won an annual award for innovation in cycling. We're all given a gingham-checked chip cone containing a banana-shaped sweet. The sweet is in honour of a new kind of miniature traffic island dubbed 'the banana' at the same crossing, which frees up the extra space needed for the chip cone.

In a PowerPoint presentation, two of the local civil servants who helped design the chip cone, Kees Vernooij and Sjoerd Linders, show how exactly they went about the task. That's handy, I think, an introductory course in crossing-point design.

First, some sociology students hung up a camera. Their photos of the square showed how cyclists in heavy traffic did all sorts of things you're not meant to do, like lining up next to each other at the red light, often on the wrong side of the central dividing line, and cycling the wrong way round the traffic island. The students also interviewed cyclists, many of whom said they found the heavy traffic and other cyclists' anarchic behaviour stressful.

The planners theorised that traffic might be more fluid if you let cyclists do their own thing, and so the workers responsible for painting traffic markings were told to position them to reflect how cyclists behave in real life. That's how the chip cone came about. The lines on the main road used by motorists continue to run parallel.

I look around the room, taken aback that so much thought has gone into designing a crossing point, and even more so that the outcome is being evaluated in such detail. Though I'd somehow expected the solution to be more technical.

'So that's how they design crossing points?' I whisper to Marco. He grins.

'No way! The normal way to design a cycle path is to follow the guidelines in traffic engineering manuals. Which aren't about people's real behaviour.'

'Eh? What *are* they about then?'

'Rules,' Marco replies.

I don't understand his point. But I will soon.

Then, a third-year student in mobility steps onto the podium. Koen Schreurs has been given the task of counting all the potentially dangerous situations in the immediate vicinity of the updated crossing point. To do this, he has applied a conflict-observation technique used in traffic planning, known as DOCTOR.

Apparently everyone in the room is familiar with the term. Googling it later, I discover that it stands for 'Dutch Objective Conflict Technique of Operation and Research' and that it's a method used to assess road design.

The DOCTOR manual contains sentences like this:

> The time-to-collision concept is based on the
> existence of a trajectory that will result in a collision.
> Where road users miss each other while moving at

high speed and without any significant adjustment in speed or trajectory, there is, strictly speaking, no such trajectory. Nonetheless, the risk of a collision in such situations remains a reality; a minor disturbance in the process could easily have resulted in a collision.[7]

For DOCTOR, then, people in motion are a type of projectile. Using this method, Schreurs has researched the behaviour of cyclists as they approach the chip cone and use it to cross. He has measured and recorded the risk of collisions and concluded that the new design leads to some pretty dangerous situations. 'This isn't the safest way to do it,' he says.

Schreurs gives some examples of the conflicts he's observed. DOCTOR's definition of a 'conflict' is a situation in which someone takes longer than is strictly necessary to do something, in order to avoid a potential collision. For example, a pedestrian on her way to the zebra crossing has to pause to let a cluster of ten or so cyclists past, all of them pedalling full tilt after crossing the road. The pedestrian loops around behind the cyclists to cross on the zebra crossing.

I hear muttering in the room. A number of attendees bombard the student with tough questions. They see something different — people cooperating with each other to make the best of the situation. Why does Schreurs view every possible interaction as a conflict to be avoided?

The student defends himself politely. He points out that he did take account of the cyclists' behaviour and the communication among them by tweaking the DOCTOR model, which was designed for drivers. And the local authorities have received some complaints about the updated crossing point from cyclists too.

'That was a hard task,' says civil servant Sjoerd Linders later. 'Cyclists in the area just before the crossing are expected to reach agreement among themselves. Schreurs's collision analysis helped the local authorities gain a better understanding of where cyclists find this difficult.'

The DOCTOR collision analysis is my first direct experience of traffic engineering. I've heard of it as a profession, of course, but up to now I thought traffic engineers were mainly concerned with designing the layout of new-build areas.

Neither have I really thought, before now, about the fact that their work is based on a specific set of logical principles, manuals, and design philosophies. I'm getting my first glimpse of this today. Collision course. Time to collision. DOCTOR. It sounds like an exact science.

The social scientists in the room have a different way of looking at the city; they see not a collection of buildings and roads, but a group of people. The urban and regional planners at the University of Amsterdam, as I gradually discover, study the interactions between human beings and the environment designed for them. A collision between two people walking along a pavement can be serendipitous: that's how William (Hugh Grant) meets Anna (Julia Roberts) in the film *Notting Hill*.

But in traffic engineering, a collision is a 'conflict' that has to be prevented. From the traffic engineer's perspective, the city isn't the sum of all the people who live and interact there, it's a set of roads via which people cross one another's routes and have to be prevented from holding each other up more than necessary.

While I'm chewing my banana sweet, it dawns on me that the chip cone is The Great Exception to the Rule: an extremely rare intersection whose design is based on the logic not of traffic engineers, but of sociologists. The chip cone is the crack in the system that reveals the system's existence.

The City as a Geometry Problem

The name 'chip cone' was a Rotterdammer's brainchild, I later discover. My city has a knack for inventing nicknames. Rotterdam is home to the new 'Kapsalon' train station (named after a hearty snack that comes in a tinfoil tray rather like the station's roof), 'Shopditch' (aka the Beurstraverse, the Netherlands' first open-air shopping centre), 'Punter's Pier' (a footbridge to what used to be the red light district), and the 'Buttplug Gnome' (a sculpture by Paul McCarthy that depicts Father Christmas holding something that might possibly be a small Christmas tree).

And now, pedalling over 'the Swan' (aka the Erasmus Bridge), I'm developing an eye for the traffic-engineering system.

There's a message in official lettering on the asphalt cycle path over the bridge that wasn't there a short time ago: 'Say BOO to cyclists riding on the wrong side.' I must admit I sometimes ride on the wrong side of the bridge; you have to wait quite a while at the lights before you can cross the road and the tram line to get to the side where you need to be. And once you've crossed the bridge over the Nieuwe Maas river, if you have to be on the left side again, you've got to wait at the lights a second time. I'm riding in the correct direction today. The person speeding towards me isn't. There's a conflict ahead: not a cyclist, but a man on a moped. He's approaching pretty fast. I move as far over to the right as I can. Should I be yelling 'BOO' now?

After the chip-cone evaluation, I wonder why there isn't a two-way cycle path on both sides of the bridge. Not only would that be easier for cyclists, it would also keep the traffic flowing more smoothly. Of course, this *is* a bridge, I think. Maybe the problem is the lack of space?

In the weeks that follow I begin to develop a new awareness of the lines painted on the asphalt, of the way streets are divided into the sections and lanes that keep people in separate channels as they race past each other. Yet human beings, with their unpredictable behaviour, often seem to cause problems within the system.

I consider my own neighbourhood, in north Rotterdam. There is a street called Zaagmolenstraat that, though not very wide, has two sets of tram rails, flows of motor traffic in both directions, and cars parked along both kerbs. Everything seems to be designed to encourage people not to spend any time there, but to arrive, drive through, and leave as fast as possible. If you need to get out of a tram with a baby buggy, you'll often find a car blocking your way, as the parking spaces are the tram stop. So you've got to pelt along the tram with your buggy to the next door, yelling 'Wait!' to the driver in their glass cabin.

The street is at least as stressful for motorists. Its layout encourages you — begs you, almost — to drive through at speed. You're allowed to do 50 km/h (just over 30 mph), and there are no sleeping policemen (speed bumps). But with all those trams, and with cyclists making odd manoeuvres to avoid getting their wheels wedged in the tram rails, and with people getting off and nipping across the street between the parked cars, you can't really drive at any speed. Yet it feels as if that's what you should be doing.

On a bike, it's a complete nightmare — so narrow, so busy, and with tram rails to look out for. I dare not cycle through Zaagmolenstraat with my older son, who's just learned how to ride.

But we do always cycle to school together along a broad, segregated cycle path running between a two-lane road with a 50 km/h speed limit and the A20 motorway. To reach my son's school we have to cross the two-lane road. I'm beginning to find this astounding too. There's no zebra crossing. No traffic lights either. There's just a narrow crossing point for cyclists, who must wait at the give-way markings for the cars to clear.

There are two more schools just behind my son's. Everyone coming by bike has to cross the road at least twice a day. Every morning, clusters of parents and children wait for a gap in the traffic. It is downright dangerous.

My four-year-old hasn't grasped the system yet. 'But we can cross here too, can't we?' he says, pedalling his little blue bike towards the left half of the cycle path, which has no give-way markings. Alarmed, I catch him up and plant my front wheel across his path. 'Stop — you can't cross over just like that!'

But why do children have to wait for a gap in the traffic rushing past? Why do drivers have priority right next to a school? Why isn't there a zebra crossing here, or at least a set of lights for the dozens of children crossing the road?

Now I'm astounded that these questions have never occurred to me before.

Traffic Lights, Give-way Markings, and Push Buttons

Traffic is such an integral part of my everyday life that I've never stopped to wonder exactly how it works. Who decides if a zebra crossing or a set of traffic lights is to be placed at a particular spot? On the face of it, this strikes me as a technical issue, a question for traffic engineers.

But once I've got to know some traffic engineers, I grasp that it isn't just a technical matter. It's a social, political, and moral issue: a question of who has most rights. That dawns on me when Luc Prinsen, a traffic management advisor at the engineering company Goudappel Coffeng, and Mark Clijsen, a specialist in traffic control from the local authority in Tilburg, take me on a tour of some of the city's traffic lights.

I beg your pardon, that should be 'TCSs', or 'traffic control systems', as Prinsen, a tall man with salt-and-pepper hair and light blue eyes, calls them. Working together with the slightly shorter, bespectacled Clijsen, he has installed quite a number of them in Tilburg.

Tilburg has about 150 TCSs: 150 intersections regulated by a computer and a set of lights, which these experts refer to not as 'red, amber, and green', but as 'red, yellow, and green'.

The first TCS on our tour, a small set of pedestrian lights, immediately raises some questions. When we press the button, the light obligingly turns green. But it goes back to red before we reach the traffic island in the middle of the road — even though the road we're crossing isn't at all wide.

That went pretty fast. Prinsen asks why that is. Straightening his glasses, Clijsen says, 'Maybe we dawdled a bit.' That's true, we strolled across, chatting. Now we have to wait for the next green light, with drivers passing us on either side.

'Are you allowed to adjust the lights?' I ask Clijsen. 'Can you set them to stay on green for longer, so people can cross at a more relaxed pace?'

'Yes, I can. That's what we do near housing for the elderly, for instance — or if someone makes a complaint.'

Wow, I think. So it really is that simple?

Prinsen adds, 'But to do that, he's got to check the logs for this set of lights to see how often that sort of thing happens. If you extend the green phase when it's actually quite rare for people to get stuck in the middle of the road, you undermine the credibility of the lights as far as all other road users are concerned. And that means drivers are less likely to take them seriously, which has a negative knock-on effect on traffic safety.'

We walk on towards a major intersection.

'Do you have to register the change officially if you adjust the lights?' I ask. 'Are there particular standards or rules you have to abide by?'

'I can make minor adjustments if I want to,' says Clijsen.

'So how often do you do that?'

'Oh, about once a week on average.'

Prinsen and Clijsen point out all kinds of features I've never noticed before. It's only once they acquire a name that I start to register them — just as with the 'chip cone' and the 'banana'. We look at virtually unnoticeable slits cut in the asphalt before the stop line on cycle paths and roads. Underneath these are vehicle detection loops that use a magnetic field to sense the vehicles above. This information is relayed to the traffic lights: someone wants the lights to turn green.

Now we're standing next to a black box on the verge alongside a major intersection. Pulling out a screwdriver, Clijsen opens a door in it. We see a computer screen surrounded by buttons, with a switchbox underneath. This is the brain of the traffic control system.

A schematic diagram of the intersection flickers on the screen. Just ahead of me, I see a motorist come to a standstill on the detection loop. On the computer screen, the patch he occupies turns black.

'Look, now the computer knows there's someone at the lights,' says Prinsen. 'And now the counting starts. There's 3,600 seconds in an hour. The amount of time vehicles take to vacate the intersection after the lights turn red totals about 600 seconds — 10 minutes — in every hour, and you have to add a safety margin on top of that. The rest of the available time has to be divided up fairly among the various streams of traffic, heading in different directions.'

But how do you do that? What does 'fairly' mean? And who does it apply to?

———

We've arrived at the 'Cityring', a happy hunting ground for anyone on a traffic light safari: it boasts a wealth of different species, all at close range. The Cityring is a one-way asphalt ring road, divided into two lanes, that runs around the city centre. Central Tilburg is encircled not by flowing water, like many historic Dutch cities, but by flowing traffic.

Completed in 2011, the Cityring is actually a series of linked-up residential streets, with pavements, like the one we're walking along at the moment; with houses, and the people who live in them; and with side streets where still more people live, work, and go to school. The only thing that marks it out as a ring road is its surface, designed for brisk traffic.

We stop at a small set of pedestrian lights that look a little out of place.

'The local authority would have preferred not to have these, but the school in this side street insisted,' says Clijsen. 'What you really need here is a zebra crossing, so pedestrians always have right of way. But that's not feasible, it would mean congestion in other parts of town.'

'We already have to turn the taps on and off,' says Prinsen. 'When it's clogged up here or it looks likely to get congested, less traffic is let in at other points.'

Water pipes as a metaphor for streets, water as a metaphor for traffic. Traffic engineers can see how much traffic can flow through the Cityring by consulting traffic models. These are flow diagrams that include all the streets in the city, with thousands of variables, such as the time it takes for the traffic lights to change, the speed limit, the expected number of cars, whether there is a bus route that needs greater priority, and so on. This makes it possible to forecast the various routes traffic will take as it flows through the streets.

Clijsen says, 'A traffic light really is a last resort, not just something to be installed any old where. That's why we turned down the application for this little TCS to begin with, but they kept on petitioning, right up to the level of the local representative responsible for traffic.'

It was a real battle, I later discover. Headteacher Bas Evers refused to accept the fact that his 450 pupils couldn't cross the road independently.

'We can't have a situation where parents have to carry on bringing their children to school right up to their last year in primary because they're worried something might happen at a dangerous crossing point,' Evers told the local radio station. 'Each time I go to school, I find myself hoping that nothing's happened — just like my colleagues and our children's parents.' He was losing sleep.[8]

Initially, the local authority announced it had no plans to install pedestrian lights. As Clijsen has already remarked, that would 'take the speed out of the Cityring'. So the headteacher and his pupils' parents decided to organise an attention-grabbing stunt. It was almost 5 December, St Nicholas's Day, so they prevailed on the jolly old Saint — a local man dressed in a white robe with a red cloak — to climb up onto a construction platform. If the local authority wasn't prepared to guarantee the safety of the school's children — of whom there were now 530 — then St Nicholas himself would just have to do the job.

'I invited all the political parties to come so we could show them the situation. I was ready to walk over to City Hall with the children,' Evers later told me by phone. 'I asked: "Don't you realise there's a school here? Why are children's interests such a low priority?"'

The message slowly got through: it wasn't fair that children couldn't cross the road safely.

In Tilburg, I press the button to operate the pedestrian

lights that Bas Evers fought for. I count on my fingers. The traffic continues for a good 30 seconds. Then the cars stop, and a few seconds later the pedestrian lights turn green.

The lights flash.

Time to clear the pedestrian crossing.

There's a narrow margin.

Then the tap's turned on again.

Further on, the Cityring causes major problems, the problems that keep Bas Evers up at night. There's a reason locals call the inner ring road 'the racetrack'. At least a hundred accidents have been reported over nine months[9] — one every three days. Does it even make sense to use the word 'accident' for such a systematic occurrence, I wonder? The official speed limit is 50 km/h (31 mph), but the ring road is so like a motorway that it's very hard for drivers to resist putting their foot down.

Prinsen, Clijsen, and I are now beside a thick black-and-white-striped traffic pole that arches over the road. This 'portal' is a particularly exotic traffic control device. It bears a speed camera and a matrix board with a smiley that can frown as well as smile.

'We call the angry smiley a frownie,' says Clijsen. He designed the light himself as a way to call out speedsters. 'Drive at a normal speed and you'll see the smiley,' he explains. 'The frownie appears if you're doing over 50 km/h, and the light stays red longer, too. So you're penalised.'

'How does that affect the motorist in the lane next to you?' I ask. 'If they've stuck to the speed limit, I mean?'

'They have to wait longer too. That's one of the drawbacks of this system.'

'What do the locals think of it?' I ask.

'They mostly support these sorts of efforts to change drivers' behaviour.'

Then a motorist drives past, breaking the speed limit, and the frownie lights up. Prinsen says, 'Hey, Mark, can you let me have the specs for those?'

What exactly is going on here? I try to look at it from all possible points of view.

People living near the ring road, schoolchildren, and other Tilburg residents crossing the Cityring on foot or by bike don't have right of way because that would slow down traffic around the city centre.

Traffic managers and civil servants like Prinsen and Clijsen are doing their very best within the limits of traffic management logic — that is, that traffic mustn't come to a standstill and conflicts must be avoided — to organise everything as fairly as possible.

Residents are mostly content with these interventions.

Yet there's a collision on the Cityring every three days.

If motorists drive too fast, they don't get a traffic fine, they just have to wait longer for the light to turn green.

And if you're a local resident who wants to get something changed, your go-to guy is St Nicholas.

'Wouldn't it be a lot easier to make this a road where you can't drive so fast?' I ask.

Clijsen nods. 'Our *wethouder* responsible for local traffic says the onus should be on the motorists to cross over at intersections, not the pedestrians. So we're doing all kinds of experiments at the moment.'

We walk over to look at one. Outside Tilburg's main theatre, saplings and shrubs in pots have been set out on patches of astroturf, so drivers are forced to slow down as they approach. The local authority likes the idea, but this time it's the local media that disapprove. 'A "minigolf course" (for €150,000) on the Cityring', complains regional newspaper *Brabants Dagblad*, reflecting the *vox pop*.[10]

Traffic calming measures outside Tilburg's main theatre.
Source: BD.nl © Bas Vermeer.

Prinsen and Clijsen want to show me one more innovative traffic light at the intersection we've just reached.

A small loudspeaker, with an explanatory sign, has been installed on the side of the road, where cyclists and pedestrians wait. It plays the music Tommy-Boy used to listen to. Thirteen-year-old Tommy-Boy was cycling along, listening to music on his mobile, when he was run over and killed by a woman driving along the provincial road near Bussum, North Holland.

'Makes you think, doesn't it?' says Clijsen.

I nod. I'm familiar with these memorial loudspeakers, which we have in Rotterdam as well: the idea was dreamed up by students at the city's art academy. Tommy-Boy didn't ride through a red light. He cycled out of the woods, his attention elsewhere, and crossed a road where he didn't have the right of way.

After his death, the crossing was altered. Now there's a fence at the end of the cycle track, so that cyclists have to dismount. If you're a motorist, you can carry on driving just as fast as ever.

'Could you put up another loudspeaker and sign for drivers?' I ask Clijsen. 'So they realise what the danger is too? That they could run over a child and kill them?'

My voice is more vehement than I would like.

There's an awkward silence.

At home, I look at my photos of the complicated intersection. Was I really being fair, with that last question?

Luc Prinsen and Mark Clijsen are doing everything they can to keep speedsters out of the system. But these specialists, with their technical backgrounds, can't make decisions about who has the right to use the road: those who live and go to school here; or those who need to pass through on their way from A to B. Within strictly defined margins, they can install and fine-tune a traffic control system. They can try to make these systems ever smarter, even have them talk to your smartphone. But the reason such things are needed in the first place is beyond their remit.

Why do headteachers have to beg for a pole with a button so that schoolchildren can cross the road, and why don't they have a seat at the table when plans for a ring road like the Cityring are under discussion, so they can say: 'If that's what you're going to do, we want a zebra crossing at the very least'?

I ring Bas Evers, the headteacher. He says he began by asking for a zebra crossing, but the local authority said that the pedestrian lights, with their short green phase, were the best that could be done. The lights are better than nothing, but as far as he's concerned they're not enough. 'Our school is a Montessori school based on principles like personal responsibility and learning to let go. But I understand why some parents of ten-year-olds still walk them to school if they have to cross a road like this one.'

I think of my son's school, which has a similar set-up. Of how I sometimes walk into the street like a lollipop lady and gesture at a motorist to stop. Of how some drivers stop of their own accord, while others behind them start honking their horns.

Could we get a set of traffic lights too? A zebra crossing, or give-way markings for motorists? Or perhaps a button for drivers to press — why is there no such thing?

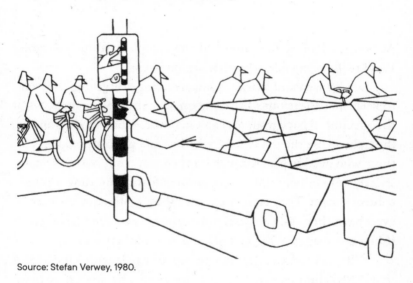

Source: Stefan Verwey, 1980.

School Drop-off Zone

Marco and I get to know each other better through private messaging on Twitter. He turns out to have a similar problem to Bas Evers in his local area. The big difference is that Marco lives in a new neighbourhood in Ede, a small town in the east of the Netherlands. The area in front of his children's school has yet to be laid out. It still has the potential to be put to all kinds of uses: it could be a playground, an area for parking bicycles, a place for people to sit, a football field.

Cycling Professor @fietsprofessor
Now they've got a plan for the area in front of our local school. They're going to turn it into a quick drop-off zone. That's a sort of roundabout where you can drop your child off safely and drive away without further ado — traffic engineers say it's safer and faster than parking your car in a space and then manoeuvring out of it.

Thalia Verkade @tverka
You don't sound too happy about that.

Cycling Professor @fietsprofessor
I'm not. It's not a drop-off zone, it's a push-off zone — you boot your kid out of the car and straight into the main entrance, and off you go. That's not what the school wants at all. My daughter's teacher has just reminded parents again that it's school policy for them to accompany their children into the classroom.

Thalia Verkade @tverka
Then how come they've already agreed on this plan?

Cycling Professor @fietsprofessor
The traffic engineer is the only expert who gets a seat at the table with the local authority.

Thalia Verkade @tverka
Why haven't they involved an urban planner?

Cycling Professor @fietsprofessor
Urban planners tend to be involved at a higher level,
in planning the new neighbourhood as a whole.
But there are no specialists in child development,
ecology, health, or psychology involved either —
even though what we're talking about here is the
area around a school.

When I visit him later, Marco shows me the space in front of the school. He lives in an area that used to belong to the viscose factory ENKA, which later became the chemical company Akzo (of AkzoNobel). In front of the school, which is to be set up next year in the former factory workers' canteen, there's a large patch of sand. What is built here will set the tone for the new neighbourhood.

This space could be transformed into an area for children to play, where they can walk, run, or cycle to school, where motorists come second. But it seems that the die is already cast: it's to become a space where we teach children to pick their way safely through traffic on their way to school.

A Barbecue in a Parking Space

While I'm learning just how much the logic of traffic engineering determines the way our residential areas are designed, a journalist colleague, Jesse Frederik, is discovering surprising things about parking spaces.[11]

There are almost as many parking spaces in the Netherlands as there are people, it turns out, which means there are twice as many parking spaces as there are cars. If you were to put all those spaces together, they would take up more room than the total surface area of Amsterdam. I later discover that the United States is even worse, with two billion parking spaces for 250 million cars; more parking space is allocated per car than housing space per person.[12]

Jesse writes: 'Over two-thirds of these parking spaces [in the Netherlands] occupy public land, and 92 per cent of them are provided totally free of charge.'

Public land. Aka the street. It's only now I'm taking a proper look at the issue that it strikes me: the street is a place that belongs to everyone, and it's there for everyone. Or it should be. It's a shared space where people should be able to do just about anything they want, provided they can agree on it.

We could use a parking space to set up a barbecue. Or, as Jesse suggests, plant a small vegetable garden. But that's not allowed. Nor can you park your bicycle or put your wheelie bin in a parking space. The only thing permitted there is a car. Why is that?

In his article, Jesse refers to various economic surveys that show how heavily parking is subsidised in Amsterdam. The market value of the land taken up by one parking space is about €3,600 a year, but an annual parking permit costs only €535. In contrast, the average cost to buy a house or flat is €5,655 per square metre.[13] The situation is similar in the London borough of Westminster, where residents pay £8,000 a year to rent living space the same size as a parking spot, but only £158 to park their cars.[14]

In Rotterdam, an annual parking permit costs even less — just €69 in 2019.[15]

'We have to make parking a lot more expensive,' writes Jesse. He reckons that's 'the solution to just about everything'. It would bring in more money for the local authority while providing the opportunity to repurpose this valuable street space.

'You could come and take a look in Ede,' says Marco, when I

send him Jesse's piece via Twitter, 'if you want to see how it works in a new neighbourhood.'

Where you could do things differently.

And so I go to Ede.

The Impact of a Guideline

On arrival at Ede-Wageningen train station, most passengers disappear into other trains: this is a junction with a direct service to Utrecht and Amsterdam every quarter of an hour. That was one of the reasons why Marco moved here recently from Amsterdam.

Cycling Professor @fietsprofessor
I can get to work within the hour. It hardly takes any longer than from Amsterdam-Osdorp. And I get a generous travel allowance into the bargain. Insane when you think about it.

Thalia Verkade @tverka
What's insane about it?

Cycling Professor @fietsprofessor
Why do we subsidise people who choose to live a long way out?

Thalia Verkade @tverka
Because not everyone can live in Amsterdam?

I touch out with my smartcard and follow Google Maps to the address Marco has sent me. He lives on the corner of a little street, newly built and still covered in sand.

There's a smell of fresh plaster indoors: the walls have just been redone because something wasn't quite right after construction. Marco fetches his three-year-old son's balance bike from the shed in the little garden and we set off for a walk round the neighbourhood, which is still a work in progress. There are piles of sand everywhere and lots of houses are still waiting for walls or a roof.

Leaving the garden, we enter the parking area that forms the centre of the block of houses. There's scarcely a car in sight: everyone who has one is clearly away from home at this time of day.

'Do you know how they decide the number of parking spaces in a new neighbourhood?' asks Marco.

'There's a standard for that,' I say. I know about it from Jesse's piece. It's a guideline set by a Dutch institute called CROW.

'Spot on,' Marco replies. 'Go on, have a guess what standard they apply here, five minutes' walk from a station used by intercity trains, with a direct service to Utrecht and Amsterdam four times an hour.'

'Hmm ... so how many cars would you need?' I ponder aloud. Turning the corner, we see metal sheeting laid on the sand to accommodate traffic.

'1.7,' says Marco. 'There are 17 parking spaces for every ten homes. Nearly everyone here can have two cars.'

I look around me at what was once the Veluwe heathlands. A hare bounds away from beneath a sapling. They have literally paved paradise to put up a parking lot. In the sections of the street that are already finished, the parking spaces are demarcated with a line of white stones. These spaces are long rectangles, slightly broader than the pavements.

'They've set aside plenty of space. Stint on parking space, they think, and you'll get complaints from residents later on,' says Marco. 'So you end up with four to five football fields worth of parking spaces, and that's without even counting all the driveways and the extra room for manoeuvring in and out.'

'Look out!' I yell abruptly.

Marco's young son has trundled off on his bike, and all of a sudden I spot a car on its way in. The little boy has already come to a standstill.

I try to imagine what possible justification there might be for 1.7 cars per home here. People need a car to reach places where the train doesn't stop, or to visit relatives living in villages, for instance, or they might have a car or van for their work. Not everyone has an office in central Amsterdam. But nearly two cars per household in a new housing estate near a major train station is definitely a lot, especially if you think what else you could do with all those hectares of public land.

'The developer targeted mainly Ede locals,' Marco explains. 'The fact that we're right next to a station with intercity services wasn't mentioned in the sales brochure. When they later found out that young families from the west of the country wanted to live here too, they added that the A12 is only a few minutes' drive from here — but not that you're only a few minutes' walk from the train.'

'But how about people from Ede who have relatives living in the villages nearby, for instance,' I ask. 'They need a car, don't they?'

'I need a car now and then too,' Marco replies. 'But why is it the norm to have nearly two cars per house? The car's parked in front of the door, the bike's in a shed. Why haven't I been allocated a parking space for my bike?'

We stroll around behind a skeletal structure with huge arches — the monumental façade of the ENKA factory, where viscose, artificial silk in the most exquisite colours, was produced for 80 years. Then we reach the fringes of the housing estate. I spot a lot more vacant parking spaces.

'No one ever parks here,' says Marco. 'Too far to walk. Soon they will put an enclosed football pitch for teenagers here, so the kids can have a kick around without damaging any cars. It's being discussed already — why not let those kids stretch their legs a bit before their game?'

'And you're against that?'

'It's noticeable that everyday activities get relegated to the edge of our neighbourhood, just so we can park our cars right in the middle. What I find strangest is how we apparently have no choice in the matter. The local authority refers to the parking standard set by CROW. But that's just a guideline. They aren't obliged to stick to it.' He points past the parking spaces at the green area beyond. 'CROW's over there, incidentally. You can walk over in no time.'

We'll be returning to CROW together. But not today. We walk back to the housing estate, towards the as-yet unbuilt area in front of the school attended by Marco's children.

'The school drop-off zone comes from a CROW recommendation too,' Marco says. 'From their computer tool for designing parking areas near schools and childcare providers.[16] The traffic engineer has to fill in all sorts of information, such as the size of the town, the position of the school catchment area, and the number of employees and visitors. Then the tool spits out the suggested number of parking spaces and recommends a zone where children can be dropped off quickly, as CROW thinks that's the safest solution. The traffic engineer adds up all the figures and presents them to the local authority — here's the blueprint for the area in front of your school, with a quick drop-off zone, just as prescribed.'

The fact that we use guidelines like these as a reference point has significant consequences, Marco explains. 'If you want to put the area in front of a school to a different use, you're not just a person who wants something else, you're someone who opposes the norm, an activist. But I really don't want this drop-off point. I'm going to see if I can start a discussion about it with the local authorities. And with the other residents.'

Bigger and Bigger Cars

Walking along my own street in Rotterdam, I decide to count the parking spaces. There are about 50 spaces for the 50-odd houses, nearly all of which are divided into two flats. That's a lot fewer than in Marco's neighbourhood. But then there is a big car park around the corner.

I search online for the parking standard that applies to this part of town: it's one car per flat.[17] That's tight. By evening, the pavements along our street often have cars illegally parked on them. And the spaces themselves are narrow. A neighbour's Tesla won't even fit into one.

Why is that? I check the requirements for parking spaces. It turns out there's a norm for these too, the Dutch NEN standard. A local authority that wants to meet this standard must ensure that parking spaces at right angles to the street are at least 2.4 (preferably 2.5) metres wide and at least 5 metres long.[18] Again, this isn't a requirement or a law, it's a guideline.

The suggested dimensions are based on a 'model vehicle'.[19] The model gets a little longer and broader every few years, because car manufacturers keep on making their vehicles bigger. Between 1973 and 2008, for instance, the Honda Civic grew from 1.5 to nearly 1.8 metres wide and from 3.55 to 4.27 metres long.[20] And just compare the old Mini with today's version.

That's why the parking spaces in Marco's new housing estate are not only more numerous, but bigger than those in my street.

Since it's over a hundred years old, the parking spaces were slotted in here decades after it was built, making the best of the space available.

The world of toys reflects these changes. Lego offers a particularly clear illustration: standard Lego cars are now six studs wide, compared with just four in the 1980s. And they take up more space in Lego City. The faint cycle lane at the side of the road has vanished, while the 'pavement' has shrunk by two studs, or even three in some versions. The space allotted to cars has been discreetly expanded, at the expense of the rest of the miniature city.

These discoveries are making my hankering after a second-hand electric Kangoo feel increasingly ill-advised. My partner's beginning to have doubts too. It would be nice to have that freedom, but do we really want to drive round and round the neighbourhood searching for a space — which would also need to have a charging point?

And just how energy-efficient is it to use a machine that's between ten and 20 times your own weight to get about? We live in the city centre. Couldn't we just use bikes, trams, and trains, and borrow or hire a car from our neighbours via peer-to-peer car-sharing platforms such as SnappCar or MyWheels when needed?

We decide to buy two children's car seats to begin with, which we can also use in any car we're borrowing. It takes a bit of extra effort, but we don't have the bother of parking, and this solution saves us a few hundred euros each month. With the money we've saved, we buy an electric cargo bike. If you line the box with long wooden panels, we discover, it has nearly the same capacity as the boot of a Lada Niva.

The Travel Time Budget (Marchetti's Constant) and its Impact

Not having a car of my own spares me another problem: I rarely find myself stuck in traffic jams. Why exactly did I think congestion was such an important issue, again? Not that I am the only one. The radio gives traffic updates at half-hourly intervals. Is that because we attach so much importance to traffic jams — or do we only think they are important because they're mentioned on the radio every 30 minutes?

And here's another odd thing: if our society is so over-aware of this problem and so over-focused on tackling it, how is it we haven't been able to find a solution? I'm keen to write about this, so I do some preparatory reading on the subject. In a book recommended to me by a reader, I find a list of predictions and vows to tackle the issue stretching back over many years. The result is a spectacular litany of broken promises:

1. In 2010, traffic jams were three times as long as in 1988, although the government of the day had vowed to reduce them to a third of the length.
2. In 1997, it was predicted that there would be no more traffic jams in 2010 than in 2000. In fact, the total number of traffic jams increased by 50 per cent.
3. In 1993, it was expected that the length of traffic jams would stay roughly the same until 2000. In fact, their total length almost doubled.[21]

Over the same decades, I discover, the Dutch motorway network expanded significantly, from about 2,100 kilometres (about 1,305 miles) in 1988 to nearly 2,500 kilometres (about 1,553 miles) today.[22] And, like parking spaces, motorways have become much broader as well. All this to resolve the congestion problem.

Yet, as we know, the tailbacks haven't got any shorter, nor are there fewer of them. Instead, there are more, and they've lengthened. There are plans to add a further 1,000 kilometres (about 621 miles) by 2030, though it is acknowledged that even this additional road surface won't suffice, so further congestion is inevitable.[23]

What's going on here?

One evening when I'm out on my bike I run into a new motorway extension. It's spring, and my partner, our children, and I are staying in what we call our dacha: an allotment with a wooden chalet in a complex called Eigen Hof ('our own garden') just north of Rotterdam, in the wedge between the two major roads, the A20 and the A13, a stone's throw from the Kleinpolderplein junction familiar from road congestion updates on the radio.

Eigen Hof is a green island with a few hundred allotments that's buffeted by the endless surf of traffic. 'Like living on the coast,' the late writer Jan Wolkers described the sound.[24] But there are no cars within the allotment area itself. Within the confines of Eigen Hof, the rights of the slowest come first — the allotment owner on his knees, worrying away at the weeds under his hedges. You can't even cycle along the paths in the growing season, or at least only if you're a child.

Once ours are in their dacha bunkbeds, I go for a spin on my old red sports bike, heading towards Delft. But I don't get very far. There's a post on the cycle path with a notice about something called De Groene Boog ('the green arc'). The notice is the work of a consortium of building companies that will be laying 11 kilometres (over 6.5 miles) of new asphalt over the next few years. The plan is to extend the A16, which runs up from the south and currently ends at the Terbregseplein junction. I ride off in the other direction, in a disappointing half-loop, then cycle back to our chalet, where I search online for information about the new motorway. Pex Langenberg, the member of the Rotterdam local executive responsible for traffic, promises that people won't be able to see, hear, or smell the motorway.[25]

This new connecting road, I read, is 'a missing link'.[26] It's going to be surfaced with the best noise-absorbing asphalt known to man, and in the near future, of course, the only cars on it will be electric ones, as the *Algemeen Dagblad* writes. 'De Groene Boog already offers a sustainable experience.'[27]

All of this has passed me by, apart from the fact that my own sustainable green experience — an evening ride on my bike — was cut short. Why are they building this in the first place? According to a brochure for local residents, 'the 11 kilometre-long A16 from Rotterdam will soon enable traffic on the A13, the A20 and nearby local roads to flow through more smoothly'.[28]

Yet another stretch of asphalt to combat congestion. But what about those broken promises?

The author of the book exposing those failures, Arie Bleijenberg, is happy to give me an explanation. We arrange to meet at Delft train station, at 9 am on a Tuesday.

There are plenty of different ways to cycle to Delft from my allotment, and it's quicker than first cycling to Rotterdam Central Station and taking the train. Besides, the weather's fine. But I leave too late and end up in a tailback of several hundred students cycling to the university: no 'chip cone' here yet. In the bike parking area under the station I hastily spray deodorant under my shirt — they should have showers here! — and pelt up the escalator to Starbucks, where we've arranged to meet.

Bleijenberg, a softly spoken man with greying hair and large spectacles, spent many years as a senior civil servant at the Ministry of Transport, Public Works, and Water Management, as it was then known. Now he's an independent mobility expert working for the research organisation TNO on replacing ageing bridges and locks.

I tell him I just don't understand why we can't find a solution to congestion, and that there are plans for yet another new section of motorway near a place where I spend a lot of time. What's going on here?

Once our espressos are ordered, Bleijenberg gives me his explanation, in a pithy soundbite that would fit nicely on a traditional blue Delftware tile. 'New infrastructure attracts new business, bringing more congestion.'

In other words, build a road or a railway line and people will settle nearby, producing more traffic. So the congestion increases.

'The fact that a motorway attracts traffic congestion is statistically proven, too,' Bleijenberg continues. 'Canadian researchers have measured this effect in several large urban regions in America. Lay 1 per cent more asphalt, and you get 1 per cent more traffic. The fundamental law of road congestion, they call it. Asphalt has been shown to attract cars: you can't get rid of congestion by building more roads.'

And then Bleijenberg launches into an account of the discovery made by Geurt Hupkes, a transport economist who, in the 1970s, researched how often, how far, and at what speed people travelled daily, all over the world.

Regardless of whether they lived in Peru or Singapore, Germany or the United States, the Netherlands or the Soviet Union, and no matter whether they had a car, a bicycle, or just their own legs, most people turned out to spend between 70 and 80 minutes a day getting about, if you added up all the trips to friends and family, work, and the shops. Hupkes called this the 'law of constant travel time and trip rates': the concept is also known as 'the travel time budget' or Marchetti's constant (after the Italian physicist Cesare Marchetti).

This aligns with what Bleijenberg explained to me about new roads attracting new business. Give people speedier transport, and they won't use it to spend less time travelling, but to move further afield. Give a company the capacity to cover a larger area, and it will use that mainly to achieve economies of scale, by establishing a single large office at one location and closing down small local branches. As a result, the places we need to travel to are increasingly far-flung. We're being scattered in all directions like particles in a centrifuge.

Between 1962 and 1972, Geurt Hupkes found that the average number of kilometres Dutch people travelled every day increased by over 50 per cent, to 32 kilometres (nearly 20 miles). It was precisely during that decade that everyone in the Netherlands acquired a car.

He also found comparable figures for a large number of cities in the United States and both Western and Eastern Europe.[29] While the average travel time remained about the same for everyone, the annual distance covered per person rose from 7,000 kilometres (nearly 4,350 miles) to 11,500 kilometres (nearly 7,146 miles) in the course of the decade.[30]

We're Travelling Further All the Time

Ever since the 1950s, we've been increasing the
distances we cover in the same length of time

Bicycle   Public transport   Plane   Car   Car
                                                        (passenger)   (driver)

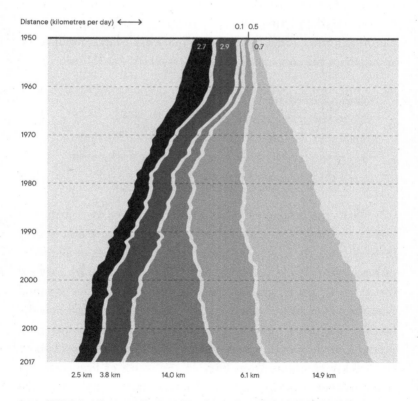

Sources: PBL Netherlands Environmental Assessment Agency (based on figures from Statistics Netherlands), Onderzoek
Verplaatsingsgedrag (Research into Mobility Behaviour), Onderzoek Verplaatsingen in Nederland (Research into Mobility
in the Netherlands), Schiphol Airport, KiM Netherlands Institute for Transport Policy Analysis.

The law of constant travel time and trip rates, and the fundamental law of road congestion, are revelations to me. They explain very clearly why those traffic jams aren't about to disappear. But what I don't get is this: why do we carry on building 'missing links' and adding more lanes to motorways when this will only increase congestion? They must know this in the ministry where Arie Bleijenberg worked for such a long time, mustn't they? Rijkswaterstaat, the organisation formally responsible for implementing the ministry's decisions, and which also directs road planning and construction, is definitely aware. As long ago as 2001, it issued a publication of 95 pages, no less, about these laws.[31] And Amsterdam University's department of urban and regional planning knows about them too. When I ask Marco about it, he summarises the concept of constant travel time as follows:

Cycling Professor @fietsprofessor
Contrary to what you might think, it's not the distances we travel that stay constant, it's the time we spend travelling, while the distances are variable: they keep on increasing.

That's the centrifugal effect I referred to. Yet we continue to build more traffic lanes and tunnels. And more metro and railway lines. Because the law of constant travel time applies to all modes of transport. Thanks to the Intercity Direct service, it's easy for me to live in Rotterdam and work in Amsterdam. Once it would have taken 16 hours to walk from one city to the other, but now the journey takes just 41 minutes by rail. More spectacularly, 'super-commuter' Kate Simon was interviewed by the *Guardian* in 2018 about her weekly commute from Nice in the south of France to her senior marketing job in London.[32] Cheap air fares, coupled with the growing use of teleconferencing tools, have put 'super-commuting' within the reach of more people than ever before.

'There's no way of saving travel time,' Bleijenberg concludes. 'The only gain you can achieve is the distance you cover. And that's why the history of mobility can be viewed as an ongoing reduction in travel friction.'

Again, that sounds like something to do with colliding particles. And indeed, 'travel friction' turns out to be a technical term. 'It means we're forever trying to travel faster, more cheaply, and more comfortably over ever-increasing distances, but in the same amount of time,' Bleijenberg says. He's currently looking into how we can do that more sustainably: if we're not going to travel any less, then at least we could be polluting less on our journeys. He is engaged in a research project on the use of synthetic kerosene, produced using wind and solar energy, as an aircraft fuel.

'But won't that just push traffic congestion into airspace?' I ask. 'Won't it mean that we'll all have to queue up to board a plane instead, and won't it result in more and more congested skies?' After all, making cars 'cleaner' hasn't done anything to ease pressure on parking spaces or reduce tailbacks. And then something extraordinary happens. In the middle of Starbucks, Arie Bleijenberg starts reciting a poem in a dreamy voice:

> I didn't come here purposefully, you know —
> I wandered here, I wandered there at will
> because the tiny flowers I so love grow
> beneath tall trees in woodlands deep and still
> But now I'm here, I'll readily concede
> that I've arrived, yes, I am here indeed.[33]

'Wow,' I say.

'Pierre Kemp,' says Bleijenberg. 'It's lovely, isn't it? It's his attitude to life I like, too. And that's something else I keep thinking about: *why* are we so focused on increasing speed and efficiency? But I don't think we can tackle all our problems at the same time.'

I recognise that train of thought: ruminating on technical solutions — bike highways, electric cars, synthetic kerosene, showers at work — then, suddenly, lines from a poem, or, in my case, memories of a blissful, carefree holiday, emerge; thoughts that we swiftly thrust aside.

Because what we do at work has to be functional, doesn't it?

The Asphalt Machine Behind our Congested Roads

I publish a long article about the laws of road congestion and constant travel time and trip rates. But I have no answer to the question of why we continue to add extra lanes to motorways in the hope of avoiding congestion, when it's so patently obvious that it will fail.

This has to wait until I get a call from Jan Korff de Gidts. He's read my piece and wants to explain why we don't stop laying more asphalt, even though we know it won't help.

Korff de Gidts has been monitoring motorway construction by Rijkswaterstaat (the executive department of the Ministry of Infrastructure and Water Management) for more than 40 years. He began when the forest he loved, Amelisweerd (in the province of Utrecht), was uprooted to lay a ten-lane motorway through the area. In the 1970s and 1980s he was one of the activists who appealed against this development to the Council of State, thereby saving more trees from being felled. In the end, the road was laid in a cutting, which helped to limit noise pollution to some extent. But they failed to prevent it from being built altogether. Now Korff de Gidts is in the process of analysing a further extension of the same road, because the fundamental law of road congestion applies in this case too. It seems even a ten-lane motorway isn't enough to absorb expanding car use.

According to Korff de Gidts, the machine that's covering the Netherlands in asphalt runs automatically: widening a road is no longer a political decision. Why is that? 'The government uses predictions of road congestion that are based on traffic models. The prognoses contain a thing they call the I/C ratio. The I stands for intensity, the expected pressure on the road, and the C for capacity, how many cars can drive through in an hour.'[34]

The government policy documents setting out these prognoses, and the papers on the state of mobility, are based on a given level of economic growth and increasing pressure on motorways, leading to an increasingly unbalanced I/C ratio. If the expected motorway capacity is too low and the intensity too high, Rijkswaterstaat gives the minister for infrastructure and water management a warning: we're on our way to gridlock.

'The politicians have linked this reasoning to policy and planning,' Korff de Gidts explains. 'We now believe the prediction, so we make sure it's fulfilled: the more roads there are, the more cars, and the more new or wider roads.' After all, as we have learned, asphalt always attracts more cars in the long term.

The Mobility Policy Document published in September 2004, based in its turn on a civil service document about the I/C ratio, shows clearly how the asphalt machine works.[35] The future the document referred to was 2020. This was the forecast:

> *Traffic delays to double*
> By 2020 there will be traffic hold-ups not just during rush hour, but also, increasingly, at times of the day that are quieter now. In the absence of any further policy measures, traffic delays on the network of

arterial roads and motorways will increase to twice
the 2000 level by 2020. That can also be seen from
trends in vehicle hours lost.[36]

This is another prediction, like those listed by Arie
Bleijenberg, about how bad things are going to get. Such fore-
casts provide the basis for policies which, while doing nothing
to mitigate road congestion, do increase the amount of asphalt
on the ground. The 2004 Mobility Policy Document advocated
the massive expansion of the entire Dutch motorway network,
including the widening of the Amelisweerd cutting.

It was also at this time that they started looking into
extending the A16 near Rotterdam, the project later christened
'De Groene Boog'. Work on this project, which I passed on
an evening bike ride from my allotment, has only recently got
underway. So the analyses on which the development is based are
now over 15 years old.

A 'vehicle hour lost' refers to a car stuck in a traffic jam for an
hour, or 60 cars stuck in a tailback for a minute each. The aim is
to reduce the number of vehicle hours lost as far as possible. 'If
the models that produce the prognoses show that traffic intensity
is going to exceed capacity by a long way, traffic engineers say the
number of vehicle hours lost is going to increase,' explains Korff
de Gidts. 'And then you get demands to make the roads wider.
The media talk about bottlenecks, gridlock and clogged arteries.'

But in a system based on the logic of vehicle hours lost,
something fails to happen that should, says Korff de Gidts.
Motorists aren't offered any alternative, such as cycling or taking
public transport, because vehicles can't make such a choice, and
vehicles are the focus of the system. 'But people aren't vehicles.'

Nor is the notion of growth for growth's sake questioned.

'The new motorway will attract more motorists again, and that, paradoxically, means it'll produce an economic profit, because road users can drive faster and new road users will be sucked in. That's how the asphalt machine keeps on going.'

So more asphalt is laid, based on a line of argument that applies to vehicles, even though we've already known for a long time how people will react to the expansion: they'll travel even longer distances.

Korff de Gidts's account reminds me of the DOCTOR evaluation: people as projectiles. Similarly, the models used by the Ministry of Infrastructure and Water Management and by Rijkswaterstaat take precious little account of human behaviour or of how people respond to and interact with their surroundings. And they take no account at all of the fact that people, unlike their vehicles, are capable of making choices.

Korff de Gidts hasn't finished what he has to say yet. 'Around cities, it gets even worse. I'll send you a diagram. Got your email open?'

'Yes, go ahead.'

The Bottleneck

If *this* is your problem...

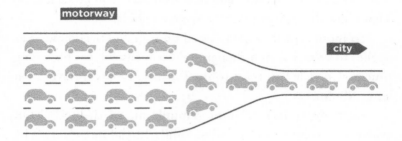

...then *this* isn't your solution

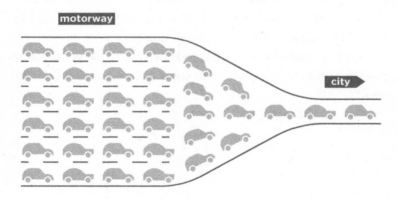

Source: Cees van de Brink, 'Kracht van Utrecht' group, adapted by *De Correspondent*.

'As you can see, traffic models represent motorways in a misleading way: they don't take any account of the motorway's environment,' says Korff de Gidts. 'But cars travelling along a major thoroughfare towards a smaller road have to go into cities and out again, don't they? And you can't usually widen the road in a built-up area. But central government just says: not our problem. So that's how you end up with bottlenecks.'

That's what the picture shows: more and more bottled-up cars forced to exit through too narrow a gap, so that their drivers instantly forfeit any travel time they may have saved on the newly widened motorway. 'So we fill up all the available space around and in cities with more and more cars,' says Korff de Gidts. 'By the way, do you know where the money comes from to build the roads which then get clogged up with even more slow-moving traffic?'

'I haven't a clue.'

'From our gas fields in Slochteren. The profits have gone into the Economic Structure Reinforcement Fund, FES. Have a look online.'

Once we've hung up, I check this. Between 1995 and 2010, the Economic Structure Reinforcement Fund invested just under €2 billion a year in facilitating longer journeys by investing in high-speed train lines and motorway expansions, some more successful than others. The money came from the sale of gas from the deposit at Slochteren.

I stare at the figures. True, using natural gas revenue to build infrastructure is a good deal more socially responsible than putting it in an overseas bank account, as happened with so much of Russia's oil revenue. It's a luxury that I can choose between three trains for my commute to Amsterdam, drive down from Rotterdam to the white cliffs of Picardy in just four hours, and order goods online that arrive the next day. It turns out that even the recreational cycle paths in Midden-Delfland, the area north of my allotment, were paid for by this Fund. I've benefited from it personally.

Yet those billions, I reflect, could also have been invested in education or social care, or in addressing the problems of the future. They could have been spent on pensions, as in Norway, or in raising the dikes further. The Delta Works, the flood defence infrastructure built to protect the land around the Rhine–Maas–Scheldt delta, were funded from gas revenues. And now, through an administrative mechanism, we've converted gas revenues into motorways, creating a heavily subsidised traffic system that's vulnerable to recurrent congestion.

Combating Congestion — A Black Hole

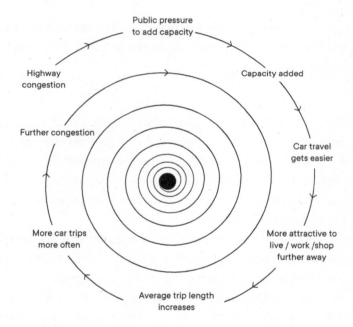

Source: D.A. Place, 'Urban transportation: policy alternatives', in Hanson & Giuliano (eds), *The Geography of Urban Transportation*, 2nd edn (Guilford Press, 1995). Reproduced with the permission of Guilford Press, adapted by *De Correspondent*.

Cycling Professor @fietsprofessor
And then people will use their cars for other trips. After all, they're conveniently parked in the allotted space at the front door.

Thanks to all the space we set aside for cars, they continue to proliferate. There are now 8.5 million in the Netherlands, a country of 17 million people.[37] The United Kingdom has a similar ratio: 31.7 million for a population of 67.22 million. In the United States, it's 108.5 million cars for 329.5 million people, and in Australia there are 19.8 million for 25.69 million people. China has 224.74 million cars — one car per three households.[38] The total number of passenger cars in the world is estimated at 1.4 billion and rising each year. Lease cars account for half of all new cars in the Netherlands.[39] A third of these new vehicles are 'four-by-fours' (SUVs), aka 'anti-social killing machines' (if knocked down by one of these, a pedestrian is between two and three times more likely to die).[40] Our roads are becoming more dangerous and more congested, while our cars are getting bigger and taking up more and more space.

And that trend costs a lot of money too — more than people imagine, as Arie Bleijenberg later tells me. If a driver knocks you down on the road, for instance, or if you develop an air-pollution-related respiratory complaint and run up medical bills, traffic engineers won't count your problems as part of the cost of car use.

Bleijenberg, however, has totted up those costs on the basis of government figures. According to his calculations, a bill for €21 billion goes unpaid every year — more than double the planned annual budget of the Ministry of Infrastructure and Water Management. 'Those costs are passed on to taxpayers, accident victims, and people with traffic-related health problems.'[41]

At the same time, accidents causing permanent injury can have certain economic benefits — albeit of a perverse kind. A person who suffers serious brain damage as a result of a traffic accident is a worker removed from the economic system. Yet the ongoing care that he or she then needs creates at least one job. And then there are all the technical devices that need to be developed for that person, as well as transport tailored to their individual needs.

How can you weigh the costs and benefits of such systems against each other? Is it even possible or ethical to do so in economic terms?

Rail travel doesn't involve the same extensive hidden costs. And since a train departs again with new passengers on board, far less public space goes to waste. That's why I initially see rail travel as a good alternative.

But then confusion strikes. Billions from the Economic Structure Reinforcement Fund were invested in rail too. As a result of the increased capacity, people are now taking trains more and travelling longer distances — and trains are increasingly oversubscribed.

Where will it end?

In the middle of Groningen's agricultural landscape, there's now to be a 3-km-long test centre for a hyperloop, the vacuum train that is Elon Musk's brainchild and which is supposed to whisk passengers within half an hour from Amsterdam to Paris or from New York to Washington. Dutch Railways are subsidising the experiment.

Should we really go on increasing speed, extending rail networks and airports, and making roads wider if the main effect of such change is to encourage people to travel even further? Will it really become second nature by 2050 to take a hyperloop or flight to work, in another country? And what then? Will we be taking interplanetary trips — to Mars with Elon Musk or Amazon's Jeff Bezos — because the conditions on this planet will no longer be bearable?

Building in the Green Heart of the Netherlands

The more I learn, the more questions arise. I talk to my colleague Jesse Frederik again. In his view, the idea that increasing speed only means that we'll cover longer distances is short-sighted: 'Land that's further away is cheaper. That's why industrial estates are always a long way out. That's why some people live in the commuter belt, so they can have a bigger home and a garden at a lower price, and others in Amsterdam, where they'll have a small home without a garden and pay a lot, but be close to their work. Mobility enables people to make these choices, based on weighing up different factors.'

That's true. But doesn't the same reasoning apply the other way round? Isn't land outside urban areas inexpensive precisely because we *made* travelling there comparatively cheap? If travel weren't cheap, land outside urban areas wouldn't be attractive — in fact, it might not even exist. Without cheap travel, we wouldn't have created the new Flevoland polder. Thanks to its construction, continued population growth hasn't obliged people in the inhabited areas of the country to live closer together.

'If a million people had decided to live in the same area, the number of people per square metre would have exploded,' says Jesse. 'Building would either have to be very high-density, or high-rise, but there are limits to how far you can take that, especially if you want to preserve green areas and historic buildings.'

Yes indeed, there is population growth to bear in mind as well. 'So are we going to allow high-rise building? Build in the countryside?' Jesse asks.

I ask Marco what he thinks.

> **Cycling Professor** @fietsprofessor
> You don't necessarily have to expand outwards or
> put up high-rise buildings to accommodate large
> numbers of people in a city. Look at De Pijp, for
> example — that's a very popular area to live in.

De Pijp, a district of Amsterdam built in the 19th century, has about 23,589 inhabitants per square kilometre.[42] These people aren't poor or disadvantaged. And the locals now live closer together than a century ago. 'In 1900, Amsterdam had an average of about 22,000 inhabitants per square kilometre. The average is only about 5,000 now,' Jesse tells me.

London has an average of 5,700 people per square kilometre. Compare that with a city like Manila (capital of the Philippines), where the figure is 43,000. Among European capitals, Paris is the most densely populated, with 21,000 people per square kilometre — a population density twice that of New York (10,000). I'm amazed to discover that the 19th-century districts of European cities, with their narrow streets and three- or four-storey houses, are home to nearly as many people per square kilometre as Manhattan, with all its skyscrapers. The explanation is that the tall buildings so typical of Manhattan are set much further apart, with far broader streets in between.[43]

The century of the car pulled us apart. Might we now be nearing the end of that century? For the last few years, De Pijp and De Nieuwe Pijp (built in 1920) have had a few streets without any demarcated parking spaces: car-owning residents have been offered a space in an underground garage. The only thing you can park in these streets now is your bike.

The Van Ostadestraat in De Nieuwe Pijp, 1981.

Source: Beeldbank Amsterdam (Amsterdam Photo Archive).

The Van Ostadestraat in De Nieuwe Pijp, 2017.

Source: Meredith Glaser.

> **Cycling Professor** @fietsprofessor
> Population growth might well be the reason we need
> to say that a standard parking space 1.7 metres long
> just isn't on any more. Making motorways wider just
> isn't on any more. The way we used to do things
> worked for a while — and now it no longer does.
> We mustn't build any new housing estates that are
> only accessible by car. And from now on, they must
> include all the basic facilities people need: schools, a
> library, a medical centre.

Marco sends me an image including two satellite photos.[44] The first of these shows the Valburg junction, an enormous four-leaf clover in the Betuwe region where the A15 and A50 motorways intertwine. The second, taken from the same altitude, shows the village of Valburg, which lies next to the junction.

You can clearly see that the junction is the same size as the village, which has nearly 2,000 inhabitants. A single motorway junction, in other words, takes up as much space as an entire village.

The Valburg junction (below) takes up the same space as Valburg village (above).

Source: Google Maps.

Could we organise our country in such a way that it would no longer be necessary to commute, as so many people have to today? I try to imagine what it might be like. The existing mega-carparks and spaghetti junctions could be replaced by residential areas, which would need to provide jobs, shops, schools, a library, and a hospital. That would give people's lives more of a local focus. But what if you wanted to change jobs, but you didn't want to or couldn't move house? Wouldn't such a change place some people at a disadvantage, particularly those with limited choice in finding new employment?

Everyone wants to be mobile: mobility is largely equated with freedom. No one wants to be bound to a particular location.

How complicated this is when you look at it in detail. I message Marco:

> **Thalia Verkade** @tverka
> It's a painful thing, changing the status quo.

> **Cycling Professor** @fietsprofessor
> That's the pain of half a century of spatial planning based on the notion that we can cut people's travel time by increasing the speed of travel. But what we're doing now hurts too, doesn't it? It's precisely by wanting to have a house and garden for everyone and, at the same time, wanting to make cities accessible to everyone, that we've already yielded up all our natural environment and open areas to motorways and housing estates that are ghost towns during the day. And that's the result of a political decision, too.

I keep losing sight of the fact that our status quo also represents a choice, with its pros and cons. What we have now seems like such a natural state of affairs. It's only after quite a while that it dawns on me why I can't work out how we might change the existing situation.

I've stumbled across one of the major issues in urban and regional planning: how space and traffic are interlinked, and how they could be interlinked.[45] That's a complex political issue on which everyone has their own views, and to which it's impossible to find a single solution.

Yet at the moment we're building motorways where a technical formula tells us we have to, to deal with bottlenecks in a pipeline system which, far from floating in thin air, lies squarely in our daily lives.

While I'm writing my article about the law of constant travel time and the fundamental law of road congestion, I make another discovery, leading to a further enigma. I find out that it's still possible to interview the man behind the law of constant travel time, transport economist Geurt Hupkes, now aged 90. Bert van Wee, who has taken over Hupkes's research at the Technical University of Delft, gives me his address and phone number.[46]

'Hupkes speaking!'

'Hello, this is Thalia Verkade. I'm a journalist at *De Correspondent.*'

'I can't really make out what you're saying ...'

A telephone conversation is too much of a strain for Geurt Hupkes, but his mind is still sharp, and he emails me to share an idea that's occurred to him recently. He thinks Marchetti's constant, the travel time budget, has been increasing for some time.

'I suspect that the time budget for journeys may well have increased considerably thanks to omnipresent communications technology,' he writes. 'These days, people make full use of the time they spend travelling, not only on public transport (WiFi in Intercity trains), but in cars as well (by using a hands-free kit or making a covert call on their mobile).'

This strikes a chord with me: ever since I've had unlimited 4G on my mobile, train journeys have seemed like less of a waste of time. I'm now just as happy to take a slower train to my employer's editorial offices in Amsterdam if it's quieter than the faster alternative. In essence, Dutch Railways provides me with a free workstation for flexible working. In Russia I sometimes used to work in our Lada with a Bluetooth earbud in.

But what does an increasing 'constant' mean? Are we spending even longer stuck in traffic jams and is rail becoming even more oversubscribed because we can now engage in other activities en route? Are we going to build even more roads and railway lines for that very reason, so we can deal with all the phone calls we're arranged to make?

And in that case, is there still any meaningful distinction between travelling and not travelling? Does 'travel time' have any meaning?

Clogged Arteries

On my bike trips from my allotment, with all these questions running through my mind, I watch the 'green arc' being built. First there's the digging: molehills 2 metres across. Then red and green pennants are planted in the soil. Then come mountains of sand. On top of these, I spot excavators that look like toys, so high up and so far above the horizon.

What a gigantic undertaking this is. The projected costs amount to almost €1 billion.[47]

It's technically advanced too. The new road will be linked with perfect precision to the other two motorways. The project is as meticulous as open-heart surgery. And that's just what it is. 'The A13/A16 will form a bypass around central Rotterdam,' in the words of the brochure aimed at local residents.

I ride through the Lage Bergse Bos, an area of urban woodland north-east of Rotterdam, under which De Groene Boog is to be laid. Long bundles of felled trees lie along the route of the future motorway. I stare at the information panel telling me that some trees had to be removed in any case because of ash dieback. What was here will be replaced by a more attractive natural environment, so they promise.

I send a photo to Marco.

Thalia Verkade @tverka
A bypass under the city's lungs.

Cycling Professor @fietsprofessor
I'm just reading Richard Sennett's *Building and Dwelling*, which discusses where the whole notion of arteries and bypasses for traffic comes from. I'll send you a summary.

I read what Marco sends me and buy the book. Richard Sennett, an American sociologist interested in towns and cities, has looked into the origins of the idea that urban settlements depend on circulation.

The fact that human blood is pumped around the body was discovered in the 18th century. From then on, circulation became a familiar metaphor for the workings of large-scale human structures like cities.

Sennett writes about Paris. After a terrible cholera epidemic and a major uprising in 1848, stemming from economic problems, the administration ordered the construction of a network of broad avenues straight through the medieval street plan. The old city, teeming with narrow, crooked streets, was streamlined, making it more difficult for rebellious Parisians to barricade the roads. The avenues provided enough room for military units on horseback, enabling them to control public space. These broad thoroughfares also provided enough space for rapid movement, which had previously been impossible and now suddenly led to dangerous situations: horses could now trot or gallop straight ahead for some way.

To regulate circulation through the city's arteries, one-way streets were brought in. In practice, that meant a ban on driving down certain streets in a particular direction: say 'Boo!' to horse-drawn carriages heading into oncoming traffic! The practice initially met with resistance. But steadily the street changed from a place for meeting other people into a place where traffic had to be able to circulate freely.

As I begin reading up on the history of traffic in the Netherlands, I discover what a strong impact the circulation metaphor has had here too. For instance, Frits Bakker Schut, head of public works in The Hague in the 1950s, ascribed 'anaemia' and 'hypertrophy' of the 'urban tissue' to the quadrupling during that decade of the number of cars on the road.[48]

Speaking about a contemporary radical plan to build two huge 'traffic arteries' through the centre of Utrecht, city councillor Wim Derks, a supporter, said: 'This diagnosis, the work of an expert, is as perfectly objective as a doctor's diagnosis of inflammation in a vital organ.'[49]

And Hendrik Kaasjager, Amsterdam chief of police, proposed in 1954 that a number of the city's canals should be filled in to create more space for motor traffic. Banning traffic from the city centre, as others had proposed in the past, would be tantamount to 'cutting off its circulation', as he put it.[50]

The idea that streets exist to channel motor vehicles, as if they were all thoroughfares, can now be seen in nearly every newspaper article that translates I/C ratios and Rijkswaterstaat's prognoses of road congestion into human language:

'The Netherlands nears gridlock'
Everywhere you look, the country's grinding to a halt.
Gridlock on roads and rail, as well as in cities and
airspace, is paralysing transport and the economy.
These harmful effects are set to snowball, says an
alarming report from the Ministry of Infrastructure.
(*De Telegraaf*, 2017)

'Randstad suffers from clogged arteries'
Gridlock. The roads are full, the trams and trains
brimming with passengers: a little longer, and the
conurbation in the west of the country will reach
paralysis unless something is done. But politicians
underestimate the problems, and the budget available
is paltry.
(*NRC Handelsblad*, 2017)

'Royal Dutch Touring Club warns — even local roads
increasingly congested, more congestion in 2019'
The number of traffic jams rose by 17 per cent in 2019.
This congestion is no longer restricted to motorways.
Even local and provincial roads are now increasingly
prone to blockages.
(*RTL Nieuws*, 2019)

The metaphors of clogged arteries and paralysis suggest a
collective problem that threatens our very lives. That's precisely
why I was so keen to help solve the issue of road congestion —
through bike highways. They call new motorways 'missing links'
and 'bypasses', but you might equally well call them 'wounds' or
'scars in the landscape'.[51] Adding more lanes to a motorway in
order to tackle road congestion is rather like a fat man loosening
his belt to combat obesity.[52]

Carrying out a bypass operation isn't risk-free. De Groene Boog rapidly develops complications. *Wethouder* Langenberg admits to the media that it's not going to be altogether feasible to make it 'inaudible and odour-free'. 'Locals will smell the A13/A16 after all', says a headline in the *Algemeen Dagblad*, meaning that they'll have to breathe polluted air.

Electric cars won't solve this problem: they'll carry on producing pollution. Car brakes produce fine particulate matter and tyre abrasion releases large quantities of microplastics into the air, the sea, and our bodies.[53] That was something I hadn't realised when I wrote my first, enthusiastic pieces on mobility about the electric car as a solution to CO_2 emissions.

It's a painful discovery that repeatedly brings a frown to my face as I watch my two little boys bounding about on the trampoline on our little green island, our allotment surrounded by the sea of asphalt.

What's Your Number Plate?

Why had I, too, viewed car ownership as the norm? Was it because my partner and I had been so dependent on our car in the vastness of Russia? In Rotterdam, we live between three supermarkets, next to a DIY store, and within cycling distance of the doctor, our childcare, the school, two hospitals, and two libraries. We don't have to drive regularly for work. Are we really still going to buy a car? We weigh up the pros and cons.

A car would make it much easier for us to visit my partner's brother, who recently moved to a place it's really hard to reach, in the 'Green Heart' of the Netherlands. Frankly, it's pretty ironic that you need a car to visit a region with that name.

It would also be easier for us to get away to the country for a weekend — that's something we enjoy. So the next time we have a holiday, we opt for an experiment. How about going to a holiday park in the rural Veluwe region, with two children who can't yet walk very far, without a car?

Although not exactly easy, the journey is interesting: my partner boards the train with his bike, laden with baby equipment, and then cycles from the Ede-Wageningen station, with our eldest son perched at the front, through the woods to the park. From the station, I take the bus, lugging the double pushchair, the trekking rucksack, and our baby, and for the last mile or so I plod uphill along a road without a pavement. 'What's your number plate?' asks the receptionist when I arrive.

Once we're settled in, we continue our ruminations: why is it that people enjoy going on holiday here so much? Isn't it because you have to slow to a walking pace if you want to drive up to your bungalow to unload your luggage? And because you then park at a distance from where you're staying, so your children can run off along the footpaths in clean air, carefree and safe, while you can enjoy a coffee or a drink in peaceful natural surroundings?

If we enjoy this so much on campsites and holiday parks, we reflect, why shouldn't we try to organise our own streets in the same way? The way things are now, many of us hurry to escape from our home environment as fast as possible in everyday life. The area around our homes is so unpleasant that we spend our holidays in bungalow parks to avoid being surrounded by cars.

After a weekend of scattering peanuts for the squirrels at our door, we come to a decision. We don't need our own car after all.

II

Caution — Children at Play

How have cars changed the environment we live in?

In its early days, my Rotterdam neighbourhood must have had the same sort of appeal as a rural holiday park does now. While I'm waiting to meet a civil servant from the local authority, I stroll along my street and try to picture how it would have looked then.

In 1906, when it was new, there were probably hardly any cars parked in front of the houses, if indeed there were any at all. And presumably there wouldn't have been many bicycles either — they, too, were just beginning to appear on the scene.[1]

Martin Guit, the local authority's mobility strategy officer, turns up on foot. He's in his forties, with fair hair and small glasses. Although it's a chilly day, he's happy to walk around with me and explain why my street looks the way it does: which aspects have developed organically, and which are the result of interventions by the local authority. 'You can see straight away that this neighbourhood wasn't built with cars in mind,' he opens.

We begin by walking to one end, where the pavement on the side with the even-numbered houses runs across the street, joining up with the pavement on the other side. If you want to drive out of the street, you have to cross this raised stretch. 'Why is there a pavement running right across the street at this end, but not at the other?' I ask.[2]

It turns out that this has a specific name in Dutch traffic-engineering jargon: it's called an '*uitritconstructie*' (which translates literally as an 'exit construction', but might be termed a 'street intersection ramp').

Street intersection ramp linking pavements on either side of the street.
Source: Thalia Verkade.

'A lot of what you're looking at is the result of 'Sustainable Safety' guidelines,' Guit explains.

Sustainable Safety (Duurzaam Veilig) is a design philosophy dating back to 1991, created by the Dutch Institute for Road Safety Research (SWOV) and further developed through CROW guidelines. (Mobility policy seems to be awash with four-letter abbreviations.)

Every year, SWOV publishes a report covering not only the number of lives lost through traffic accidents, but also risks such as elderly people riding electric bikes, or motorists using phone apps while driving. It then offers recommendations on how to make our streets safer. In 2017, the managing director, Peter van der Knaap, stressed the need for traffic safety to be made a national priority.[3] According to SWOV, driving over 30 km/h (slightly under 20 mph) in residential areas is dangerous and should be made impossible.[4]

The thinking behind Sustainable Safety is that, given human fallibility, the traffic environment needs to be engineered to rule out serious accidents. One of the essential aspects is biomechanics, the definition of which again suggests an exact science involving elementary particles: 'Aligning the speed, direction, mass, dimensions and protection of traffic participants.' Humans are seen as a collection of vulnerable molecules that need to be protected and to protect each other by technological means to avoid damage.

Guit explains that Sustainable Safety ranks streets from lower to higher 'orders'. 'Your street is a lower-order 30 km/h zone, as you can see from the sign in front of the intersection ramp,' he says, pointing at the raised stretch of pavement I had been so curious about. 'And you can tell this from the speed bumps as well.'

We walk round the corner and Guit points out the roads ranked as higher-order. 'At the end of your street there's a road with a speed limit of 50 km/h, the Bergselaan, a "stroomstraat" ("flow street"). This in its turn leads into another "flow street", the Gordelweg, which then links up with the slip roads to and from the motorway.' The motorway, which belongs to the highest 'order', is classed as a 'stroomweg' ('flow road'), that is, a road whose function is to allow traffic to flow through at speed. It's by analogy with the motorway and the concept of 'flow roads' that urban traffic engineers and local civil servants speak of 'flow streets' running through the city. These are streets that channel plenty of traffic and have few other 'functions'; that is, they are not designed to be places where people want to spend any length of time.[5]

We've walked around the corner, where the intersection ramp at the end of our street links up with a pavement which continues onto a second intersection ramp at the end of the street parallel.

Suddenly a man without a coat on appears in front of us. 'From the council, are you?' he asks Guit and me.

Guit nods.

'I've been trying to get through to them for the last 18 months about how it's all going to pot here. I live on the ground floor and my office is up there.' He points at the first floor of his house. 'Nothing escapes me. Not long ago someone was run over and killed up there.' Now he's pointing at the Gordelweg, the 'flow street' towards the slip road to the motorway. I recall that one of my neighbours, a 70-year-old lady, was run over and killed there last summer, together with her dog. 'And this is where we'll have the next fatal accident, you mark my words! There's cars using our pavement as a rat run!'

There's no need for Mr Vos (he doesn't give his first name) to give any further explanation. While we're talking, one motorist after another drives over the intersection ramp without stopping. People use this residential street as a cut-through — you can avoid an intersection and a set of traffic lights by turning off here. But that means you have to drive over Mr Vos's pavement.

'Ten children from this row of houses play here, and other local kids as well,' he says. 'I put out one of those big green tortoises to warn drivers, but I can guarantee there's going to be an accident one of these days.'

The hi-vis green plastic tortoise, 1.70 metres tall (nearly five foot six), holding a red flag, is known as 'Victor Veilig' ('veilig' meaning 'safe'). It warns drivers that there are children playing nearby. Some Victors are battered from having been run over.

'The best advice I can give you,' Guit tells Mr Vos, 'is to carry on nagging the council. I'm not responsible for this area, but get in touch with the civil servants who are, and with local politicians.'

'I've been going to every neighbourhood council meeting for the last year and a half!' retorts Mr Vos, his voice rising. 'But there hasn't been a blind bit of change!'

An Audi rumbles up onto the street intersection ramp at speed. I gesture — slower, please! The driver raises a hand and brakes.

'He hasn't much choice now there's three of us here,' snaps Mr Vos. 'But I did the same thing the other day when I was here on my own, and the fellow got out and threatened to punch me.'

'Carry on reporting these incidents,' says Guit. He explains that the official structures are complex and that there aren't necessarily enough funds available to do everything that needs doing.

Guit and I stroll to the other end of my street. At the very end we walk on to a road classed as a higher 'order', the Bergweg, another 'flow street'. There's no street intersection ramp here, but a zebra crossing. Guit doesn't know why it's different at this end any more than I do. 'For international road users, zebra crossings are clearer than street intersection ramps,' he guesses. 'They know it means pedestrians have right of way.' But is it safer?

'A bit further along the Bergweg, another person was run over and killed last year, on the zebra crossing,' I say, feeling a cold shiver down my spine. The victim had been a young man, 19 years old, just out of high school.

Strolling back towards my house, we pass a junction where my street crosses a narrow side street. 'Why isn't there an intersection ramp here?' I ask.

'Because this junction involves two streets with a 30 km/h speed limit,' says Guit. 'So you can't lay any extra paving here, according to the Sustainable Safety rules.'

'Is that really so out of the question?' I ask. It would be such an improvement. If the pavement ran across the road to the opposite side, my children would be able to cross to play with the neighbours' children, and vice versa.

'You'd have to prove it was safer than the existing situation,' Guit says. 'But it might be confusing. And anything that might cause confusion is rated as less safe. What traffic engineers want is predictability.'

When I later raise the subject with a local mother, I see what he means. 'I think it would be dangerous,' she says. 'The kids would think it was a pavement, but drivers would just carry on regardless.' Then we'd have the same problem as Mr Vos.

'Isn't it strange to think there was hardly any traffic in 1906, when all this was new?' I remark to Guit.

'Maybe we should go back to that,' he replies. 'Sustainable Safety was a big improvement after cars were introduced, though. Until the sixties or seventies there weren't even any traffic bumps and you could do 50.' 50 km/h here? With no traffic bumps? In the street where I live? Compared with that, it's much safer now.

'But maybe it's time to take the next step,' says Guit. 'Reduce the limit to 15 km/h (just under 10 mph) or 10 km/h (just over 6 mph) in residential areas.'

At such low speeds, there'd be no need for pavements or street intersection ramps.

I point at the play area over the street, with its chicken 'springer' and slide. 'Our sons and the little girl from next door like playing there, and they don't need to be supervised. But they can't cross the road to get to the playground on their own.'

Guit nods. He's keen to have quiet streets with little traffic, but first you need a council that's willing to take that sort of action. Which in turn depends on people voting for parties that include such proposals in their manifestos — the street as a space for people first, then traffic. 'We're gradually seeing more parties starting to think that way,' he says.

We say goodbye at my front door and I go in. It's so strange.

'The country's reaching gridlock', newspapers warn: we see this as a huge threat, traffic must keep on flowing. And that's why I have to squeeze my toddler's hand so tightly that he can't slip out of my grasp on his way over to his favourite chicken ride.

This Is How Long it Takes a Car to Stop

If you brake at 35 km/h (just over 21.5 mph), you'll cover a further 16 metres (about 17.5 yards) before coming to a standstill

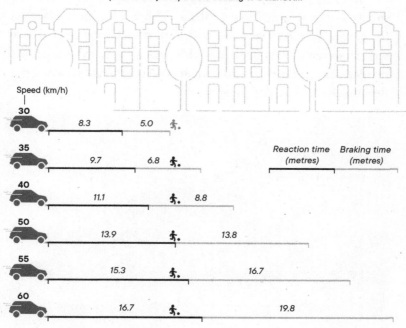

Source: Verkeer & Meer (https://www.verkeerenmeer.nl).

Mr Correct

That evening, I search the web for old photos of my street. The most interesting ones show the Bergweg at the point where it meets another flow street, the Benthuizerstraat. The two paved roads meet at the point where they run out of the city under the A20, like the two prongs of a cake fork pointing upwards.

In 1908, when my street had just been built, the area around the cake fork was just like a village. There was a post office on the corner, with a coffeehouse called Transvalia next door. These streets weren't through roads: this was an area where people strolled about, and there was a small tram that trundled along the Benthuizerstraat to the River Maas.

The junction of the Benthuizerstraat and the Bergweg in Rotterdam, 1908. My house is close by, in a side street running off the Bergweg.

Source: Antiquariaat Voet.

The same junction in 1932.

Source: Antiquariaat Voet.

By 1932 the Bergweg had acquired tram rails. The coffee-house had grown by a couple of storeys and become the Victoria Theatre, later converted into a cinema. This part of the city was known for its cultural life and there were plenty of people out and about on foot. What I find most striking in the photo from 1932 is the little boy, about the same age as my eldest son, crossing the street on his own. That's unimaginable today. This is now one of Rotterdam's ten most dangerous junctions.[6]

The junction in 2020, with the boarded-up Correct
building on the corner.

Source: Boudewijn Bollmann.

I know the building that was once a theatre as the gigantic
electronics store Correct, which took up the corner until
recently. Driving into Rotterdam, one of the first things you'd see
would be its oversized orange sign. Correct was one of the city's
best-known shops in the 1980s and 1990s, a huge emporium that
attracted people from all over, in search of the latest gadgets.

I come across an interesting interview with 'Mr Correct',
as the owner, Harry de Jong senior, was known. In 1988, he
told *Het Vrije Volk* newspaper how he saw electronics as a major
contributor to resolving the traffic congestion problem. 'First and
foremost, telecommunications enable people to complete their
work wherever they happen to be, so they don't have to go out.
You can see this from the massive demand for fax systems of all
kinds. Computers and photocopiers are linked via telephone lines
or satellites. Increasingly, meetings will be held via videophone,
saving precious travel time.'[7]

Mr Correct also correctly predicted that cars would one day
have a system to locate traffic jams and propose an alternative

route. A smart forecast. The visionary never predicted what the internet would mean for his own company, though. In recent years, Correct has lost ground to Coolblue, another Rotterdam firm that sells similar products online. The building on the corner is empty now. Local media came up with suggestions — couldn't it be turned into a cinema again? Project developers had ideas of their own — couldn't they convert it into apartments?

I take another look at the photo of the coffeehouse, with the men chatting in the street in front of it. At the theatre and its lively surroundings a quarter of a century later.

Then, going outside, I gaze at the dilapidated corner building and the roads flanking it, where motor traffic predominates. This was once a really attractive area. How could we have handed over control of the place where we live to this extent?

How the Car Conquered America

It wasn't a foregone conclusion, I soon discover. When cars were still a novelty, drivers were expected to conduct themselves with humility. This is made clear in advice written in 1908 by the president of a Chicago motorists' association and published by several newspapers, including the Dutch *Algemeen Handelsblad*.[8]

If you were at the wheel of an automobile, it was incumbent on you as a motorist to abide by the customs of the town you were in. And just like at my allotment, the rights of the slowest were prioritised:

> Never drive around a corner without giving a warning signal.
> In crowded streets, it is folly to attempt to drive past others. The few moments gained are but a paltry compensation for the danger incurred.

Drivers were expected to conduct themselves with modesty and gallantry:

> It is better to drive very slowly or to stop than to trust your own ability to avoid others.
> Whenever, in a moment of great danger, the choice falls between a fellow human being and your own automobile, it is always the latter that must be sacrificed.

Finally, the last tip reveals a profound conviction that this was an ethical issue:

> You must always remember that although a pedestrian weighs one hundred and fifty pounds and your motorcar three thousand, this is not one of the cases in which might is right.

Those were the prevailing mores in my neighbourhood's early years, too. So what happened?

Marco recommends another book to me, Peter Norton's *Fighting Traffic*. Norton, an American historian of technology, writes about opposition to the rise of mass car use in 1920s America.

I had already spent some time researching the period when Henry Ford's new production line first made cars affordable in the United States. The number of Ford Model Ts grew by the day.[9] (Fun fact: they were all black because that was the colour that dried fastest.)[10] But at the same time, more and more people were being knocked down and killed. Motor vehicles had been supposed to solve the problems associated with horse-drawn vehicles — which had caused numerous accidents, and were noisy and smelly[11] — but cars' speed, compact mass, and popularity soon led to far more problems.

Between 1920 and 1930, Norton writes, 200,000 people died in motor traffic accidents in the United States. There were fatal accidents with horse-drawn vehicles too: around 2,500 a year in England and Wales between 1901 and 1905.[12] Fatalities involving horse-drawn conveyances also ran into the thousands in the United States.[13] But American statistics from those early years show how the 'pleasure automobile' perpetuated and aggravated the problem: while the number of fatal accidents involving horse-drawn vehicles remained high but stationary between 1907 and 1911, the number of recorded fatalities involving cars increased four-fold over the same period.[14]

With their intimidating speed, cars caused chaos, disrupting normal urban life. The police thought motor vehicles should be banned from built-up areas. Parents, particularly mothers who had lost children, protested with posters portraying the car as a monster. 'DON'T KILL A CHILD' screamed billboards erected by the Illinois authorities.

But Ford, the only really sizeable automotive manufacturer in the early days, continued to produce growing numbers of cars, accompanied by growing numbers of drivers. What goes for roads applies equally to cars, it seems: build more, and more people will use them. And the American people divided into two camps. Some maintained that cars had no place in the streets of a town or city. Others, however, concluded that the problem was the city itself, that streets must be restructured in the interests of safety and efficiency. In many American cities, streetcars (trams) were less than satisfactory: too slow, too expensive, and too infrequent. Now there was a cheap, liberating alternative — and to accommodate it, the city must adapt.

Perhaps these new drivers experienced the same sense of freedom that I felt when the internet first appeared. Suddenly I no longer had to wait for information or make my way to the library in all weathers, and boredom became a thing of the past. Later, the World Wide Web made its way onto our mobiles, in the form of 4G, then 5G — total freedom! But that made us dependent on our phones and the companies that provide us with mobile access.

Similarly, 100 years ago people came to depend on car companies for their transport. And just as we couldn't live without the internet now we have it, the newfound freedom brought by the car and enjoyed by many had to be facilitated.

I continue reading Norton's book, and Marco gives me a summary of another he's just read, David Prytherch's *Law, Engineering and the American Right-of-Way*, which reveals that the first people to address the problems caused by cars in cities were plumbing engineers. In the past they had installed water pipes, now they turned their attention to roads; these could also be viewed as a kind of pipe, through which motor traffic needs to flow smoothly and unimpeded. Circulation was more than just a metaphor, then.

Putting free mobility for cars before the needs of pedestrians converted the street into 'vehicular space'. Even the pavements, the margins to which pedestrians were now consigned, were part of this vehicular space, following the engineers' geometric logic.[15]

More and more Americans, Norton writes, came to embrace this logic. Where people had once been urged not to kill anyone, they were now urged not to get themselves killed. The authorities began to instil this message in their citizens: if you were on foot, you were to keep to the side of the road. In this way, responsibility for safety was transferred to the most vulnerable road user. Children who had previously played out in the street were now assigned a space of their own, in playgrounds.

———

Norton uses one particular word to demonstrate how American public opinion reversed in the space of ten years.

Originally, 'jaywalker' was the term used for someone wandering about in the street like a country bumpkin or 'jay', out of sync with modern times; today, it means a pedestrian crossing a road at the wrong place. It was a little-used word until the city of San Francisco included it in a public information campaign about traffic in 1920. The campaign instructed pedestrians on 'the dangers of jaywalking'. But was it walking in the street that caused the danger? Wasn't it the driving of vehicles?

In 1925, the police, who had argued just a few years before that motorists had no business driving in cities, arrested no fewer than 83 people in Washington DC for jaywalking. These people escaped prison on condition that they became co-founders of a Careful Walkers' Club. Their membership was publicly announced.

Views were starting to change. After 1930, Norton shows, the prevailing opinion was that people who simply walked out into the road were jaywalkers, and that they, rather than motorists, needed to adjust their behaviour. More and more cities and states began to make the act of spontaneously crossing the road a punishable offence.

Never before had I realised that language could play so crucial a role in the acceptance of radical change.

At the same time, encouraged by the automotive industry, a shift took place in the popular imagination, from driving as 'a danger to the city' to driving as 'a question of freedom'. That notion still underpins most car advertisements. And the car did bring freedom and adventure. Unlike the train or the tram, it could take you just about anywhere at any time of day. Particularly if roads could be further adjusted to accommodate drivers even more.

The installation of parking meters, writes Norton, shored up the idea that cars were an integral part of city life. Sure, you now had to pay to be allowed to park your car next to the pavement, but at least that brought an end to the discussion about whether it was really such a good idea for everyone to be able to drive their car into town. You were paying for the privilege, weren't you? Excise duty on petrol had the same effect; you were now paying the state to be allowed to use your car, which ended the discussion about whether it was really such a good thing to drive everywhere. Street space, once a public good, had become an economic commodity.

Traffic Engineers Arrive in the Netherlands

'Do you know how the road traffic system in this country came to be the way it is?'

During a break at one of the many mobility events I now attend, a tall man with round spectacles comes over to me. He immediately answers his own question: 'It was the Marshall Plan.'

He introduces himself as Marcus Popkema and tells me he wrote his doctoral thesis on the origins of traffic engineering as an academic discipline in the Netherlands.[16] Now he teaches at the Windesheim University of Applied Sciences in Zwolle, on the very course taken by the student who had offered the DOCTOR analysis of chip cones.

'I'd like to hear all about it,' I say.

So one Friday morning I catch the train to Zwolle. What I'd learned about Marshall aid in my secondary school history lessons was this: much of Europe lay in ruins after World War II, and the United States came to help us rebuild.

What I hadn't been taught, and what Popkema's thesis makes clear, is that this was also a means to boost America's economy by greasing the wheels for US businesses that were keen to offer their services and market their products in Europe.

The Windesheim University of Applied Sciences isn't far from the train station in Zwolle: walk through a subway under a motorway and you're there. Popkema shakes my hand and leads me into an empty room with a list of the full names of all the lecturers hanging on the wall. Totting them up, I see about half are women and half men.

'Does that reflect the gender breakdown among the students, too?' I ask.

'No, there are a lot more men,' Popkema says. 'Incidentally, the course isn't called Traffic Engineering any more, but Spatial Planning — Mobility. The word "mobility" is supposed to attract more female students.'

'Does it?'

'We've gone up from one to two female students a year now,' says Popkema, with a poker face. 'Not statistically significant.'

We sit down at a white table, and he starts to talk: 'The interests of the petrol, car and tyre manufacturers crossed the Atlantic along with the Marshall Plan. Dutch engineers, people with a technical background, were funded by the Americans to attend conferences held by the IRF, the International Road Federation.'

Although the name sounds neutral, the IRF was set up in 1948 — the year the Marshall Plan got under way — by a number of petrol companies and an association of American car manufacturers and tyre producers.

The IRF's raison d'être, Popkema says, was to boost US industry: to promote car use and the building of road infrastructure, both in the United States and elsewhere. Offices opened in London and Paris. And Dutch professionals went to the United States to learn from traffic engineers, a professional group that didn't yet exist in the Netherlands. 'There were courses, congresses and journals there, and once you had a qualification you could now call yourself a traffic engineer,' Popkema explains. The professionalisation of this niche area gave it authority and influence. 'The Dutch delegations that attended the American conferences came home convinced that the Netherlands needed traffic engineers too.'

By now, the Americans had set out their vision of traffic engineering in works such as the *Highway Capacity Manual*, which explained how to build a maximum-efficiency highway network. The manual was published by the Transportation Research Board (TRB) of the National Academy of Sciences in 1950. The TRB still exists, Marco later tells me. Every year it hosts the world's biggest international conferences on mobility, with many thousands of attendees. Dutch traffic engineers continue to take part.

In the lecturers' staffroom in Zwolle, Popkema gives me an example of how motorway logic took over the streets of the Netherlands: 'In the mid-1960s, the Ministry of Transport and Water Management set up its own traffic engineering service. This produced a manual called *Motorway Design Guidelines*, a Dutch version of the *Highway Capacity Manual*. Then they came out with the *Non-Motorway Design Guidelines*, which was based on the first manual. See how it works?'

'You mean, if a road wasn't a motorway, it was now a "non-motorway"?'

'Exactly. The mindset that puts efficiency and traffic flow first — which is so much in evidence in motorway design — also came to dominate the design of other traffic situations. Including those in ordinary residential streets. Ever heard the term "under-lying road network"?'

I'd come across the expression in the report 'Bypasses voor bereikbaarheid' (Bypasses for Accessibility), produced by the TNO, the Dutch Organisation for Applied Science. The 'underlying road network' means all the roads and streets in the country apart from motorways. According to the report's authors, the underlying road network can be used to absorb traffic from congested motorways: streets where people live reduced to run-off collectors to relieve an overflowing drain.

'So a sort of template has been created, based on motorways, and it now determines the way we look at roads and streets in general?' I ask.

'Yes. And even you unconsciously think in the same way. "Bike highways" — I thought that was an interesting choice of word in your "cycling versus congestion" articles ... It's a term derived from motor traffic, when you think about it.'

'I realise that now,' I say. I've since come across similar terms used internationally: 'bicycle motorways' in Germany, 'cycle superhighways' in Britain (now 'cycleways').

'The sheer diversity of the terms in use for this type of cycle path shows we're still conceptualising them in different ways', says Popkema. 'Is the main point of these cycle routes that they're fast, that you can cycle without interruption, or something else? Anyway, at some point a coinage crystallises and becomes standard. Once that happens, there's no longer any flexibility in how you interpret what you see in real life. And then you get guidelines with terms like "non-motorways", and we construct reality based on that.'

Popkema accompanies me out of the building. In front of the university, we stop at a fence about 200 metres long. 'They put up this fence a few days ago to keep the various streams of traffic separate, to sort them more efficiently and guarantee a higher level of safety,' he says.

The fence ensures that students walking to Windesheim can't cross the road here and hold up the traffic in the IJsselallee behind it, which might eventually result in congestion on the A28.

Amsterdam Slams on the Brakes

In a full-page article headed 'Roads Crisis', which appeared in a 1965 issue of the *Gereformeerd Gezinsblad* newspaper, I spy a familiar metaphor about how our infrastructure's increasingly clogged arteries are threatening to kill us. Here, though, it isn't just life in the cities, but the economy as a whole that is in mortal danger. 'Roads, especially our national roads, are the arteries that channel traffic and transport. But if they clog up and traffic flows are seriously obstructed, that will hold back the healthy development of our country and a healthy economy.' The newspaper italicises the last sentence of the article: *'If our roads become clogged up, it will cost time and money.'*

By now, economic growth and the success of US lobbying meant that over a million Dutch owned a car. Cities had to adapt.

Then an American urban planner, David Jokinen from Detroit, who had turned up in The Hague in the late 1950s thanks to the United Nations, and who was now a technical adviser to the province of South Holland, expressed some radical ideas.[17] He argued that, following the successful Delta Plan that defended the country against flooding, a vision of equal scope and ambition was needed for our roads.

David Jokinen, the young 'master planner', 'traffic engineer', and 'spatial planning expert' from America: it's fascinating to read in old newspapers how this man, under all kinds of titles, managed to find journalists ready to provide a platform for his 'revolutionary ideas' from the United States. I think back to my own enthusiastic articles about Elon Musk's vision for the future of mobility.[18] It's striking how willing we are to have Americans determine the future of our country.

Jokinen published books, of which the best-known was *Geef de stad een kans* (Give the City a Chance), funded by the Dutch importer of Fiat and brought to politicians' attention by the Road Foundation (Stichting Weg).

The Road Foundation is another of those supposedly neutral names. It sounds like an association working for the common good, but was actually an organisation set up in 1968 by oil companies, car dealers, and a number of other businesses and groups with a vested interest in the automobile industry.[19]

So Jokinen seems to have been a pawn of the developing Dutch car lobby, and his ideas were imbued with American convictions about the nature of a city, which would have a central business district that people used cars and motorways to reach, later to return to their homes on the periphery.

Rotterdam was the biggest Dutch city to get a kind of central business district — the office blocks around the train station, where street life is conspicuous by its absence. Jokinen thought that Amsterdam, too, should modernise and free up space for a central business district. But the locals rebelled.

The battle for the streets of Amsterdam at the beginning of the 1970s: the more I discover, the more astounded I am that I've never heard of it before. I did know about the car-free Sundays of the time, and that in 1973 you could roller-skate along the motorway, thanks to the oil crisis in the Middle East. But that there had been a genuine revolution in central Amsterdam, with locals ranging from the lowest to the highest social stratum and from Left to Right, opposing the demolition of city neighbourhoods to make way for a new metro line and highway — that was something I'd never been taught at school.

By 1967, Jokinen had a plan for the Dutch capital:

> The proposals for Amsterdam will result in a brand-
> new system of six broad access roads, large sections
> of which will run through the existing urban fabric
> of the neighbourhoods due for regeneration, such as
> the Kinkerbuurt and De Pijp. These 'city highways'
> will channel traffic to the rim of Amsterdam's inner
> canal district, to the historic heart of the city, the
> Singelgracht, and will end, for the time being, in large
> purpose-built parking garages.[20]

Jokinen rejected the idea for a metro, which was mooted by the Amsterdam municipal authority, as far too costly. What he envisaged was a light railway running level with the city, along-side the new highways. But many of the locals were against his proposals.[21] What they wanted were affordable homes, conservation of historic buildings, and safe streets for their children.[22] An unexpected alliance emerged between conservative citizens, long-established residents, and the protest generation.

Film footage exists of the revolt against plans to demolish the Nieuwmarkt neighbourhood to build a new highway, and it is amazing.[23] To protect houses, squatters strung rope bridges across the street from the upper storey of one house to another, while residents protested at ground level. One man obtained listed building status for a house in the middle of the planned highway route, protecting it from demolition.

Nieuwmarkt: the rope bridge over the Kranboomsloot, 9 March 1975.
Source: Bert Verhoeff/Anefo.

I think of Jan Korff de Gidts, the man who explained to me
the impact of calculating I/C ratios, who had played a leading role
in similar protests against the construction of the Amelisweerd
cutting near Utrecht, a decade later.[24] The footage of this is
equally striking, I discover. The riot police, acting on government
instructions, dragged the 'Friends of Amelisweerd' out of the
treetop huts they'd built to save the trees from felling. While the
Friends' interim injunction against the forest clearance was still
before the court, the authorities ordered the trees to be bulldozed.
It took just a few hours.

In the 1970s, the Dutch public refused simply to accept unpop-
ular decisions imposed from above. This was part of a wider
trend in much of Western Europe towards questioning and often
opposing traditional authority, and in the Netherlands it had a
big impact. Again and again, journalists single this resistance out

as *the* reason our transport infrastructure is so different to that elsewhere in the world.

In the summer of 2019 *The Guardian* published a spectacular collection of Dutch anti-car and pro-cycling posters from the 1960s to the 1980s.[25] Many of them were the work of the ENWB (standing for the Real Dutch Touring Club, though the initial E can also stand for 'First', 'Only', or 'Fair'), now the Dutch Cyclists' Union, which was set up in 1975 and remains one of the world's biggest and most influential cycling associations. The name ENWB was a sarcastic reference to the ANWB, the Royal Dutch Touring Club. Originally an association for cyclists, under pressure from organisations representing motorists' rights, the ANWB had morphed in the mid-1920s into an interest group for people who saw roads and streets as places where you should be able to drive at speed.[26] Today, it's the Netherlands' main lobby for motorists.

On YouTube, I discover a documentary — again British-made — about the White Bicycle Plan, featuring an in-depth interview with Robert Jasper Grootveld of the Provo counter-culture movement about his ideas on mobility.[27] I had heard of the white bicycle idea, a hippyish plan for bike-sharing. It was made world-famous by John Lennon and Yoko Ono, who were photographed at the Amsterdam Hilton with a white bike, given to them by a Provo activist, on their bed.[28] But I hadn't realised that the plan was also a protest against capitalism and that it was intended to provide 'liberation from the car-monster'.

Browsing the Web, I discover more and more. A photo of a 1977 die-in, for instance: 8,000 people, many of them parents with their young children, cycled to Amsterdam's Museumplein square to protest against the violence resulting from car use in their city.[29] That image, Marco later tells me, still inspires activists worldwide to hold similar die-ins.

———

So what happened to Jokinen's proposals?

In the end, only a tiny majority in the Amsterdam City Council (23 to 22) voted against pursuing his city highway plan.[30] But it was still a majority.

You can see the result where the Jodenbreestraat runs into the Sint Antoniebreestraat: the street narrows abruptly and becomes more crooked again, winding through a centuries-old plot of land. There's also a small memorial to the battle for Amsterdam — a boundary post resting on the back of a tortoise, the whole made up of recycled fragments taken from broken monuments. The pillar bears the following lines:

> *De tijd kruipt met het bouwwerk heen,*
> What's built must yield to time's slow plod,
> *van hier, vandaar rest soms een steen.*
> Here lies a stone and there a clod.

In the years that followed, what had started as a protest against the status quo gradually became part of the established order.

The ENWB was obliged to rename itself, following legal action by the ANWB, and later finally became the Dutch Cyclists' Union. It is this movement, which came together at local and national level to defend and spearhead cyclists' interests, that the Netherlands has to thank for its network of interlinked cycle paths, which took shape from 1982 on.

I had not known that many of our cycle paths are so recent, younger than I am. They are actually sections of road reclaimed from motor vehicles because of these activists.

David vs Goliath

Having never realised that the battle for our streets had been so hard fought, I had not reflected during my 'cycling versus congestion' project on how extraordinary it is that we're even in a position to advocate for a network of bike highways at all. Most countries wouldn't have the infrastructure, they would have to start from scratch; for us, it would just be a case of extending what we already have.

But the Netherlands is so different from other countries. That always strikes me when I return home from abroad.

It's different from Britain, for example, where cycling in most cities takes guts, and where the number of children walking to school on their own has dwindled from four out of five in the early 1970s to virtually none at the time of writing.[31] Britain had no mass protests against cars.

It's different from Belgium, where *moordstrookje* ('murder strip') was the Flemish word of the year in 2018, referring to the far-too-narrow cycle paths demarcated by lines of white paint on provincial roads. Or Australia, where some drivers see cyclists as 'less than human'.[32]

'See an American walking, and you'll likely hear the beeping of his car lock within a few seconds,' wrote Arjen van Veelen in his book *Amerikanen lopen niet* (Americans Don't Walk). There are some roads in Florida where pedestrians are now supposed to pick up a flag hanging from a post and wave it while they walk (or run) across the road, when they can put it back in a holder.[33] And shame on you if you don't cross the road at the assigned spot — then you're a jaywalker.

The majority of industrialised countries are now designed with the car in mind. You don't walk to the supermarket if it has a huge car park and is a kilometre away, on a thoroughfare. And if you're to be able to drive there at a decent speed, there'd better not be any pedestrians to slow you down.

The Netherlands is different. Thanks to the country's 37,000 kilometres (over 22,990 miles) of cycle paths, Dutch people make more than a quarter of all journeys by bike.[34] And although the number of children walking to school on their own has fallen considerably over the last few decades and many parents are very concerned about how unsafe the areas around schools now are — rightly so, given that over 10,000 traffic accidents were recorded in a three-year period[35] — at least children cycle to school here.

What we have in the Netherlands is unique, but Dutch people are not particularly aware of that. 'A bike is something, though almost nothing' ('Een fiets is iets, maar bijna niets'), to quote the slogan popularised by the Dutch counter-culture movement Provo in the 1960s.[36] In other words, although bikes are not obviously expensive or impressive vehicles, they can help people connect and experience travel in a uniquely positive way.

Prove It!

Why did the Netherlands see widespread resistance to cars in the 1960s and 1970s, when other countries didn't? Why didn't we introduce a law against jaywalking? What stopped us becoming as totally car-fixated as people in other countries that had once also been full of keen cyclists?[37]

After reading Peter Norton's book I browse through old Dutch newspapers to find out how cars were viewed here in the 1920s. And I make a remarkable discovery. There was a battle of opposing views in the Netherlands too. But the outcome was the opposite of what happened elsewhere.

At the time that the Ford Model T was conquering America, the Netherlands still had few cars: in the 1930s, car journeys between the four big cities in the west of the country totalled around 4,000 a day. Outside that region, the number of car journeys came to no more than a few hundred.[38] Yet cars were rapidly claiming many victims in the Netherlands, just as in other countries. This is clear from the nicknames they were given by the newspapers of the time, including 'the terror of the highways', 'death on wheels', 'the death-dealing monster that brings ruin', 'the flying peril', and 'motoridiocy'.[39]

In the Netherlands, as elsewhere, a heated discussion flared up on how to deal with this issue. Until 1924, a person hit by a car in the street was required to prove that the driver had made a mistake or been careless. But then a member of the Dutch House of Representatives decided that was unfair.

In 1924, Alexander van Sasse van Ysselt tabled an amendment to the new Motor and Bicycle Act, proposing that the following should apply:

> The owner or holder of a motor vehicle who drives the said vehicle or has it driven shall be liable for any damage caused to persons or goods not transported by him through an accident involving a collision or by the said vehicle hitting or running over such persons or goods, unless such damage is attributable to *force majeure* or to the parties adversely affected.[40]

This amounted to a reversal of the burden of proof. It was the opposite of the notion of jaywalking. Van Sasse van Ysselt was determined to provide legal protection for pedestrians and cyclists. *De Maasbode* newspaper wrote: 'The drivers of these motor-cars and similar vehicles are likely to take rather greater care if they can be obliged to pay a sizeable sum in fines.'

The proposed amendment sparked off a debate in Parliament that would continue for months. Just as in the United States, there were people who thought that everyone should be able to move about as fast as possible and that the country should adapt the roads for that purpose. Henri Polak, a member of the Senate, noted the existence of 'literally poor motorists who need a car for professional reasons. The speaker has in mind the medical doctors, road haulage operators, and so on, whose livelihood will be seriously affected by Section 25a.'[41] In Polak's view, it was pedestrians unwilling to cooperate to improve traffic safety who were the problem. 'Eighty percent of traffic accidents can be attributed to the dull pigheadedness — so typically Dutch — of non-motorists who fail to abide by the highway code. I shall vote against this bill!'

But a member of Polak's own party, Maup Mendels, agreed with Van Sasse van Ysselt. 'Why do the Honourable Members not object to the fact that a pedestrian or cyclist disabled by an inebriated motorist is required to prove that the other party is guilty?' he asked. 'This injustice has prevailed hitherto, but it will be abolished by this Act.'[42] Fast vehicles already had right of way; surely that was enough.

The House of Representatives adopted Van Sasse Van Ysselt's amendment by 44 votes to 30.[43] In the Senate, however, there was a majority against.[44] A compromise was reached that, in the event of a traffic accident involving a driver and a cyclist or pedestrian, the onus lay on the motorist to prove that they were not responsible. This laid the foundation for what the Dutch call 'the liability law'.

The traffic liability law gradually acquired more substance through court judgments. In the last quarter of the 20th century, for instance, the Netherlands Supreme Court ruled that in the event of a collision between a motor vehicle and a non-motor vehicle, or with a pedestrian, the motorist automatically bears 50 per cent liability. In collisions involving children up to the age of 14, the motorist's liability rises to 100 per cent, regardless of the degree of responsibility of the victim.[45] That is the rule today.[46]

The liability law remains a subject of debate in the Netherlands. How fair is it, after all, that a motorist is considered to be liable and is thus required to bear any medical costs incurred by a person who walks through a red light?

But the rationale for this rule is that a road user with a car is in a privileged position the moment they get behind the wheel; they can go faster. It's only fair for this privilege to bear a price. By reversing the burden of proof, the Dutch — in contrast to the Americans — opted to protect a person who is not operating a dangerous vehicle in public space from those who are.

But the fact that the burden of proof had been placed on the motorist so early on didn't mean that Dutch streets remained the province of walkers. While Van Sasse van Ysselt's amendment was being debated in Parliament, the *Algemeen Handelsblad* newspaper published 'ten commandments for the pedestrian', drawn up by the traffic commission of Paris, that medieval city teeming with narrow, crooked streets which had built broad avenues a few decades previously. Twelve years after the newspaper had first printed the advice provided by a Chicago motoring club for drivers, it now dispensed very different educational 'command-ments' to those of its readers who got about on foot:

1. Cross the street at a right angle.
2. Look right and left before stepping off the pavement.
3. In the event of danger, stay in the middle of the road.
4. Don't stand on the edge of the pavement.
5. Walk along the right-hand side of the pavement.
6. Don't stand in the road.

7. Don't step out of a moving vehicle.
8. Don't cross at an intersection where traffic is being regulated until the way ahead is free.
9. When walking across a square without a traffic island, make sure you cross at a right angle to the kerb.
10. Don't interfere with the work of police officers engaged in regulating traffic.[47]

The term 'pedestrian' acquired legal status in 1936. Anyone walking in the streets could now be classed as a road traffic participant. Whenever you walked out of a building, you were no longer entering a shared public space, but traffic, a world of fast machines you had to avoid.

The Story Behind the Scar

Now that I must teach my children to look left, then right, then left again, I'm piqued by curiosity: what was it like to grow up in the Netherlands in the 1950s, when motor traffic started to take over the streets? Vigilance is second nature now, but what about back then?

As a child, my father had been knocked down by a moped, I knew. It had left him with a noticeable scar on his left knee. When, as a child myself, I'd asked him how he'd got it, a guilty look came over his face. It was from when he was a boy in Arnhem and ran out into the road, he said.

Back at my parents' kitchen table in Leiden, I ask my father for the full story behind the scar. 'I think I was seven or eight, so it must have been in 1950 or 1951,' he says. 'My father, your grandpa, was at the bus stop on the other side of the road, waiting for me. I was so happy to see him, so euphoric, that I ran into the street without looking. And then that moped came along ...'

'Moped' wasn't the word they used back then. It was still known as a 'motorised bicycle', according to my father. They had gained popularity rapidly — in 1947, there were none in the Netherlands, while by 1951, the probable year of my father's accident, there were 200,000.[48]

The number of families with their own car also grew fast in the 1950s. In 1950 there were 121,000 cars in the Netherlands, while by 1960 there were already four times that number.[49] Within a short space of time, cars and mopeds became accessible to everyone and ownership expanded fast. 'I had a Solex too,' my mother says. 'Got it on my sixteenth birthday.' That was just ten years or so after my father's accident.

'Your grandpa was standing at the trolleybus stop reading the paper, so he didn't see me arrive,' my father continues. 'Make sure you don't do that when you're waiting for your children!' He gives me a warning look.

'Of course, I shouldn't just have run out into the road without looking,' he adds. 'Make sure your children get that into their heads.'

I nod.

'It was terribly painful,' my father recalls. 'I suppose it was your grandpa who picked me up. But I can't remember what happened next, or if we went to the doctor.'

The accident made the newspaper. Although he no longer has the cutting, my father remembers exactly how the article began: 'Yesterday, out of the blue, a little boy stepped out into the Bakenbergseweg ...'

Back home at my computer, I search for the cutting in an online archive of Dutch newspapers. My father was almost childishly proud of having been in the paper: it would be nice, I thought, if I could email him the article. But it turns out that the relevant editions of the *Arnhemse Courant* haven't yet been digitised.

A few weeks later I find myself pedalling up the Bakenbergseweg; the street where my father's accident took place runs right over two hills. It's a wide, busy road. Drivers whoosh past me at full speed — I can feel the wind as they pass. The bus stop is still there, but the trolleybus is no longer in service.

I find old black-and-white photos of this road online. It's now divided by a central reservation which didn't exist at the time of my father's accident.

I cycle over to the Gelderland Archive and leaf through the collections of the *Arnhemse Courant*. How voluminous newspapers were back then. The first pages are mostly dedicated to the start of the Cold War, so I flick forward to the pages focused on local news, scanning the short pieces for the letter B of Bakenbergseweg.

There we have it!

> An eight-year-old girl stepped off a trolleybus in the Bakenbergseweg and was on her way to the motorbus when she ran into a van. Fortunately, the consequences were limited to minor injuries, which were attended to on the spot by public health service staff.

Not my father after all. A child the same age.

Over the next few hours I find dozens of news items about accidents involving young children. Countless pieces about little boys and girls who, just like my father, were crossing the road when they were hit by a motor vehicle: 'out of the blue', 'suddenly', 'unexpectedly', or 'presumably without paying attention'. Even toddlers were expected to be vigilant in traffic: 'Yesterday a three-year-old, crossing the Vosdijk without paying due attention, ran into a moped.'

Accidents were frequent on this road in particular: 'After the fatal crash at the Bakenbergseweg–Schelmseweg crossroads on 16 December, there had been five further accidents, Mr R.P.L.A. Hoedt remarked during the question and answer session following the council meeting. He reiterated that the situation needed to be remedied.'

The same stories recurred again and again. One weekend, five people walking in the streets around the region had ended up in hospital. Then:

> At about 3 pm yesterday, the four-year-old daughter of Mr and Mrs Lamers ... of Groesbeek was run over and killed. Young Petronella Lamers was walking heedlessly over the Wylerbaan road, presumably following her father, who had set off on horseback. The driver ... did his best to avoid the child, one of the Lamers family's twins. He was unable to do so, and his car hit the little girl, who was killed almost instantaneously.

Four years old. The same age as my eldest son.

> The child's body was returned to her parents' home. The driver, who was in shock after this tragic accident, has not yet been questioned by the police.

I walk out of the archive and cross the road running through the industrial district, ending up on the banks of the Rhine. A barge passes by. So that little girl was *heedless* to follow her father, who had set off *on horseback* all those years ago. And *she* was the one who had behaved heedlessly? And why had my father blamed himself for his accident, when the numbers of mopeds had multiplied overnight? When the Bakenbergseweg was such a dangerous road?

'Couldn't find the article,' I tell my father on my return from Arnhem.[50] 'But I wouldn't say you ran into a moped — I'd say a moped-rider ran into you.'

'True, but I was in the wrong too,' my father replies. 'My generation, and my parents' generation, weren't assertive enough to protest at the growing dangers on the roads. I hope my parents had civil liability insurance that covered the moped rider — he had a fall too.'

Then our conversation turns to the delight that accompanied the arrival of a car. 'When someone in the street bought one, all the neighbours would drop in to congratulate them.'

Of course they did. How happy, proud even, I'd been when I drove off in my own brand-new Lada Niva from the Moscow dealership. Now I could literally go my own way in Russia.

It's strange how these two things can coexist: euphoria at new freedom — and the fact that that freedom can mean you have to pick your own child up from the road, bleeding and screaming, as my grandpa had had to do with his youngest son.

Learning to Cope with Street Sharks

Prosperity — that was the main thing that the arrival of the car had meant to my parents' generation. But it went hand in hand with discipline: making sure you didn't end up under the wheels. After all, the liability law, although on the side of the pedestrian, isn't much comfort if you are dead.

Following the ten commandments for pedestrians published in the *Algemeen Handelsblad* newspaper in the 1920s, a film was shown in cinemas, produced by an association set up 'to combat undisciplined behaviour and strengthen national moral fibre', of which the Royal Dutch Touring Club was a member.

The film, which you can see on YouTube, shows Amsterdam's

bustling, disorderly street life,[51] backed by a cheerfully tinkling soundtrack. The sequences, filmed from a moving tram, are interspersed with admonitions such as 'Take care! Why are children playing in the road, as if there weren't enough room for them to play in our parks and green areas?', and 'It is preferable to refrain from learning how to RIDE A BICYCLE in the road!'

From the 1950s on, you could practise in real life. In 1951, a 'Safety Avenue' was set up for a week in Arnhem, in an area next to the theatre — a street where actors purposely made traffic mistakes so that members of the public could point them out.[52]

Traffic Safety Netherlands produced countless games for children. In the 1950s, the cartoonist Maarten Toonder created a splendid board game for the organisation. The spaces on the board said things like: 'Don't play football in the road. Look out for traffic. Put 5 chips in the pool.' Or: 'The Youth Traffic Brigade helps you cross the street safely. Roll the dice again.'[53]

My father emails me about his experiences of traffic-safety education: 'We had lessons about traffic safety at school, supervised by Traffic Safety Netherlands, then you had to take a cycling test with someone following you, and you got a certificate. It was the same for you, wasn't it?'

Yes, I'd taken a traffic-safety test too. I'd learnt about traffic signals by playing a card game called 'Traffic and Me'. These days, children read a book about a dog called Spot and the Street Sharks, also published by Traffic Safety Netherlands.

Learning to be vigilant: what alternative is there? I, too, teach my children to look around and to stand still before crossing the street. Stop, Look, Listen, as the campaigns in the UK and Australia advise.[54]

'Look right, look left, look right again': that's still a mystery to my younger son, aged two. Strolling past the old Correct building on my way to the supermarket, holding his little hand tightly in mine, I feel as if I'm walking through a negative of my neighbourhood. Thanks to the old photos, I know what the original looked like and I can't let it go.

'Hunting Small Game — Open Season All Year Round'

Once upon a time there was an alternative to Traffic Safety Netherlands, the organisation that teaches you how to cross the road safely. An association that demanded action to make such concerns unnecessary.

I discover this almost by accident. Its name sounds like an anti-abortion movement: *Stop de Kindermoord* ('Stop Murdering Children'). This was the organisation that resisted car culture most strongly in the 1970s, through pamphlets, demonstrations, posters — all conveying a hard-hitting message.

One includes a black-and-white drawing of a child's bicycle, smashed up in a road accident. Underneath is the tagline 'Hunting small game — open season all year round'.

Another depicts three broad black motorways scrawled over a blue background. A child's face, barely visible under the brush-strokes, pipes up: 'But what about me?'

The statement announcing the foundation of this move-ment in 1972 was a far cry from the language of Traffic Safety Netherlands:

> In Eindhoven and Helmond, a few people have
> decided to cast off the resignation with which the
> Dutch people accept the daily massacre of children
> in road traffic. ... It is high time we put an end to the
> ignorance, carelessness or cynicism that determine
> the setting of priorities in this country. This is no
> marginal issue; it's about whether we want to be a

civilised nation. All those statements about humanity, human rights, the human habitat — the Treaty of Rome, the Stockholm Declaration (and let's not even talk about two thousand years of Christianity) — are just hollow phrases if we're not prepared to draw the necessary conclusions.

Then the author, journalist Vic Langenhoff, switches to a personal note: 'One of the 3,000 people killed in traffic accidents in 1971 was my youngest child, just six years old, run over on the way to school by someone racing full tilt around a blind bend. (The fine was 150 guilders — criminal driving is cheaper than you might think.)'

In this father's view, the driver should not be absolved of guilt just because he paid a fine. But there was another point Langenhoff wanted to make. Motorists had been given free rein to use public space in a way that caused 400 children's deaths annually. It was high time to put a stop to this. You could contact Langenhoff if you, too, had had enough of the prevailing indifference: he put his address under the appeal and continued to publish pieces about the reactions he received. The response was overwhelming.

What started as a pressure group soon developed into an organisation with grassroots activists all over the country, who fought for residential streets to be places where children could play and live carefree lives, as they had before the advent of motor traffic.

Maartje van Putten from Amsterdam became the chair of Stop Murdering Children. One Saturday morning she and a group of a few dozen parents and children cycled to the home of the then prime minister Joop den Uyl. In a recent British documentary, *Stop Killing Our Children* (2019), Van Putten talks about the experience: 'He opened the door himself and we talked for twenty minutes or so. He handed out sweets to the children and said, "Come and see me in my office during working hours".[55] By now, Vic Langenhoff had made forceful criticisms of Traffic Safety Netherlands, which in its turn attacked Stop Murdering Children, putting the onus on children and their parents to take care of their own safety.[56] Stop Murdering Children eventually garnered widespread public support, including from the Dutch royal family.[57] It also helped set up the cycling pressure group ENWB.

And gradually the number of victims began to fall. The change was also thanks in part to Tjerk Westerterp, the minister for transport. He, too, had lost a child in a car accident. According to some it was this that pushed the government into taking action, one example being the introduction in 1975 of seatbelts, a lifesaving measure for people in cars.

But most of the initiatives that made street life less hazardous were local. The *woonerf* or 'home zone', a phenomenon I would learn much more about later on, made its first appearance. Many cities began to install segregated cycle paths and implement traffic-calming measures. Rotterdam introduced a million-guilder 'bump budget' to fund speed bumps: any citizen could apply to have one installed in the street in front of their home.[58] Like the ENWB, Stop Murdering Children changed its name — now calling itself Priority for Children! — and became a trusted partner of government.

Then I was born, and I came to know the Netherlands of the early 1980s as a reasonably people-friendly country. Sure, you couldn't cross the road alone as a young child. You had to look right, then left, then right again. You had to take your cycling proficiency test. But I could play with friends who lived in home zones, and just about every other country in the world was more dangerous for cyclists. The worst was over. I had no idea that it had taken place, or how it had been stopped.

I was wholly ignorant of the suffering caused by injury or death on the roads.

III

The Story That's Never Told

Who are the victims of this system?

Accidents. That was what Marco had hoped to discuss with me that day we met for the first time in Amsterdam. 'Know what you really ought to do a piece on? Traffic accidents!' he'd burst out half-way through our conversation.

I was struck by his passion, but didn't dwell on it. It is only months later that I begin to pay more attention to this issue and am reminded of our conversation. Under one of my own articles, I comment that 400 children were killed by cars in 1972, provoking Marco to retort: 'Killed by drivers, you mean. You don't say someone's been shot and killed by a gun, do you?'

He drops a further hint in a subsequent exchange of messages on Twitter:

Cycling Professor @fietsprofessor
One good thing — I've been through too much to be blind to the problem.

Thalia Verkade @tverka
You've been involved in an accident yourself?

Radio silence.

The unspoken answer lingers between us. We touch on it in our Twitter exchanges. Marco lets slip that there is something he wants to tell me about, but he doesn't say what it is. Awkwardly, we reach a tacit agreement that I will ask him the next time we meet.

This is on a café terrace in Amsterdam. After a long conversation about the pleasures of travel, I cautiously ask him what happened.

'I haven't talked about it for nearly 30 years, and I'm not sure what'll happen if I do,' Marco begins. 'What it'll do to me, I mean.'

This is followed by a disclaimer: 'Most of the people around me don't even know that anything happened. So I'm quite worried that if my colleagues or journalists or policymakers know, they'll say: oh, so he's just an activist suffering from a trauma. And that doesn't cut the mustard, because it means you're not an objective scientist. The only thing that counts is measurable phenomena, and emotions just get in the way.'

I nod. 'Do you want to talk about it?'

'What do you want to know?'

'What happened?'

There's a moment's silence. Then he starts to speak.

'I was nine. It was a Wednesday afternoon and I was playing outside with two friends. My mother was out for a few minutes; she'd popped over to the shop. We lived in a quiet cul-de-sac, in Ulft, a small village in eastern Gelderland. There was a through road running past our cul-de-sac. My friend Dion and I asked my older sister if we could go out through the gate at the back. She said that was fine. We wanted to slip through a gap in the hedge onto the road beyond to hide from our other friend, Niels. So we ran out through the gate, towards the gap.'

Pausing momentarily, Marco shifts into the present tense.

'Niels is waiting next to the house. Dion and Niels catch sight of each other, and then Dion gives a little jump and lands on the edge of the road. A driver comes along, can't brake in time. Screeching tyres. The ball Dion's holding bounces into the road.'

Marco stops again. I see what an effort it is for him to talk about this.

It's only a year and a half later that he tells me in detail about what he experienced in the first seconds and minutes after it happened. How Dion's body landed about eight metres away, next to the path up to the neighbouring house, and how the windscreen of the car was shattered. How he'd run towards Dion, who lay inert, half of his body on the verge.

'There was blood gushing out of his head. I started to scream and ran indoors, panicking, looking for someone who could help. The only person at home was my 12-year-old sister. We ran out together, belted past Dion and shot over to the neighbour's. She was already on the phone. She'd heard me scream and realised she had to ring emergency services even before she saw what had happened.'

Marco doesn't tell me all this on the café terrace. What he does tell me comes out in fits and starts.

'A lot of things I can't remember at all any more, but others still stand out in my memory. For instance, I was in the front seat of a police car because I had to give a statement, and suddenly a screech of tyres made me jump out of my skin. The police were doing a braking test with another car, presumably to measure the braking distance and establish how fast the first car had been travelling.

'My mother and my other sister were on their way back from the shop when they spotted the ambulance behind our house. But our family couldn't get any information from the hospital when we phoned, as we're not related to Dion.

'Dion's mother rode past Dion on her bike, with her other

son on the back: she was taking him to football practice, a hundred metres away. Can you imagine?

'They picked on me at school. I got called a murderer. "Marco shoved him in front of the car," they'd say. I felt guilty for years. I should have gone first, with the ball. It was a kind of politeness thing — he'd been playing round at my house, so I should have been out in front.

'After the funeral, we never really talked about it again properly, not in school and not at home either. What we did do was sit on the sofa with damp hair watching a TV programme about all sorts of different road accidents and what is was like for the people involved. I still wonder if that was on someone or other's advice. It did do me some good to watch it with the rest of my family: the presenters were always pointing out that accidents involve a series of coincidences ...'

Then Marco shifts from the particular to the general. 'Do you see? Twice a day, in this country, someone's involved in a traffic accident and never makes it back home. That's six or seven hundred times a year. Since Dion's death — on 3 October 1990 — it's happened 18,000 times. And next year there'll be another 600 deaths or more. And think about all the people with serious injuries, that's five times the number of deaths: people whose lives are changed forever, which generally means a huge deterioration in their quality of life. This just keeps on happening, year after year after year. Then there are all the people suffering from trauma. All the people who attend the funerals — relatives, friends, colleagues. The people working in the emergency services.'

There's also the driver who's killed someone without warning, accidentally, out of the blue. 'Imagine you're driving around without a care in the world, and the next moment your windscreen's smashed, there's a child lying in the road, another child screaming and running around, and everything else is deathly silent.' It had been a small car that had hit Dion. 'The woman driving must have been in shock.'

During our first ever conversation, Marco had wanted to raise this issue — the fact that there was more at stake than traffic jams and bike highways. He'd agreed to be interviewed by me because he'd thought he would be able to have a proper conversation with a journalist from *De Correspondent*.

But I had been too focused on keeping traffic flowing smoothly and saving travel time, just like everyone else. Mobility and the economy were a machine, and I was a tiny cog keen to make that machine run even faster and more efficiently. As a journalist, I wanted to be of use to our country. I was like a robot. And Marco, who'd known since he was nine years old that there was something fundamentally wrong with our mobility system beyond traffic jams, had had to explain to a robot why he wasn't interested in showers at work.

Only now did I understand why our conversation had been so awkward.

Involuntarily Complicit

A few months later, Marco and I publish a joint appeal: 'How does our society deal with traffic accidents?'

It's only now that I really learn about an issue I have been blind to for so many years, and which I've never focused on as a journalist. Hundreds of comments flood in, both under the original article and by email.

In some cases, the main emphasis is on technical solutions. Better mirrors. Rearview cameras. External airbags. Self-driving vehicles, maybe?

Then there's the personal stories of traffic-related suffering. Most of these come in by email. My inbox starts to resemble a war correspondent's; 'A traffic-related death is a violent death', as journalists Gerard van Westerloo and Elma Verhey wrote back in 1971.[1]

I immerse myself in these stories and talk to dozens of people. Much of the trauma is long-term. One man, Niels van der Wal, tells me how he's still recovering after an accident that took place eight years earlier, when he was hit by a motorist while out on his bicycle.

'The motorist was responsible for paying my income, but I exchanged that for a lump sum so I could buy the kind of home I needed, which had to be quiet — brain damage has made me ultra-sensitive to noise. Now, eight years on, I'm retraining and hoping to get back into paid employment. I'm volunteering in the field I used to work in, and it's going pretty well. Hopefully I can go back to having a job again next year.'

The father of a young girl writes to me. Things seemed to be all right straight after her accident (nothing was broken), but his daughter was left with permanent headaches and brain damage in the long term. 'We're not just parents any more, we're full-time carers.' This father doesn't want his daughter to be identifiable from my description. 'I don't want her to be "labelled", as that might saddle her with problems in future. She'll probably have enough difficulties to cope with as it is.'

Writer Fleur van der Bij, now 38, tells me about the tragic death of her sister Ylse at the age of 12. Fleur was 15 at the time. It was only much later on, when she was travelling in Africa for a book, that the grief she'd repressed came to the surface, manifesting itself in a mental illness with manic and psychotic episodes. 'It took me five years to recover.' She ended up writing two books about her experiences.[2]

I learn about the inadequacy of the language we use. A crash is often called an accident — but why do we call something an accident if it is the predictable result of policy? We could also call it systemic violence.

A mother from Flanders who knocked down and killed a child tells me she was unable to work for four years afterwards. She couldn't give her children the love they deserved; all she could do was cry and reproach herself and feel deeply ashamed that she'd been unable to prevent what happened. 'I call myself a culprit, because you have to use some label or other.' What else could you call her? A victim-cum-culprit? Involuntarily complicit?

The daughter of a driver who killed a 12-year-old girl wrote: 'My father never spoke about it. My mother told me what had happened, and after that the lid went back on. It's on for good now and has been for 20 years. I was the same age as the girl who died that day. It took a long time for me to understand that something awful had happened and that it had affected me a lot too. One of the reasons for that is the terrible taboo.'

I interview her later, having arranged to meet her at her home. She's had therapy to process her trauma: the feeling that everything good she'd once taken for granted could vanish in an instant, that she no longer had the right to exist. This isn't a thing she can ever explain to her father, so she chooses to remain anonymous. He must never know the story has been made public.[3]

This is how I learn how deep the trauma caused by traffic violence is and how far it extends. Four hundred and thirty Europeans die this way every week.[4] Dying or killing another person in public space, on your way from A to B, by accident — that is not comparable with any other kind of death, and for many of those affected it's impossible to come to terms with.

How great is the cumulative suffering, I wonder? I add up the total number of traffic deaths in the Netherlands since the catastrophic North Sea flood of 1953 and conclude that there has been the equivalent of a flood disaster every two to three years on average, bringing the total number of traffic deaths to over 110,000. More Americans have died in car accidents in the past 20 years than in both world wars.[5] According to the World Health Organization, upwards of 1.3 million people die this way each year: it is the main cause of death among the young (15–29-year-olds).[6]

What if you were to add them all up? Since my first article on traffic jams, at least four million people have been killed worldwide. Since 2000, we have lost 24 million people in traffic. That's more than the number of people allegedly killed under Joseph Stalin's 30-year regime – counting only the last 20 years of traffic fatalities. The total death toll since the first ever fatal car accident remains unknown. But it probably at least equals the current population of the UK. [7]

It makes sense to do these sums. A death on the roads isn't a single isolated tragedy. People whose mother or father was run over and killed in 1953 are still alive today and still miss the parent they lost.

And every week sees a further 10–15 cremations and funerals in the Netherlands alone, which can permanently take the shine off life for parents, children, loved ones, and friends.

Then there are the people whose lives are permanently changed by accidents. People whose loved ones become full-time carers. There are those working in emergency services who have to ring people's doorbells, and those who saw it happen and still wake in terror at night. What do we have to offer these people?

At the World Day of Remembrance for Road Traffic Victims

When Marco and I highlight the issue of the suffering caused by death and injury on the roads in my article, we receive a brief round of applause: morally speaking, we are in the right. But where do we go from here? What else can be done? You'd have to take all the cars off the road to eliminate the risk altogether, which isn't going to happen.

But can we really accept the existing state of affairs? I ask people this question and see divided opinions. Some offer technical innovations to shore up the status quo: 'We can solve this.' And others say: 'No, we can't allow this to continue.'

Peter Mak, who works in the Ministry of Infrastructure on the national traffic accident database, says: 'My job is just analysing the figures. Personally speaking, though, I think it's unacceptable. Two deaths every day.'

'We think it's socially acceptable for over 600 people to die in traffic accidents each year,' says Nikolai Lieshout. He's a traffic-accident analyst from the Zeeland-West-Brabant police unit, one of the members of the special police service that deals with serious accidents.

'What do *you* think?' I ask.

'It's not acceptable as far as I'm concerned.'

I get chatting to Lieshout at the annual remembrance event held in Middelburg, Zeeland, by the national organisation for traffic victims. On his very first day as a police officer, he says, he had to ring a doorbell and tell the woman who answered that her husband would never be coming home again. Now he's been a forensic researcher for ten years. He sees dead and seriously injured people immediately after collisions. 'You never get used to it.'

'How many traffic-accident analysts are there?' I ask.

'One hundred and seventy-five in the whole of the country, 13 in Zeeland-West-Brabant.'

We employ 175 people to analyse the violence on our roads.

The National Organisation for Traffic Victims, run by Elly Winkel, used to hold get-togethers several times a year for the people affected.[8] Once a year they would meet in Middelburg on the World Day of Remembrance for Traffic Victims — in a hotel that's hard to get to except by car.

'Get-togethers of survivors and the bereaved are among the few events you can attend for support if you've lost someone you loved,' says Fleur van de Bij, explaining how she came to be involved in Winkel's organisation. She went to her first event 21 years after her younger sister Ylse was knocked off her bike and killed at the age of 12. 'The fact that traffic accidents are so sudden leaves many bereaved people in shock afterwards,' she says. 'It may be much later before you process the grief and mourn the person you've lost. And it also depends on the nature of your relationship with the victim. When a child dies, it's often the parents who get all the attention. That makes sense, or it seems to make sense, but as the victim's sister I was over-shadowed by my parents' grief, and there was hardly any support available for me. When it's only years later that you discover you're suffering from what happened, it's even harder to deal with. That's something everyone at these events understands. Your experiences are acknowledged, and you can connect with people.'

The mayor of Middelburg gives a sympathetic address to the several hundred people in the room who have lost loved ones. I gaze at the heads of the people in front of me. Parents of children who are no longer alive. People who've been given their first opportunity to talk about their pain. Their first opportunity to meet others like them. To avoid having to explain for once, to have the depth of their grief understood — by everyone in the room, apart from one journalist who's had the good fortune to be spared such knowledge.

A white-haired woman called Marian Kreemers goes up to the podium. Her son Etienne, she tells us, was killed 20 years ago cycling along a dike with his scouting pals. He fell off his bike, and suddenly a motorist was there. He was 17.

Marian talks about how she now tours schools speaking about her loss. 'The best thing,' she says, 'is the children who tell me afterwards, "I'm going to be a lot more careful now".'

Gazing at the huge white vases of flowers that flank the stage, I feel a wave of indignation rise within me. Rather than a mother seeking space for her grief, what I hear is a mother unconsciously blaming her son for his death by urging other young people to be more careful.

I bite my tongue. It feels as if these victims have been punished twice: first by the tragedy itself, then by the way society talks about it, putting the onus on vulnerable road-users to be more careful. This mother really is saving children's lives — it may genuinely help if people remain alert when they're out and about. But why has no one here said it's insane that it is so easy to die in the streets around your own home, the streets where you hang out, the streets you walk or cycle through on your way to wherever you want to be?

The reason is that there's only one narrative, repeated again and again: we have to get rid of dangerous drivers and pay more attention when we're out and about. The next speaker up is a man from Traffic Safety Netherlands who does what the organisation has been doing since 1932 — talks about how we can teach children to behave in a 'safe' way.

The Messaging Ban for Cyclists

Once upon a time in America there was a man who texted 'I love you' to his wife while driving. In that instant, he crashed into an Amish family's horse-drawn wagon, killing a 17-year-old boy, a five-year-old girl, and a boy of three. His story was included in a film about the dangers of texting when driving.[9] The film doesn't deal with the inherent dangers of driving, with the amount of concentration and attention that it demands, or with the fact that human beings' ability to concentrate is limited.

There's nothing intrinsically dangerous in sending a text, but there is in driving a car. Yet what we talk about is the danger of texting. The Dutch have now decided that you can't text on a bike, even though it's not cyclists sending messages who run people over and kill them.

I have an awkward conversation with Peter van der Knaap, the managing director of the Dutch Institute for Road Safety Research (SWOV), about Sustainable Safety's principle of human fallibility. 'You must never have a situation where human error could result in serious injury or death,' says Van der Knaap. 'What you need to be aiming for is a safe system that will replace all the millions of decisions individuals take. In sustainably safe road traffic, dangerous situations should ideally be made physically impossible, so people never even face them.' According to Sustainable Safety, that means sorting people into separate streams, depending on whether they're moving fast or slowly.

'But isn't being tired or distracted only a problem because people insist on travelling through public areas in heavy machines moving at high speeds — and are obliged to do so?' I ask.

Van der Knaap says, 'Messaging — or kissing — is absolutely lethal in combination with driving. The same applies to looking after small children while peeling an apple. We just shouldn't combine such different activities at the same time ... It's like taking part in a conversation, you can't text at the same time. You can only focus on one thing at a time.'

True, you can only focus on one thing at a time. But if you text during a conversation or drink yourself into a stupor at a party, you may well be anti-social, but you're hardly going to kill someone.

In the hotel in Middelburg, I look at the photos on the wall behind the stage: 70 or 80 individuals who people at today's event have lost. A picture of a proud young man with his first car, the one he drove off the road, hangs next to a photo of a little girl who was out on her bike when she was run over. I step outside, into the car park, which is bigger than the hotel itself.

Now I understand what the philosopher Ivan Illich called 'the radical monopoly': 'when one product exercises an exclusive control over the satisfaction of a given need, and excludes other products from competition'. In everyday language, that means that we allow everything in our lives to depend on cars, even if we destroy each other in the process. It also means that we can't escape from such dependence.[10]

Victims of road violence come by car to an event commemorating victims of road violence, and no one sees how crazy that is. It's just a case of 'there is no alternative'. We can send rockets to Mars, we can clone animals, and we can electrify the whole world. But transforming traffic is beyond us.

So we pour our energies into saving lives. Caringly, tenderly, we instruct our children to stay safe, just as we ourselves learned to do: stick to the zebra crossing, don't stand in the blind spot behind that lorry, learn to estimate the distance a braking car takes to stop. And please make sure you wear a helmet on your bike, even though there's never been any research into whether it will help in a collision with a motor vehicle.[11]

In my neighbourhood, parents aren't allowed to volunteer as lollipop men or women at schools any more. It's too dangerous.

Van Rams Car

Cars' radical monopoly has also affected the way we report traffic accidents, as I discover in the months that follow.

In 1930, it was still possible to read about what a violent impact did to the human body, and you knew the identity of the people involved:

> On 21 October 1930 young H. Vijgen from Heerlen was engaged in conversation while standing on a footpath alongside the Heerlen–Schaesberg public highway in Heerlen. He was standing next to some trees when J.J.S., a commercial traveller from Beek (near Sittard), drove past in a motor-car. The latter was driving too far to the right and consequently crashed into young Vijgen. The unfortunate youth was hurled against a tree and killed instantly. Portions of his brain and hair stuck to the tree, and his intestines spilled out of his body. Part of his skull was retrieved from the ground by bystanders, who wrapped it in newspaper and handed it over to the police.[12]

Ninety years later, here is a similar incident:

> This evening, a van turned over after a collision near the Hoograven slip road off the A12 in Utrecht. The accident took place around 8.45 pm, at the start of the

Laagravenseweg towards Nieuwegein. On leaving the roundabout, the van, a Renault, crashed into a car. It then hit the metal crash barrier, flew into the air and landed on its side. A total of four people were involved in the accident. [13]

The person who tweets this news item writes: 'It's almost funny — as if a deranged self-driving van ran amok with four people inside.'

Marco and I set up a dedicated website for these kinds of reports: roaddanger.org. Here, with readers' help, we collect the short news items that appear each day in dozens of local media outlets: reports comprising five or six sentences, with headlines like 'Van rams car' or 'Cyclist dies in accident'. [14]

One week, we receive 70 news items each day. It strikes us that we are uncovering a vast mosaic of everyday suffering. Reports on road accidents are scattered piecemeal throughout the country's local newspapers. Sometimes they're even dispersed within a single paper. Over two days, the *Algemeen Dagblad* carries three short items about three separate collisions involving cars in the same small town:

Cyclist hit by car in Veenendaal.
Cyclist injured in Veenendaal.
Injured racing cyclist taken to hospital after collision in Veenendaal.

No one looks at the broader context; there is no article analysing how this could have happened in Veenendaal — Dutch cycling capital of the year. The atomisation of the news is one of the main reasons, I now realise, for my failure to perceive traffic violence as a major issue. The suffering it causes is hidden away in short reports in regional newspapers — if a piece even appears in the first place. Many of these articles merely outline the trajectory of the vehicle concerned and the state of affairs once everything has reached a standstill and everyone has been sawn out of the vehicle and taken to hospital. They are couched in boilerplate terms, like those you see in a stock exchange report or a weather forecast.

People
— lose 'control of the wheel';
— 'fail to notice' someone;
— are 'hit by a vehicle';
— are 'taken to hospital with unspecified injuries';
— and often 'have a narrow escape'.

Why don't we hear more about the human beings involved?

'The paper makes sure victims can't be identified — it's a matter of respect,' says journalist Job van der Meer from regional newspaper *De Gelderlander*. Nobody wants to find out from a newspaper that a friend or colleague has died on the road.

Jasper van Reenen, a freelance photographer of traffic crashes working for various regional outlets, explains that more rigorous privacy rules are the reason you now see fewer people in photos of accidents. 'These days a photographer can get into trouble just for having bystanders in a photo.'

What gets covered is also determined by how photogenic an accident scene is and whether the photographer can get there quickly enough to photograph it — that's one reason that the news tends to focus more on accidents involving cars. Two cars in a collision, with dented bodywork and cracked windscreens, are likely to stay where they are for a while. But a child's crushed bike will be taken away by the police.

Van der Meer explains how dependent his paper is these days

on freelance accident and emergency photographers. 'Reporters don't go to emergency scenes systematically now, so they don't get to talk to witnesses or victims. These days there's no time for that. Sometimes reporters are sent to cover more serious accidents. It depends a bit on what impact an incident has: if there are several cars, if a lorry's involved, or if roads or motorways are closed off for a long time.'

That's how we define impact.

The website edestad.nl carried the following headline above an item about a 74-year-old pedestrian knocked down by a driver: 'Serious traffic delays — pedestrian run over'.[15] What a pain, another traffic jam! The victim died of his injuries.

With motorway collisions, it's even more common for traffic obstruction to be the main focus:

> Delay after pile-up on A20.
> Serious traffic obstruction after accident on A4
> between Amsterdam and The Hague.
> Traffic misery after successive accidents on A50.

Traffic misery. In this piece, there's a passing mention of a person being taken to hospital. What happened to them? We don't know. Human misery doesn't get a look-in.

Traffic Delays — Pedestrian Run Over

It must affect readers, the fact that accident reports these days hardly ever tell them anything about the people involved. We experiment on our new website. What if we were to make the headlines more human? 'Man kills 21-year-old man with a tanker

— seriously injures himself'. 'Two people won't return home after a car collision on the A50.' What if we saw 70 news items like that every day? Then we'd grasp what a crisis this is — and we'd realise that the suffering it causes is systemic, not incidental.

Then there are the other people involved, the ones belonging to a category it's hard to find an appropriate name for, who are often neglected by the media as well. The people commonly referred to as 'culprits' and 'perpetrators'. The ones without any serious physical injuries; the ones being questioned as the emergency helicopter lands. The news headlines often leave them out altogether: 'Deaths in accident on A50 near Heteren.' 'Cyclist dies in front of Amersfoort police station.' No, that cyclist didn't die of a heart attack.

Newspapers don't publish how many drivers have been responsible for someone's death in their annual round-ups. Such figures are incomplete police data, consigned to page six of a traffic safety report issued by the Dutch Institute for Road Safety Research.

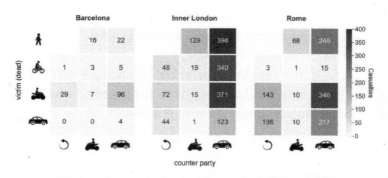

Casualties by type of road user in three major European cities in 2018.

Source: Klanjčić, M., Gauvin, L., Tizzoni, M., & Szell, M., 'Identifying urban features for vulnerable road user safety in Europe', SocArXiv (2021). https://doi.org/10.31235/osf.io/89cyu

The 15-year-old Bike Courier

On 10 January 2019, the following news item was published in the *Algemeen Dagblad* newspaper:

> *Food courier dead after collision on Amsterdamsestraatweg*
> A bicycle courier who was seriously injured in a
> collision on the Amsterdamsestraatweg in Utrecht
> on Wednesday evening has died of his injuries. This
> information was provided by the school he attended.[16]

The name of the editor who wrote the piece catches my eye —
Peter Koop, a fellow student from my journalism course. A nice guy
who got a job at the *Algemeen Dagblad*. Later, he emails me to say
that though his name appears above the news item, it was actually
written jointly with other editors, as is often the case. 'I only wrote
the passages mentioning the school (which shared the news).'

What exactly did the editors write?

The piece that bears Koop's name starts by focusing on the
young cyclist and his job as a food courier. 'The 15-year-old boy,
who appears to have crossed the road from between two parked
cars, apparently failed to spot a passing car.' The focus here is on
the victim and what he could have done differently. The bike
courier *failed to spot* the car that hit him.

'The collision was so violent that the boy's bicycle broke in
two.' Clearly the driver had his foot down.

'The driver, a 21-year-old man from Breukelen, was detained
after the accident. "We have questioned him and taken his car
in for examination,"' says a police spokeswoman quoted in the
article. "It's still too early to say exactly what role he played. That
will depend on the technical investigation, in combination with
his statement. The Public Prosecutor will decide on that basis
whether he was in any way to blame."'

In other words, let's not jump to any conclusions about the driver being at fault.

This is followed by a few paragraphs that go beyond a police press release or the accident photographer's notes. They reflect the profound grief expressed by the courier's school and his employer. There's also a mention of a bystander who tried to help before the emergency helicopter arrived.

This story is unusually human and detailed in comparison with most of the impersonal news items that Marco and I collect. Yet it still implicitly blames the victim: *he failed to spot the car.*

The news gets about and people tweet their reactions. Marieke Dubbelman, a columnist at the same newspaper, writes:

> **Marieke Dubbelman** @enkelvrouw
> 15! What a tragedy. I so often see them pass on their racing bikes, ear buds in, mobile in hand because they don't know the way. Alone in the dark on their way through the city.

Saskia Kluit, director of the Dutch Cyclists' Union, responds:

> **Saskia Kluit** @saskiakluit
> I was thinking just the same thing. Often their employers pay them by delivery and don't provide enough insurance. We don't know exactly what happened, of course, but what a waste of a young life.

It seems clear-cut: the courier was hurrying to get a job done and failed to pay enough attention.

This analysis has certain consequences.

Several major courier services announce that they're sending their delivery staff for traffic training.[17]

A criminal investigation is held into Burgerme, the courier's employer: had he been working too late?[18]

The trade union FNV declares that delivering food is too dangerous for youngsters.[19]

Six weeks later the *Algemeen Dagblad* publishes a profile of the courier.[20] We get to know his name, Ruiz Meijer. 'Some thought he might go into politics. But his real dream was to study dolphins or sharks.' The article stresses how extraordinary it was that he should have been killed this way: 'He was punctual, but he was also a cautious cyclist, very alert and careful not to take risks. That's why it's so hard for his colleagues, friends and family to understand how Ruiz, of all people, could have died in a traffic accident.'

The paper also investigates the driver, who 'was unable to brake in time'. His lawyer says there were no drugs or drink involved.[21] That turns out to be untrue. The court case, also reported by the *Algemeen Dagblad*, reveals what actually happened.

It turns out that the 21-year-old driver, Thomas, had visited a 'coffee shop'[22] with three of his friends.[23] He smoked some weed, and later the same day he got behind the wheel of his father's Volvo. He was doing 80 km/h (nearly 50 mph) when he ran into Ruiz — in a street with a 50 km/h (slightly over 30 mph) speed limit.

Ruiz had just finished his shift and was on his way home. He would have reached the other side of the street if Thomas hadn't been driving so fast.

Yet the focus on the victim and his behaviour had limited the discussion to careless bike couriers, who were now required to take traffic training, and were banned from delivering meals if under 16 years old.[24]

Driving was not dangerous, delivering food was. Not a word

about how Thomas was even able to do 80 km/h in a street in Utrecht.

It's up to victims to take action to avoid becoming victims. A senior civil servant working on traffic safety does a shocked double-take when it dawns on him how deeply that attitude is embedded, even in his own mindset. We're talking about a young couple on bicycles who were recently killed by a motorist. 'The first thing that came into my mind when I heard about it,' he says, 'was to wonder if they had light-coloured clothes on. Sometimes it's so hard to see cyclists.'

'So are you saying it was their fault?' I ask.

'No, I take that back,' he replies instantly.

It later transpires that the motorist was drunk and driving at 100 km/h (over 60 mph) in a 50 km/h (just over 30 mph) zone, and that he'd already had his licence taken off him on one previous occasion.[25] The victims, Alice Dessi and Miki Trpkovski, were 33 and 30 respectively when they died.

Even those whose children were run over and killed focus on what the most vulnerable road users could do differently, and they do it time and again. When I point this out to Marian Kreemers, the mother of traffic victim Etienne, who visits schools to tell her story, she says: 'It would be better if there were no need for such precautions. But there is.'

Ruiz's death, and the mistakes we made in the way we framed it, won't let me go. As I read about him on the memorial website his parents have created, the tears well up.

In a text his parents included in their victim statement, he wrote: 'I see myself playing in the fields again, tossing a snowball at a girl ...'

He also wrote: 'Another thing I think about is how I'm working towards a great future. I think about how I can channel my philosophy into influencing society and reducing inequality. I feel angry about inequality, and there are times when I feel invincible, too.'[26]

We let this boy die on the road in the middle of Utrecht. And then, as a society, we just sat around talking about careless bike couriers.

Thomas, the motorist who killed the boy, is given a three-month prison sentence and a six-month suspended sentence. The Council for the Judiciary provides an explanation on its website, as no one in the whole country can make any sense of the verdict: judicially speaking, a motorist is guilty of criminal recklessness only if he plays cat and mouse with another driver, each trying to overtake the other. In such cases the sentence is doubled.[27]

But what if you tear through the streets drunk or stoned? That isn't classed as criminal recklessness, apparently. A person who maims or crushes someone on a zebra crossing when drunk gets a few hundred hours of community service and is banned from driving for a while.[28] Someone with serious epilepsy who causes eight accidents, gets back in the car and carries on driving until she runs two people over, killing them, gets a six-month suspended sentence.[29]

These penalties are so lenient, they are now being increased slightly: anyone who does what Thomas did will soon get a year's prison sentence.

The injustice of over-leniency in cases of reckless driving has inspired an epigram that's become common currency: 'If you want to get away with murder, buy a car.'[30]

Incredulity at over-lenient penalties for careless driving absorbs most of journalists' attention, including mine initially.

But then I realise that these are exceptions. And exceptions always occupy a disproportionate share of the news. Two-thirds of traffic accidents involve people who rarely or never break a speed limit.[31] It's the system itself that's lethal. The man who killed Etienne Kreemers had lost his own son one and a half years previously in an accident in which he was the sole victim. 'He's never got over it,' says Marian Kreemers. 'And every time I get in the car, I think about how it could happen to me, too.'

I later hear about a case in the UK in which a cyclist is jailed for 18 months for hitting and killing a woman on his bike,[32] a rare type of accident that attracts disproportionate media coverage: one cyclist sadly runs over and kills one woman, compared to almost daily unintentional killings of cyclists by motorists. A man from Kent shares a long list of similar cases 'for the pundits lining up to wring their hands about dangerous cycling and light sentencing in the wake of the Alliston case' — a litany of incidents in which children were killed or badly injured by drivers who received light sentences.[33] Another example of the way in which we simply accept the idea that cars are killing machines.

A Formula for Traffic Deaths

Niek Mouter, a transport economist and philosopher, has done some interesting research into traffic fatalities. He and two other researchers asked people how many extra minutes they would be prepared to spend travelling to save one person from dying in traffic.

There is a method governments use to calculate this: a social cost–benefit analysis or SCBA. In essence, this is simply a spreadsheet in which the value of time spent travelling and the value of a human life — which economists have set at €2.6 million — are offset against one another. To calculate how much 1 minute of travel time is worth, researchers conducted a survey in which several hundred people at train stations and motorway services answered a series of multiple-choice questions on how much money they would be willing to spend to reduce their journey time. This was followed by a larger online survey. Together, these produced a figure that could be used in the SCBA: 1 hour in a car is worth €9.25 to a commuter.[34]

According to Mouter, politicians are told that the SCBA shows that a gain of 45 seconds per traveller on an average motorway produces more economic benefits than preventing one traffic fatality a year. After all, if a few thousand motorists save 45 seconds of the time they spend on the road each day, that adds up to a fair bit in the course of a year. So fewer vehicle hours are lost.

And this was how, in 2011, a department of the Ministry of Infrastructure and Water Management calculated the additional traffic fatalities that would occur with the raising of the maximum speed limit to 130 km/h (just over 80 mph). With a few compensatory measures, it would all be quite acceptable.[35]

'But if you ask people how long they're prepared to wait to avoid a death in traffic — that is, how we should deal with this collectively — they'll immediately say they'd have no problem waiting a quarter of an hour,' says Mouter. 'Which is 20 times as long.'

In other words, if a delivery driver runs over a five-year-old boy in the street, just about everyone would say they'd be quite happy for the parcel to be delivered more safely later in the day, as long as no one was killed in the process.[36] Yet we are only asked our views in our capacity as consumers of speed. We are treated as Homo economicus, not as the social species we are.

And politicians refer to a statistical model built on this to justify expanding motorways or to raising the speed limit. A model which turns a five-year-old boy — indeed, every human being — into a 'statistical human life'.

We don't speak of actual deaths, but of risks, which we can calculate. Even I have grown so used to this that I no longer think about how dehumanising it is. I discover this when searching for the source of a graph showing that the chance of killing someone if you drive at or above a given speed grows exponentially with each additional kilometre.

I find the figures in an online article issued by the Dutch Institute for Road Safety Research (SWOV). They've applied a mathematical formula that shows how the risk of a fatality rises steeply after 50 km/h (just over 30 mph), reaching 100% at a speed of 120 km/h (just under 75 mph).[37] But then I discover a study showing that the risk also rises very rapidly from 30 km/h (slightly under 20 mph), and that an impact occurring at 60 km/h (nearly 40 mph) is nearly always fatal.[38] This is half the speed deemed fatal by SWOV.

So now, as a journalist, I'm faced with the following questions: which graph is correct, which one do we print, and why did SWOV pick the highest estimate in its report for the Ministry of Infrastructure, rather than the lowest — safest — one?

I make enquiries. Patrick Rugebregt, spokesman for SWOV, tells me in an email that the answer lies in a more recent study. I ask Marco what he thinks.

Cycling Professor @fietsprofessor
In purely scientific terms, the Institute's approach makes sense. But if I were a 9–year-old boy, it wouldn't matter to me. I'd just wonder why people are trying to produce mathematical formulae for the relative probability of a child dying in the streets.

It's only when he puts it this way that I grasp how bizarre it all is: that I don't even blink now when engineers come up with mathematical formulae to predict the speed at which one member of the public will kill another — formulae a traffic expert can use to calculate whether a higher maximum speed is acceptable before reporting back to politicians.

This is it — the mathematical formula that produces a rising curve along which you can measure the probability P that a person will be killed if hit by a vehicle travelling at velocity v, expressed in kilometres per hour. At a speed of 120 km/h (just under 75 mph), everyone dies.

$$P(v) = \frac{1}{1 + \exp(6.9 - 0.09v)}$$

This is the less cautious of the two ways of calculating the probability of a fatal outcome. It looks entirely objective, but it diverts attention from the political choice to allow us to continue killing each other in the streets. Dion was killed on a road where drivers could do 50 km/h and still can, although hordes of children cross that road every day on their way to football practice.

Blame the Bushes

While I am seeing things I couldn't see before and now cannot unsee, Marco talks to his parents and Dion's for the first time about what happened nearly 30 years ago. They are joined later by Chiel, Dion's younger brother, now aged 35. There's a tension to these conversations 'because you don't know how it's going to affect you if you acknowledge your grief and anger, and you're also anxious about how it might affect the other person,' says

Marco afterwards. 'It seems so much easier not to talk about it, to keep your eyes shut and carry on.'

They all discover how much they are still suffering from what happened. How often both families were on the verge of getting in touch. All that time it was too painful to talk about, and their main concern was to leave each other be. Yet Marco's mother had been volunteering with Dion's for years at the local retirement home.

'I've got a feeling that everyone still feels guilty,' Marco tells me, 'at least to some extent: for being away from home for a moment, or because we had a gate we'd made ourselves, or because we kids were allowed to go out that way, or because I didn't go out first.'

Marco heard from his father that the police report referred to the bushes, which the local authority should supposedly have kept better trimmed.

He heard for the first time from Dion's mother Rita what she'd gone through when she turned up on her bike with Chiel, not knowing anything had happened. Every time she sees an ambulance she relives that moment. She saw a car with a shattered windscreen and some bystanders, including a woman she knew well. The latter's dog had gone over to Dion and lain down next to him. 'So Rita's first impression was that the dog had been struck. When she went over to see, the woman said, "Careful, Rita, it's Dion."' She had to get into the ambulance with Dion. Chiel, then aged five, was looked after by bystanders.

Dion's parents heard from Marco what had happened in the last few seconds of their son's life: that Dion probably never knew what had happened; that it wasn't Dion who'd cried out for his mother, as they'd always thought, but Marco.

As he tells me about their conversations, I wonder what the

local newspaper wrote about Dion's death. Had a little boy run into the road out of the blue again? Then I wonder whether it really matters how the paper reported what happened. Had I been about to let the media determine my view of reality again?

I decide to leave things be.

But when Ruiz dies and the media tell his story, I change my mind. What they wrote about Dion does matter. Newspapers don't necessarily report what is important, but what is considered important, or what people think others will consider important.

> **Thalia Verkade** @tverka
> Do you know what the newspapers wrote about Dion back then, by any chance?

> **Cycling Professor** @fietsprofessor
> No.

And so I end up in an archive in Arnhem once more. The newspapers from 1990 are stored in the city's heritage centre, underneath the public library. But once I get there I discover that they're not on microfiches after all. The paper volumes are in the other premises on the opposite side of the Rhine.

This results in an unexpectedly rewarding trip: I fetch a public transport bike from the station, and a little later I'm cycling over to the other archive building with librarian Ferry Reurink, alongside the A325, via the Gelredome football stadium. This is the official bike highway from Arnhem to Nijmegen, and it's nice and broad. There's no stress here, no bicycle congestion; apparently the commuters haven't really discovered this cycle path yet. We enjoy a pleasant conversation while we ride.

In the stacks, with Reurink's help, I leaf through the thick ledgers full of bound copies of daily newspapers. This time, I do find what I'm looking for, in *De Gelderlander*, dated 5 October 1990.

> *Child from Ulft dies after accident*
> Nine-year-old Dion le Comte has died after being hit
> by a car in the Anton Tijdinklaan, Ulft. The child
> emerged from a garden along Zuiderkruis Street
> and dashed across the road. On his way over he
> was knocked down by a car driven by a 27-year-old
> woman from Steenderen. Because the child came out
> of the bushes, she was unable to avoid him in time.
> He suffered serious brain damage and was taken by
> ambulance to Saint Joseph's Hospital in Doetinchem,
> where he died from his injuries.

'Dion le Comte'. His name is mentioned. I haven't seen that in recent media reports written immediately after an accident.

Dashed across the road. Focus on the victim.

Out of the bushes. Like a young deer, bolting out of the woods.

I find another short item, almost identical, in another local newspaper. And that's all.

No mention of the child who cried out for his mother.

Nor can anyone read about how Dion's parents had to decide in a hospital corridor in Doetinchem whether to make their son's organs available for donation. Or about what it was like in Dion's class next day, where his chair stayed empty, or for the football team, which had suddenly lost one of its top players. Or about what happened to the other boy who'd been playing hide and seek with Dion. Or the boy who'd lost his big brother and now had to play on his own.

The news item about Dion is at the back of the regional pullout, next to a series of classified ads placed by Opel Kadett owners keen to sell their cars. In between the obituaries, there's a big ad placed by *De Gelderlander* itself directing readers to its pages selling second-hand cars: 'From veteran cars to turbodiesel.' They buried Dion among car ads.

DION LE COMTE
30 May 1981 — 3 October 1990
He was nine years old, with a heart of gold.

**Dion with his little brother Chiel, four years his junior,
four weeks before his death.**

Source: the Le Comte family.

IV

On Automatic Pilot

Where will we end up if
we carry on this way?

One rainy February evening, I'm sitting in a car with three friends, feeling cheerful. After weeks of cycling in blustery conditions every day, it is wonderful to travel in comfort, in the warm and dry, without having to exert myself. But I can't stop thinking: this luxury comes at a high price — and I'm not talking about an unexpectedly hefty bill after an MOT.

If someone invented the car today, it would never be allowed on the roads. Think about it — a machine that kills thousands, contributes to respiratory and cardiovascular diseases, and requires more than half of public space in towns.[1]

Yet we carry on defending our use of it. This reminds me of the firearms debate in the United States, where many maintain that gun ownership is a fundamental right and that these deadly weapons have their uses, despite all the disasters they lead to. Other countries cannot understand this: 'Why does nothing get done about gun control?', writes UK newspaper *The Independent* after another mass shooting at a university.[2] It's crazy to continue allowing something that is so dangerous, right?

But let's compare the figures. In the United States, just under 500 people die each year from firearm-related accidents, while a further 14,500 are intentionally shot dead — so 15,000 annual deaths caused by guns and the people who point them.[3] Compare that with the number of people who die in traffic accidents every year: 1.3 million worldwide, nearly 38,000 in the United States.[4]

Yet not a single country has a national debate about whether car ownership is a good thing.

The fact that we no longer dare to imagine a world not dominated by the car intrigues me.

The Great Disappearing Act

Where will we end up if we continue to view mobility as a problem for which technical fixes, such as electric cars, bike highways, and increased speed limits, will automatically provide solutions? I want to explore this question.

But first I want to know: why have I never thought about all this before? Why did I just accept the status quo? In school, I learned how to safely cross the road, but not about the 1970s protests that made the Netherlands the cycling-friendly country it is today — why was this?

I find the answer in Delft, at Janneke Zomervrucht's kitchen table. Though retired now, she's been working in traffic safety since 1995.

One of her roles was as a policy officer for Priority for Children! (Kinderen Voorrang!), the successor to Stop Murdering Children. Zomervrucht tells me how Priority for Children! was swallowed up by the far bigger Traffic Safety Netherlands, which teaches children to be vigilant and to follow the Highway Code closely, as opposed to questioning whether they should have to. This is a cautionary tale, of interest to anyone who wants to better understand how a pressure group can be sidelined by the established order.

'The name was changed in 1994 because of the misleading associations with the anti-abortion movement,' Zomervrucht tells
me, sitting in her kitchen, where a letter from one of her grand-
children is displayed in the window. 'The number of children
killed on the roads was also beginning to decline, partly because
of improvements in street design.' Another reason, however, was
that parents were now waiting until their children were older
before allowing them out on their own. The negative impact on
child development of these restrictions on independent mobility
worried Priority for Children!

'We used to organise National Street Play Days', Zomervrucht
says. 'Our supporters would close off hundreds of streets across
the country to motor traffic so children could play outdoors all
day long.' The number of streets involved increased over the years
to over 2,000.

But then it all went wrong.

In 2000, the Cyclists' Union, Priority for Children! and the
organisation at which Zomervrucht had started her career, the
Pedestrians' Association (Voetgangersvereniging), were obliged to
merge with the far larger Traffic Safety Netherlands or lose their
access to national subsidies.

The Cyclists' Union managed to stay out of the merger, but
the other two organisations were too small and too dependent
on grants. And so a new era began: that of 3VO, a confusing
abbreviation dreamed up by a marketing consultancy for the
'three united traffic-safety organisations'. The new Minister for
Transport urged Traffic Safety Netherlands to ensure that the
ideas and principles of the two smaller partner organisations
remained recognisable.[5]

'It was hard for us to find our place,' Zomervrucht continues.
'What Traffic Safety Netherlands wanted was for children to
learn that traffic is dangerous, and how to deal with it. That's not
wrong, but it's one-sided. We emphasised the need to put more

effort into good street design.'

Jan Torenstra, a member of the Delft local executive at the time, who supported Priority for Children! and who is now sitting with us in Zomervrucht's kitchen, gives this explanation: 'Traffic Safety Netherlands said cars have to be able to keep on moving, and then they added that everyone should be safe in the streets. Whereas we looked at the pedestrians first. How do you make sure public space is accessible to pedestrians? Is there even enough space for cars?'

For Traffic Safety Netherlands, a child was like a deer running across the road. For Zomervrucht, Torenstra, and their colleagues, it was the road that ran through the child's living space.

'Some sections of Traffic Safety Netherlands didn't "get" the Street Play Day and refused to be involved,' says Zomervrucht. 'They thought that playing in the street was giving children the wrong idea altogether.'

So Street Play Day was replaced by Outdoor Play Day. In agreement with Traffic Safety Netherlands, the children's TV channel Nickelodeon even went off air for an afternoon to encourage children to go outside. It was a nice idea, says Torenstra. 'Though the emphasis was on playing outdoors, not on the issue of whether the street was a place for kids to play in.'

Then a decision was taken at the top to change the name of the organisation, since '3VO' had little appeal. 'Traffic Safety Netherlands' was reinstated, the other two merger partners rendered irrelevant.

There were further frictions behind the scenes and, by 2012, Zomervrucht was the only person left from the smaller organisations that had merged with the old Traffic Safety Netherlands. She worked until her retirement on projects that weren't too out of line with her principles.

'Now there aren't any professional advocacy groups left to represent pedestrians and children, nor is there any funding,' she says. 'The small grants that Priority for Children! and the Pedestrians Association once received go to Traffic Safety Netherlands. And just as in pre-merger times, it has a one-sided focus.'

Traffic Safety Netherlands again bears the name Traffic Safety Netherlands, as if nothing happened. The only change is that the new constitution gives the year of the merger, 2000, as the date on which the organisation was founded, instead of 1932. This constitution makes no mention of the two smaller partners.[6]

Rob Stomphorst, Traffic Safety Netherlands' spokesperson, ushers me into the organisation's premises next to the train station in Amersfoort, where Janneke Zomervrucht's old desk still stands. It was difficult, he says. 'The other merger partners were organisations representing very specific constituencies. Our philosophy is that *everyone* should be safe in the streets.'

Stomphorst is also in charge of Traffic Safety Netherlands' political contacts and sponsorships. He enthuses to me about a deal he recently made with Total. The oil company.

'There's a children's book that revolves around "escaping from the blind spot". The idea is that glancing in the mirror transports you to a parallel universe — it's all very exciting. The author was already planning to write an afterword about the dangers of the blind spot in traffic. So I thought, this is just what we need. Total wanted to do something on the dangers of the blind spot — would they be prepared to fund a big print run? We ended up providing every school that gives a lesson on the blind spot — 900 a year — with a pile of these books for their library. All funded by Total.'

Stomphorst also collaborated with Shell to create a mobile roundabout which schools use to teach their pupils the Highway Code.

Priority for Children! would never have accepted cash from petrol companies, whose lifeblood is motorism, I think. And although it's sensible to learn about the blind spot behind a vehicle, the real question is whether it makes sense to have juggernauts thundering through busy urban streets at all times of day.

'Can you see why the other merger partners may have found it hard to fit into your organisation?' I ask.

'I think you have to look at things realistically and objectively,' says Stomphorst.

'Yes, what we do is prepare children to cope with traffic as it is today,' agrees Hermy Grapperhaus, the in-house lawyer I'd originally arranged to meet, who hasn't said much up to now.

'It's just a fact of life,' Stomphorst continues. 'We've been developing materials for primary schools based on our principles since 1932. Over 75 per cent of schools use them.'

'Isn't there any alternative? I mean, to imposing all these constraints on children?' I ask.

'Yes, there is, but it would mean living in a commune or a hut in the middle of a heath,' says Stomphorst.

We talk about the Street Play Day. He's adamant: 'Teach kids they can play in the street, and you're teaching them the wrong kind of behaviour. Then the next day you've got to explain why it's not sensible to play in the street.' No forest for young deer.

I find it hard to listen to all this. The values of Traffic Safety Netherlands are so different from those of Priority for Children! Is it even possible to defend the interests of all street users, as Traffic Safety Netherlands claims? Peter R. de Vries, the crime reporter, twice caught members of the organisation speeding — a spokesperson and the director. That's a bit like catching a member of the Vegetarian Society sinking their teeth into a T-bone steak.

Wasn't Traffic Safety Netherlands merely an apologist for the status quo?

Back in the organisation's office, we talk about the future. They are optimistic. Walking away for a moment, Stomphorst returns with a vision that delights him. It's a drawing of a broad bicycle highway flanked by a motorway. I nod. I would once have been excited by this too — now I just see the same traffic segregated into different streams. As we get to our feet, he enthuses about how great he thinks it is that we can cycle so easily in our country, 'from Zeeland in the south to Groningen in the north'. Though our children can't walk to school on their own.

Showing me to the door, he gives me a picture book about traffic in which he's had a hand. Something to read aloud to my little boys. 'There's traffic everywhere, so be careful. Keep your eyes peeled and your ears open!'

Crystallised in Guidelines

This is why I'd never realised that there was any other way of thinking about traffic safety. The alternative organisations that could have pointed out a different path had been devoured by the monolith.

Then another question occurs to me: why is it that I'd had no views at all on the design and layout of my street and my city until now? I know the answer to that one: it is because street design is viewed as a technical matter for traffic experts, rather than a political issue that concerns us all.

That was a development in which CROW, the institute based in Ede that Marco had pointed out during our tour of his neighbourhood's parking spaces, had played a major role. I'd come across the name dozens of times since.

It's a CROW computer tool that prescribes 17 parking spaces

per 10 homes in Marco's new neighbourhood. It's also CROW recommendations that say his children's school has to have a drop-off zone.

CROW guidelines enable traffic engineers in my home city, Rotterdam, to decide whether a street intersection ramp is needed when two roads meet.[7]

The CROW module on traffic lights explains when to put a set of lights at a crossroads and when to build a roundabout instead. This, together with other modules, is part of a professional course in traffic engineering.

Whatever the street-related issue at stake, CROW has a technical solution. It's the machine room behind the street design that we all take for granted.

The fact that CROW has its head office in Ede isn't as arbitrary as it might appear. Any urban planning specialist will instantly identify Ede as an ideal location — it's in the middle of the country, on the edge of one of the Netherlands' largest areas of natural beauty, but still just 25 minutes from Utrecht by road and rail.

'We were set up in 1987 by government bodies and market participants active in road construction, traffic technology and the design of public space. The idea was that standardisation would both save money and avoid reinventing the wheel', I read on the organisation's website, which features a shopping trolley in its top right-hand corner. CROW pays for itself by selling its guidelines to local and provincial 'road maintenance authorities', which use them to organise public space with the help of traffic engineers. How extraordinary. Although what's at stake here is the use of public space — something that by definition belongs to us all — anyone who wants to understand why it is so often converted into space for vehicles — vehicular space — must pay tens and sometimes hundreds of euros. It's astounding that an institution so few people know about should play such a key role in designing our streets and cities, when members of the public can't easily access its guidelines.

How does CROW itself see its influential role, I wonder.

Marco and I decide to pay a visit together. We arrange to meet the director, Pieter Litjens, who's been working there for a year, having previously been the member of the Amsterdam local executive responsible for traffic and transport. I rent a bike at Ede-Wageningen train station, type 'CROW' into Google Maps and follow the arrows to a lovely stretch of woodland, where I see a sign indicating a business park. Those Ede folks have done a fine job. Marco turns up on his bike just as I arrive.

Inside CROW's headquarters, a large building surrounded by tall trees, we shake Litjens' hand. Although he's in his early fifties, there's still something about him that recalls the Amsterdam University student of political science he once was.

'Did you two come via the roundabout too?' he asks. We did. All three of us arrived this morning via a roundabout that marks an intersection between roads with speed limits of 60 km/h (almost 40 mph) and 80 km/h (nearly 50 mph). This roundabout, situated on the boundary between the town of Ede and the surrounding area, turns out to be a perfect illustration of how traffic guidelines operate and what dilemmas they lead to.

The roundabout lies on the outer edge of the built-up area. Drivers have priority over cyclists here, unlike in urban areas. That was decided by the Ministry of Transport, on the advice of the Dutch Institute for Road Safety Research (SWOV) and CROW. The roundabout itself was then designed on the basis of CROW guidelines.[8]

'When I arrive at the roundabout by car,' Litjens says, 'I always find it hard to tell what I'm supposed to be doing. Because it's right on the edge of the built-up area. You mostly get more cyclists than cars there in practice.'

Cyclists have right of way on roundabouts in urban areas, but it's the opposite here. So everyone using this roundabout has to do things that run counter to what they are used to: drivers must carry on driving instead of giving way, although that feels unsafe with all the cyclists, and cyclists have to give way at a place where they would usually have right of way.

'But if cyclists were given right of way outside urban areas, there'd soon be safety issues because you normally get far fewer cyclists out of town,' Litjens explains. 'So drivers might just carry on without giving way in some cases, as they wouldn't expect there to be any cyclists. You can imagine the result.'

Why was this roundabout outside the urban zone anyway? 'If they put the sign for "Ede" on the other side, the problem would be solved. Then it would be within the built-up area and drivers would have to give way,' says Marco, who's familiar with the roundabout, as he cycles around it regularly with his daughter on the way to her athletics club. 'But according to the traffic model, that would lead to congestion, which drivers would make a detour through residential neighbourhoods to avoid. That's why they've put the "Ede" sign on the inner side of the roundabout, so it's now automatically a roundabout with right of way for drivers, in line with the guidelines.'

The fact that motor traffic now has right of way means that Marco's daughter, at seven years old, can't cycle to her athletics class on her own — a ten-minute bike ride. Every evening the club is full of parents who've had to ferry their children to their sports lessons by car.

Although it appears impartial, the way this roundabout is designed and positioned is based on a choice. And in this case, the choice is to ensure that motor traffic can flow unimpeded.

Is there really any such thing as an impartial model, guideline, or standard? That question keeps cropping up. Litjens says that drawing up impartial guidelines is CROW's whole raison d'être. 'We do our best to stay out of political debates.'

But is this actually feasible?

Marco says it's not. 'Let's take safety as an example — no one's going to object to that. So you could draft a guideline stating that trees have to be positioned a given number of metres away from the verge to avoid accidents. But you could equally recommend that all provincial roads flanked by trees have to have lower speed limits. It always comes down to a political choice, doesn't it?

'It's feasible to come up with a standard that corresponds fairly closely to what the sector wants,' Litjens replies.

'Who or what is the sector?' I ask.

The sector, Litjens explains, means 'the road maintenance authorities', the local authorities where traffic-engineering measures are taken, and the contractors, engineers, and advisors who implement them. He stresses several times that CROW just implements what the sector wants. 'We don't impose anything on anyone. Standards are established according to a common need,' he says. 'They're something you can fall back on and they make it easier to put what the sector wants into practice.'

'Who are the people who need standards to fall back on?' I ask.

'Those responsible for implementing decisions, for designing roads. And politicians too. I saw this myself when I was on the Amsterdam city council. Sometimes there'd be disagreements about how to restructure an intersection or a roundabout, with groups that wanted things done differently. As the person responsible for traffic, I'd sometimes slip in the remark: "This is based on CROW guidelines, you know." There'd be far less discussion after that.'

So guidelines can be used to silence people?

'But both politicians and members of the public can raise objections, as long as they provide reasons,' says Litjens. 'Guidelines can be set aside if there are sound arguments to do so.'

'Lots of people don't know that, though,' says Marco. 'They're just told that there's a standard, and that a particular design is going to be used because it's the safest one.' And you can't just check it out online — you have to pay for the privilege.

Marco tells Litjens about the planned school drop-off zone in his neighbourhood and how the parents and the headteacher were unaware that it was a boilerplate model from CROW's computer tool,[9] let alone that they were free to express any view they wanted on its design.

Headteacher Leo Trommel confirms this: 'I didn't know that the standards they applied were just guidelines, not binding regulations.'

Was the situation similar in other countries, I wondered?

Traffic Engineering and 'Stroads'

I immerse myself in Charles Marohn's *Confessions of a Recovering Engineer*. Marohn, from the United States — the birthplace of traffic engineering — writes of the time he spent as a civil engineer in Minnesota trying to apply what he had learned during his academic training — what the manuals prescribed.

What happened, Marohn says, is that the logic applicable to *roads* was applied to *streets* with people's homes on either side. For example, one of the tasks that fell to him was to persuade residents that widening the street in front of their house would improve safety. The idea behind this is that a driver who makes a minor error doesn't drive straight onto the verge or pavement, or swerve onto the other side of the road. Sounds sensible, right? But this technical solution is problematic, even in the case of motorways. While a wider road may appear to be safer, people take more risks on an apparently safer road. And the problem doesn't end there. In residential areas, this design guideline results in the kind of street Marohn calls a 'stroad' — a street that owes its existence to the homes on either side of it, but whose layout reflects the guidelines for roads set up to convey people as fast as possible from A to B.

State Street in Springfield, Massachusetts, is a typical stroad. It's one of the city's main streets and home to the Central Library, yet you can drive along it at 40 km/h (25 mph). To cross, pedestrians need to walk more than 80 metres to reach a junction with a set of lights.

Marohn's book focuses on a mother of two children who took a chance and started crossing the road directly in front of the library, instead of walking to the lights. The subsequent collision cost her her daughter. And that isn't her fault, says Marohn. It's the fault of engineers like himself who design streets in such a way that they're dangerous and then go on to justify their designs by referring to guidelines for roads that should never be applied to streets like this in the first place.

Marohn has stopped working as a civil engineer. He's the founder of an organisation called Strong Towns, which has been working for over ten years now to equip people with knowledge that will benefit the community as a whole, not traffic.

'It's no different with us,' says Canadian Tom Flood from Hamilton, near Toronto, who I speak to on a video call. 'Getting traffic calming measures [put in place] is a monumental process. But why does the entire city council have to consider one intervention, to make motorists drive slower in one place?'

For Flood, 'the lightbulb went on' when he was cycling to school with his kids. 'All of a sudden I couldn't not see the utter absurdity of the fact that children can't walk to school on their own without the risk of dying.'

Flood found a grateful audience on Twitter to share his personal frustrations with. A former advertising executive, he cuts clips from car advertisements showing people driving fast and recklessly and mixes them with home videos of his own children cycling through the city.

He also tweets — writing this after attending a ghost bike ride, a memorial for an 18-year-old killed by a driver in Toronto while cycling:

> **Tom Flood** @tomflood1
> For God's sake we need non-profit organizations to advocate to adults in leadership positions to provide safe routes for people (kids) on bikes and those who walk. Think about that. My god what have we done?

'Road violence is not accidental, it is a direct result of our city's choices,' says Flood. 'Our cities have shown time and time again that the only thing that matters is the expedient and unobstructed movement of vehicular traffic — no matter what the cost. All the staff reports and other bureaucratic and technical procedures you have to go through if you want to change something are just more ways of masking the fact that our cities continue to prioritise the movement of the driver over everything else, including the lives of its residents. As I've said before: these aren't *accidents*, these are *results*.'

Fighting for a Child-Friendly School Environment

Back in the Netherlands, shortly after our visit to CROW, Marco sends me some news about the land in front of his children's school.

> **Cycling Professor** @fietsprofessor
> Just got back from the meeting I'd requested to consult residents on possible alternative uses for the land in front of the school. What a tough evening. There were three people who insisted on their rights as motorists, regardless of all other aspects. And their main argument was that the guidelines prescribe a drop-off zone. That was what was agreed, they said!

> **Cycling Professor** @fietsprofessor
> And then the people from the local authority pushed me forward to provide the counter-arguments. They don't have to make a choice — after all, it's just a few locals making demands. It's so obvious that the majority would like to see the space used differently, in a way that would be good both for the children and for our neighbourhood. Yet we have this battle against what the guidelines dictate.

> **Thalia Verkade** @tverka
> So what happens next?

> **Cycling Professor** @fietsprofessor
> Well, at least there's a new opportunity. The next
> thing we've got to do is organise a local opinion
> poll. There's no need for that if you want to fill the
> neighbourhood with parking spaces or put in a
> drop-off zone, because those things are standard
> according to the guidelines. But there is if you want
> to create a safe and pleasant environment for the
> kids and the neighbourhood as a whole.

What a battle. Over a small area in front of a school in Ede. But at least Marco can try to make changes, as he lives in a new neighbourhood. There's still sand in front of the entrance to the school. And he has the knowledge, the network, and the skills to effect those changes.

By now, I'd read his letter to the local authority. To back up his arguments, he'd referred to a crucial difference between his situation and mine: 'Recent research by Wageningen University shows that parents are often willing to change their behaviour (by reducing car use to bring their children to school, parking further away from the school, and so on), but that the only point at which such change is really feasible is when a new school opens.'[10]

All that Tilburg headteacher Bas Evers can do — like everyone else who thinks the approach to their local school is too dangerous — is fight what's already set in asphalt and concrete: the existing infrastructure, on which parents and teachers base their habitual behaviour. And to make any changes, you have to call into question guidelines and traffic models that appear to be impartial, though they are anything but.

That's the Direction Things Are Going In

'That's the direction things are going in.' This is a recurrent phrase I hear during my investigations. As if the future of mobility were itself autonomous. Maybe it is. When so much is determined by formulas, guidelines, and models, isn't the situation comparable to, say, a self-driving vehicle? The algorithm operates, and human beings step in only when things go wrong.

Although algorithms and guidelines are, of course, written by people, who have made certain choices.

When I started writing about mobility, scepticism about electric cars was still widespread. But more than three years of climate angst later, not a single country in Europe seems to harbour any remaining doubts. 'That's the direction things are going in.'

The Netherlands — perhaps partly because of enthusiastic articles by journalists like myself — is now the world's most tax-friendly country for electric cars. Even the automotive industry wants to be involved, provided that the transition is subsidised: the RAI Association of car and bike sellers; the Royal Dutch Touring Club (ANWB); the garage owners represented by BOVAG; and the car leasing firms of the VNA have all signed a 'Climate Agreement', 'to which all modes of transport will make a contribution, thereby avoiding a situation in which the entire cost is borne by motorists'. In other words, we're all going to pay.

I'd once thought that cutting CO_2 emissions by making cars run on batteries was a sound, principled choice to slow climate change. It hadn't occurred to me that there might be perverse aspects to the transition. Such as the fact that €700 million in subsidies, provided by the Dutch taxpayer, would go to already wealthy people.[11] Tax incentives to speed up the transition to electric vehicles are now being created in many other countries, including the United States and the United Kingdom. (Norway and the Netherlands were among the first.) Starting in 2011, UK residents could avail themselves of a 'plug-in car grant' covering 25 per cent of the purchase cost of a car (up to a maximum of £5,000; now reduced to £2,500 and due to be phased out completely) and 20 per cent of the cost of a van (up to a maximum of £8,000). This was the biggest incentive available for private vehicles in the UK, reducing the total cost of electric vehicles below the cost of conventional cars in some cases.[12]

Now I'm becoming increasingly sceptical of the innovations I used to enthuse about blindly. Do electric bikes really get more people out of their cars? Or are people who used to ride ordinary bikes now riding electric ones? Both: people with e-bikes are spending less time on ordinary bikes and in cars.[13] Who are the people using the various hire vehicles, including taxis, scattered around my own city, Rotterdam? People who used to drive, or people who used to walk and take public transport? According to a poll conducted by journalists in Brussels (among 150 people) and academic research from France (among 4,000 people), a mere 3 per cent of all trips taken by e-scooter would otherwise have been taken by car. Most people would otherwise have walked (59 per cent in Brussels, 44 per cent in France), taken public transport (16 and 30 per cent, respectively), or cycled (15 and 12 per cent, respectively).[14] In the United States, Uber and Lyft have dealt public transport a crushing blow and created even more congestion than before.[15]

In Rotterdam, the only area where you can pick up a Felyx (electric moped) for hire is what is known as 'the service zone', in the wealthier parts of the city north of the River Maas. If you live further to the south, where housing is cheaper, the cycle paths are also far less good. That's the essence of transport poverty — being unable to go where you want because of the unequal distribution of mobility resources.

As regards bike highways, the bicycle traffic on the way to

my eldest son's school has got busier and faster over the last year, with growing numbers of people riding e-bikes, speed pedelecs, and electric cargo bikes, including us from time to time. When we're on our ordinary bikes, we now sometimes cycle along the dog-walking strip that flanks the cycle path, where a small child can still wobble about. I give the dog owners a slightly sheepish smile; I'm hoping to stay on good terms with them. Since 2020, there's been an affordable leasing plan in place for expensive-to-buy electric bikes, designed to get 200,000 commuters out of public transport and their cars. These new cyclists, pedalling fast with the help of their batteries, are making the cycle paths even busier than before.[16]

How satisfied am I with this change, three years after I backed precisely the same idea as a journalist, with my 'cycling vs congestion' project? Marco sends me a new draft proposal from CROW, and I gulp. The idea is to divide cycle paths with a bright blue centre line, to prevent cyclists from overtaking other cyclists. Just like the dividing line on a dangerous road designed for motor traffic.[17]

What I'd viewed as a revolutionary future now looks to me more and more like a souped-up version of what we have now: more and more mobility, more journeys to cover increasingly long distances. The fastest traffic participant still has most rights. The street is still a traffic pipeline, with increasingly bulky cars and increasingly fast bicycles, which are beginning more and more to resemble two-wheeled cars.

Where will it all end if we carry on this way if it's left to engineers to come up with solutions? It's enough to inspire an episode of British dystopian TV series *Black Mirror*. Are you sitting comfortably? Then I'll begin.

The Service 'Utopia' of the Future

It's 2030. Your e-car, which has been travelling through your neighbourhood at 6 km/h (nearly 5 mph), draws up outside your home. It then chauffeurs you to the motorway, where it continues at a smart pace of 150 km/h (over 90 mph) — the number of traffic victims at this speed is the same as when more fallible humans drive at 130 km/h (about 80 mph). It drops your youngest child off in the zone next to his school, 8 kilometres (nearly 5 miles) from your home.

Although this has never been officially acknowledged, autonomous cars learned to drive on their own thanks to technologies including reCAPTCHA. This is the system some websites use to enable people to prove they're not robots by clicking on all the photos that include images of traffic lights, cyclists, or cars. By doing this, they've unwittingly trained Google's self-driving cars.[18]

Your child has just moved up a class in primary school. Later on you'll see a photo of the class, which the teacher will send using an app. But now you have to join a work conference call via the windscreen of your steering-wheel-free car.

The algorithms used by super-conglomerates Uble and Metazon are designed to resolve the congestion problem by ensuring that people are picked up from their homes in shifts. Sometimes you start work at 9 am, sometimes at 2 pm. It's also cheaper to travel when there is not much traffic.

If you can afford a private ride, you can have videoconferences, TV shows, or films projected onto the inside of the car windows. If that's beyond your means, you get to see ads, just as on your e-reader.

If you're less well-off, you can share a ride via Uble. More people per car is more efficient; it saves road space. There are virtual reality headsets hanging above the seats, though, so you're not obliged to talk to each other — an invention thought up by Mercedes.[19]

By 2030, mobility has become an all-inclusive service. No one owns a private vehicle any more. If you want access to public roads you have to pay for Uble's or Metazon's services; there's no alternative. If you really must have the same car in front of your house all the time, you have to pay heavily for the privilege, and the car remains the property of your mobility provider.

For an additional charge, you can ride in a car with the latest high-efficiency particulate absorbing (HEPA) filters. These days it's healthier to be inside a car than outside — at least as far as your lungs are concerned. The government has declared war on obesity: with growing numbers of cars and electric bikes, excess body fat is now public health enemy number one. The McDrive serves only low-calorie products.

After the traffic-jam updates on the radio — they're still with us — there's news that the strikes in the mines in the Democratic Republic of Congo where the cobalt for these cars is sourced have run their course peacefully, thanks to a massive police presence. This is followed by a cheerful news item: in the country's centrally located wild boar reservation, where the boar have been placed so that they can no longer cause economic losses by getting run over by cars, the first piglet has been born.[20] 'How sweet,' you think, noticing that your self-driving car is now attempting to move over into the 15th lane, where it's allowed to do 180 km/h (over 110 mph) for an additional charge.

Now and then you go to work by speed pedelec, because you need to lose a few kilos yourself. Then you take a quick shower: thanks to the efforts of crusading journalists, all employers are now obliged to provide shower facilities. For trips in town, you use an app to access your Swapfiets hire bike (Swapfiets was taken over by Uble in 2023). No one has their own bike any more; you don't want to overload the bike parking system.

If your bike has a mechanical failing, a Uble e-van will pop over at night (to avoid even more road congestion) and bring you a new one. It still isn't possible to automate this service completely, so it provides a rare job for someone.

Simson's black, white, and red bicycle-repair kits now disappear from Dutch shops after nearly one and a half centuries. Expressions such as 'tyre lever' and 'travel time' are archaisms from the olden days when people still used fossil fuels.

The papers have a new topic to debate: should it be a requirement for eight-year-old children who've passed their first cycling test (run by Uble, of which Traffic Safety Netherlands is now a subsidiary) to have their bike microchipped before they're allowed out onto cycle paths?

They'll have to be subject to even more rules. No texting, of course. No riding two abreast. No calling out to each other. No taking their hands off the handlebars — that old rule, imposed on Dutch cyclists during the German occupation in World War II, is back again.[21] No daydreaming. A minimum speed requirement — 13 km/h (over 8 mph). Your six-year-old daughter can just about manage that, thanks to her battery-powered bike.

At the weekend, a self-driving car takes you and your family through the new tunnel to the North Sea island of Terschelling. You hark back nostalgically to the time when the wind used to ruffle your hair on the ferry crossing. The windscreen plays adverts encouraging you to go on holiday by hyperloop this summer to Los Angeles, where the tech entrepreneur who once advocated for electric vehicles has managed to build 100 tunnels, one above the other. A statue of him has been unveiled on the spot where the tunnels cross one another.

Your life is fast, comfortable, and friction-free. Mobility is no longer a source of frustration, but a service for the ever-more efficient *Homo economicus* of the future. But there are also many things it isn't — spontaneous, autonomous, peaceful. Those values are not part of the algorithms that shape your mobility. And that's just as well, because you don't know what you're missing.

Fortunately, this is just a story. But why not compare it with the predictions of the Mobility Alliance, which represents various motorists' groups in the Netherlands? The vision for 2030, issued in 2019, contains the following paragraph:

> Wouldn't it be nice if a journey in 2030 were like this? In the morning you get a pop-up message in your diary to tell you your itinerary is ready. That's right, you have some meetings in The Hague today. While your car is quietly manoeuvring out of its parking space, you check your automatically generated travel schedule for the day. The itinerary is integrated with the route planner in your car. At the street corner you turn off the 'self-drive' mode and take the wheel yourself. Once you're on the regional road, you switch over to auto-pilot again. In line with the instructions received, you drive to the travel hub near Amersfoort, where a parking space has been reserved for you. You get out before reaching the open area around the hub, and the car parks itself. You fetch your favourite kind of coffee, which you've ordered while you were in the car. You board the train, and during your journey you receive a message telling you that your meeting has now been moved to a venue in the city centre. The itinerary adjusts automatically. So you cancel the hired car you've booked and opt for a hire bike, which will enable you to reach your destination more quickly and easily. When you reach The Hague Central Station, your smartphone tells you where the

hire bike is waiting for you. You arrive relaxed and in good time for your first meeting.

To achieve this, the Mobility Alliance notes that investment in mobility is an 'urgent necessity' — an additional €3 billion a year is required until 2040, according to the Alliance's website, totalling €57 billion over the next 19 years.

Car advertisements reflect the same image. A Hyundai gets stuck in a morning traffic jam: the woman at the wheel (the car still has one) scans her watch (travel time!), gets out, unfolds a Hyundai e-scooter, and covers the last kilometre to her office in Amsterdam's 'financial mile' this way, skimming past cars crawling bumper to bumper. Looking out of her tall office building, she smiles as she watches her car park itself.[22]

A utopia to some, a dystopia to others. Then I hear about a tragedy that shows how an episode of *Black Mirror* can become reality.

More Machines, Fewer People

On 18 March 2018, a self-driving car belonging to Uber kills a woman in Arizona. This is the first time an autonomous car has ever killed a person. Grainy images are released a few days later. YouTube allows the whole world to witness the accidental death of a human being.

The highway, illuminated in the dark, rolls on beneath the camera. But then, suddenly, a distant spot in the image morphs into a woman pushing a red bicycle with shopping bags suspended from the handlebars. The dashcam shows the face of the Uber back-up driver who is supposed to be on standby in case the robot makes a mistake.

At the moment when the collision becomes unavoidable,

the back-up driver looks up, startled, from her lap, where — it later transpires — she was streaming a TV show (*The Voice*) on a smartphone.

Elaine Herzberg was the name of the woman with the bike. She was 49. She was crossing the road at a point used by pedestrians in the absence of a zebra crossing. No St Nicholas had climbed onto a construction platform to sort this problem out.

Once the video was posted online, the media focused all their attention on the Uber employee. It was clear that she hadn't been paying attention. But then the spotlight returned to the company itself. The woman didn't have the right professional background to bear such a responsibility, so why had she been given it?

A further bitter irony was the fact that the victim was homeless. She was killed by a multibillionaire's experimental robotic toy, which he'd let loose in public space. What a power gap between rich and poor. While Uber came in for criticism, no criminal proceedings were brought in the end.[23]

I wrote an article about this: 'A self-driving car killed a woman this week. Why was it allowed on the road?'

People asked me why that one death shocked me so much. After all, self-driving cars would make everything much safer in the long run — the research (conducted by the car industry) said so. At that moment I wasn't yet able to explain. But I later realised that it was the feeling that our streets are being taken over by machines and that people are forfeiting their freedom, their ability to affect what goes on around them, their very humanity, and becoming slavish consumers of speed.

Elaine Herzberg disappeared from the news. And then KPMG, the accountancy firm, announced that the Netherlands would be the first country to be ready for the self-driving car. The only remaining problem was Dutch cyclists, who were still so unpredictable that autonomous vehicles would be unable to cope.

A representative of KPMG drew a comparison with the

arrival of ordinary cars over a century ago. In the early days, a car would be preceded by a man with a flag, to warn people to move aside. Something like that was on the way now, he said.[24]

Are we going to have traffic engineers design the best possible 'smart streets' for self-driving cars? Will we be allowed to walk or cycle in places where no raised pavement or segregated path has been installed? Will the algorithm that operates the self-driving car be so conservative that the car will have to stop for every leaf blowing across the road, or will people have to change their behaviour once again to accommodate these vehicles?

There are other, even more pressing, questions to which I also can't find any answers: what exactly are the interests of the corporations and organisations that are developing self-driving cars? Why is DARPA, the Pentagon's Defense Advanced Research Projects Agency, so heavily invested in developing them? For a military agency, a self-driving car is a four-wheeled drone.

I'm assailed by ever-greater doubts. Why are so many experts so convinced that this is the one and only future, and why is how to 'prepare for it' all that we discuss? Why are so few really critical questions asked in our public debate, on television and in newspapers? Why do we all become so besotted with each new promise of seamless mobility? Where are human beings in all this?

'Fewer autonomous cars, more autonomous children,' Marco tweets. He adds a video clip of a father on a home-made cargo bike, with two babies in children's padded seats on a plank, and a third young child at the front. According to KPMG, the algorithm used by self-driving cars is incapable of coping with this. Which means that cyclists like this have to get off the road.

It's clear to me now that all the models, guidelines, manuals, and algorithms we use to allocate priority to our fastest road users are underpinned by a strategy that's seemingly set in stone, in our streets. We could continue in the same way as before. That would mean opting to prioritise the rights of the most rapid, efficient and comfortable modes of transport.

It also means opting out of everything else. The right to get about unassisted by technology or a corporation. The right to be in the streets with a child, without fear. The right to peace and quiet in public space. The right to clean air. The right not to be killed or to kill another person *by accident*. The right to equality in our streets.

What happens if you opt *for* all these things? If you choose something other than travelling faster and further all the time? That's the subject of our final chapter.

V

Public Space as if People Mattered

What happens if you try to do things differently?

No more pavements, restricted parking, strategically placed railway sleepers, tubs of flowers set out like barricades — welcome to the *woonerf*. Journalist Tijs van den Boomen's description of this type of neighbourhood design hits the nail on the head: 'It was often an accumulation of as many items of street furniture as possible, as if a child had been told to use every single building block in the box.'[1]

Just as I had once taken zebra crossings and pedestrian crossing buttons for granted, I'd always viewed the woonerf as a typically Dutch phenomenon that had presumably existed since time immemorial and was probably the result of spontaneous generation. Yet woonerfs, too, turn out to be an invention, I discover. In the 1970s, when this revolution in urban design began to attract international attention, they were a new development thought to herald the country's future.

The woonerf had made its first appearance in Emmen in the early 1960s, where the box of building blocks was turned upside down by Niek de Boer, an urban planner commissioned to design a neighbourhood for workers at a new viscose factory. The word 'woonerf' (which translates literally as 'residential plot') was a spontaneous coinage from that time.[2] A cluster of woonerfs constituted another innovation, known to the Dutch as a 'cauliflower neighbourhood', although the illustration that inspired that expression was the brainchild of a German, Walter

Schwagenscheidt. Nowadays, about a million Dutch houses are
part of 'cauliflower neighbourhoods'.[3]

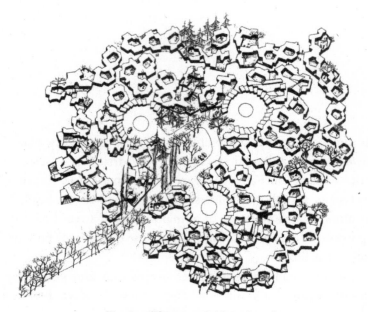

The 'cauliflower neighbourhood'.

Source: Walter Schwagenscheidt, *Ein Mensch wandert durch die Stadt / Un homme se
promène par la ville/A Wanderer in the City* (Verlag H. Müller-Wellborn/Die Planung, 1957),
pp. 77–78.

At the time, the ideal model for the city was modernist and
functional, a place where people didn't walk, but were moved
around as fast as possible by car and rail.[4] When it became clear
that it was hardly possible to cross a street on foot any more,
zebra crossings were introduced. The zebra crossing made its first
ever appearance on a drawing board in Britain. Soon, it became a
reality, painted in white on tarmac or concrete. The first Dutch
zebra crossing was installed in 1949 in Breda by the Royal Dutch
Touring Club. But the latter saw fit to make a chastening observation: 'The crossing shouldn't be too inviting for pedestrians.'[5]

To ensure uniformity and visibility, it is essential to mark out
all pedestrian crossings exclusively in the Zebra pattern.

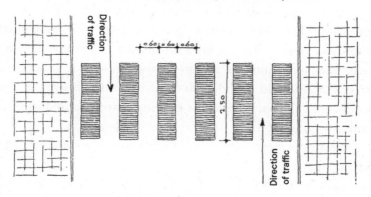

Fig. 15. The Zebra pattern.

Illustration from *Memorandum No. 6*, Royal Dutch Touring Club (ANWB).

Now zebra crossings worldwide determine how we move about in the streets and interact with each other. The city model of the time is also recognisable in neighbourhoods such as the Bijlmer (part of Amsterdam) and Amsterdam Nieuw-West, as well as in new urban municipalities such as Zoetermeer and Nieuwegein. These have a relatively large amount of space for cars, both on the roads and in parking areas.[6]

The woonerf was a reaction to this model. It was a new ideal focusing on play, equality, and social cohesion, rather than on traffic flow, speed, and efficiency. Although cars were allowed into woonerfs, the speed limit was expressed in human terms: a walking speed. That's just 6 km/h (slightly under 4 mph). The pedestrian also always had right of way over other street users.

From the 1970s on, there were both older residential areas that had been converted into woonerfs and new neighbourhoods designed using the woonerf model; rather than being tubes for rapid transit, the streets here were designed to spend time in.

Beyond the Netherlands, woonerfs were emulated in many countries. They were known as 'complete streets' in the United States and 'home zones' in Britain.[7] 'Instead of politely ignoring each other, as Londoners tend to do, the residents ... now throw street parties, hold rounders and softball tournaments in the nearby park and socialize in the evenings,' wrote journalist Carl Honoré in 2016.[8]

But in the meantime, things had started to go wrong in the Netherlands.

Niek de Boer's first woonerf is still in good shape. However, John Schoorl, writing in De Volkskrant in 2015, described the 'cauliflower neighbourhood' of Emmerhout as very down-at-heel. High-rise buildings had been added, no one was looking after the grass properly, the area was crime-ridden, and turnover among residents was high.

I cycle around Tanthof, a small 1980s neighbourhood of Delft that's a collection of interlinked woonerfs, rows of houses separated by alleyways to prevent the spread of fire, and narrow passages. Pedestrians and cyclists can get around the neighbourhood from any angle, but there's only one way drivers can get in.

The main thing that strikes me is how many cars are parked here. What grass and plants there are don't look very well maintained. Although it is a school holiday, there aren't any children playing outdoors. Everyone's inside. There are various possible explanations for this. But these days Tanthof isn't a shining example to be shown off to foreign delegations.

'The residents are older now,' says André Pettinga. As a traffic planner for the local authority, he has an insider's view of how the woonerf has changed. 'So people do sit down and walk about in Tanthof, but there are far fewer children playing outside than in the early days, when it was all new.' Because of the shrinking numbers of children in the neighbourhood,

Tanthof's schools are set for a compulsory merger.[9]

This may be partly due to natural changes in demographic structure: my own street has gone the opposite way in recent years and now has younger residents. Yet I can't seem to find a genuinely vibrant woonerf built in the 1970s or 1980s. In Rotterdam, I come across a woonerf sign in a 1930s neighbourhood. It's unclear what distinguishes this little side street from those running parallel to it. There's no difference in street furniture or any other aspects of its design: no plants or trees, no chicanes, no tubs of flowers. Is a small sign enough to make motorists drive at walking speed?

When I tell Marco about my ride around Tanthof, he replies:

> **Cycling Professor** @fietsprofessor
> I live in a post-cauliflower neighbourhood. There are narrow, meandering streets here too. But drivers regularly do 39 km/h (over 24 mph).[10]

And my colleague Gwen Martèl, aged 32, says: 'I used to live in the Galvanistraat in The Hague, a street built before the war. When I lived there it was a woonerf, with a special street sign. There weren't any pavements. Cars were only allowed to park in a zigzag pattern, which left quite large areas free for children to play, while drivers had to wait if there was a car coming from the opposite direction. But now it's a zone with a 30 km/h (almost 20 mph) speed limit, and it's become a one-way street.'

What's happened?

The 30 km/h Sign

According to André Pettinga, the 30 km/h zones introduced in 1984 brought an end to woonerfs in the newer neighbourhoods. 'The idea of a 30 km/h limit came to us from Germany. Put a 30 km/h sign on a German road and the locals will stick to it. It's not the same here.'

Little by little, Pettinga says, the woonerf — once a robust concept in urban planning and social improvement — gave way to a far less ambitious model focused on technical traffic issues, with far less emphasis on the street as a place to spend time in.

Besides, it's much cheaper and easier to lay straight streets with the odd speed bump. This can even be done mechanically, rolling out the paving stones like a carpet. Such streets are far easier to maintain and keep clear of dirt and snow, enabling local authorities to save money. And according to Sustainable Safety's philosophy, this design was actually safer.[11] Children would once again learn that they had to stick to the pavement.[12]

The word 'woonerf' disappeared from the Dutch Highway Code at the end of the 1980s: now all that remains is the word 'erf' (literally 'yard'), which includes industrial estates and shopping streets. 'I do think it's progress that we can extend the concept to cover other urban areas, not just residential streets and neighbourhoods,' says Pettinga. 'It's a good thing that we can think about this without putting cars first, which used to be the default approach.'

Yet the idea of the street as a place to spend time in faded away in many residential neighbourhoods. Sustainable Safety has nothing to say about woonerfs.

According to Janneke Zomervrucht, who, as an advocate of the interests of children and pedestrians, favours woonerfs, some local authorities still use this model in their plans for new-build areas. But the term used for the speed limit applicable

to woonerfs, *stapvoets* (at a walking pace), was deleted from the
Highway Code in 2013, and many people no longer know what it
means.[13] In the last few years, several local authorities have added
a sticker indicating a 15 km/h speed limit (slightly less than 10
mph) to the rectangular blue woonerf sign depicting a house, an
adult, a child with a ball, and a car.[14]

Fifteen kilometres an hour. That's the average speed of an
adult cyclist. Not a walking pace.

According to Statistics Netherlands, the country lost over
2,500 woonerfs in the second half of the 1990s, leaving just over
4,000.[15] How many still exist today, and how exactly are they
counted? I search Statistics Netherlands' website for the latest
figures. When I can't find them, I ring the information service.
'Woonerfs? What exactly do you mean? Haven't heard the word
before. Do we keep figures on them?' a member of staff replies.
Later, Statistics Netherlands emails me a set of statistics on farm-
yards (one of the primary meanings of 'erf'). 'Was this what you
were looking for?'

And so the term 'woonerf' has vanished from the Highway Code,
manuals, design principles, and statistics, and ultimately from
human memory.

At the same time, special status has been conferred on zones
with a 30 km/h speed limit, while the speed bump has been
honoured with an official CROW design module.[16] It's now a tool
available to traffic engineers designing local streets or roads that
have to accommodate both slow road users and motor traffic.
Members of the public, though, have a hard job getting a speed
bump installed, and compared with a woonerf, it is just a sticking
plaster on an open wound, a solution designed from the motorist's perspective.

Just as with traffic lights, members of the public have to take the trouble of lobbying local newspapers and members of the local executive if they want a speed bump.[17] You won't get one even if measurements show that 15 per cent of drivers exceed 39 km/h (well over 24 mph) in an area with a 30 km/h speed limit. That's not considered dangerous enough.

The last example comes from Marco's new neighbourhood in Ede, where other key prerequisites for a safe 'cauliflower neighbourhood' have also disappeared.

Cycling Professor @fietsprofessor
Though the streets end in cul-de-sacs, they're very wide, and ample space has been provided for parking and manoeuvring out of parking spaces. The speed limit for the first 500 metres of the neighbourhood access road is 50 km/h (over 30 mph). This is probably because a traffic model says that makes it easier for cars to turn off the 'higher order' flow street faster. And it's far easier to drive fast in today's cars, which are bigger, faster and more comfortable than their 1980s counterparts. There's bound to be an accident here sooner or later. Then we're sure to get a speed bump.

Niek de Boer was disappointed when the principle that neighbourhoods should be designed as places in which to spend time was abandoned. John Schoorl wrote: 'He spoke of "a miserable compromise, a caricature": there was now a "disastrous mix of different types of traffic, together with children at play".' The woonerf principle had been sacrificed to efficiency and the cult of speed.

Yet it *is* possible, as this historical story shows, to design streets, squares, neighbourhoods, districts, and towns according to a completely different model — and to put these designs into practice.

Strolling Along the Banks of the Seine

Anne Hidalgo, the mayor of Paris, is trying to turn a city with several million inhabitants into a place where people can once more go about their business in a carefree way, without needing to travel at high speed or to use heavy machines to reach their destinations.

This mayor isn't intimidated by the threat of gridlock. In the summer of 2016, after a few experiments, she closed a road alongside the Seine to motor traffic. Before that, it had accommodated 2,600 cars an hour during rush hour. It's now again possible to cycle and stroll along what used to be a two-lane asphalt highway, laid through the city in the 1960s, or to enjoy an aperitif at one of the picnic tables there.

I borrowed my parents' car for my last visit to Paris. Just one day before leaving I discovered the existence of the 'vignette Crit'Air' or air quality certificate. Since 2016 it's been mandatory to have one on your windscreen to drive into the city. The cost (€4) wasn't the problem. But the procedure for ordering the sticker online — the only way to get it — would take ten days. *Merde!*

Fortunately it turned out to be possible to drive into Paris without the sticker between 8 pm and 8 am. So I arranged to arrive in the evening, and once I reached the city the Citroën Picasso went straight into a parking garage, at €35 a day, a few Métro stations away from my hotel. When the alarm clock went off at 6 am on departure day, I got out of bed cursing: if only I'd booked a ticket for the high-speed train, Thalys, I could have enjoyed breakfast in Paris and still arrived in Rotterdam at the same time, and it would have cost me hardly any more. Now I had to leave Paris before 8 am — all because of the air quality certificate.

A year and a half later I visit Paris again with a friend and discover the other ways in which the city is trying to break its car habit. This time we hop on the Thalys. On arrival at the Gare du Nord, I enter my credit card details into a terminal at a bike-docking station, and we help ourselves to two identical rental bikes.

Now we both have a Vélib', a portmanteau word combining *vélo* (bicycle) and *liberté* (freedom). The first half hour is free. You pay a euro for the next hour, and then a further euro for each additional half hour. If you swap your bike at another docking station within half an hour, you can continue to ride around for nothing. Each Vélib' is used an average of six times daily, and 300,000 Parisians have a subscription. This is one of the world's biggest bike share schemes.[18]

Shortly after our visit, the system collapses when a new operator decides to electrify all the docking stations. It goes hopelessly wrong,[19] dogged by a series of technical problems. But during our stay we see plenty of people on Vélibs. Cycling through Paris is exciting and fun. At each intersection, suggested bike lanes are marked out: dashed lines down the right side of the street, with an outline of a bike at intervals. And there are traffic signs depicting bikes everywhere.

I feel welcome. As a tourist, I find this far more relaxing than driving around and trying to find somewhere to park. We can cycle just about everywhere, and we can even ride in the opposite direction to motor traffic along the bus lane, which has a dual function as both bus and cycle lane. Parisians on bikes, both Vélibs and their own, ride with easy nonchalance, letting motor traffic stop for them. We cycle cheerily over one crossroads after the other, along the grand boulevards, past little cafés serving espresso and croissants, towards the car-free highway beside the Seine. Cycling beneath the now-redundant signs for motor traffic, we find ourselves at the river.

Now, suddenly, we are the fastest road users. Lots of café terraces and lively goings-on here. We look for a docking station, where we will pick up our next bikes in due course. I notice the docking station isn't on the pavement, but on the road itself. A space the size of one car now accommodates six Vélibs.

Hidalgo earned both plaudits and brickbats for handing the bank of the Seine back to pedestrians. A pressure group called '40 millions d'automobilistes' ('40 million drivers', a name reflecting the number of driving licence holders in France) brought a court case against the mayor, arguing that her actions had jeopardised mobility. She was accused of having fudged numbers to show that closing the highway alongside the Seine had reduced motor traffic in the city centre. Her private telephone number was shared online in 2017.

Can removing a road make it easier to drive more freely elsewhere? A major study of 63 roads and squares closed to motor traffic in various European cities (mainly in Britain and Germany) suggests that it does.[20] In many cases, cars disappeared altogether, rather than being displaced into parallel streets, lessening the dreaded congestion.

Hidalgo made the same claim, but the court disagreed, holding that the research was inadequate. However, actual measures of traffic levels before and after the road closure along the Seine, announced the week the court handed down its decision, did indicate a reduction in motor traffic in the areas nearby.[21]

Whatever the situation, Paris provides its residents with ample alternatives to cars, something traffic models fail to take into account. When my friend and I get on the Métro after a concert, we are struck by how busy it is. Five years after Anne Hidalgo became mayor, people make 200,000 more trips by Métro than before — every day.[22]

Being determined to take the long-term view, Hidalgo continued her battle. When the court denied that there had been a drop in motor traffic in the area around the road she closed, she switched to a different approach based on more fundamental principles — the need to protect Paris's cultural heritage. She won her case: people can continue to stroll unhindered along the banks of the Seine today.[23]

Rather than enabling more people to travel around, Hidalgo wants to bring their destinations closer together. She's keen to organise Paris on the principle of 'hyper-proximity'.[24] People must have the right to engage in all the meaningful activities necessary to fulfil their needs and wishes without being dependent on rapid modes of transport — that's the message of the '15-minute-city'.[25]

Having won the 2020 municipal elections, Hidalgo took advantage of the COVID-19 pandemic to speed up her plan to make Paris a more human city. Pop-up cycle paths have appeared city-wide and additional funds have been made available for similar infrastructure in the outlying districts, the *banlieues*. She has promised to cut 72 per cent of street parking spaces — that's 60,000 spaces. Her ultimate aim is for people to be able to reach any point in Paris by bike or on foot: the City of Light as a patchwork of '15-minute communities', with the Champs-Élysées transformed from a highway into an urban garden.

Paris reopens my eyes to my own country. On the highways along the Seine, cars have made way for picnic tables. Could we make the same changes?

The contrast with my home city of Rotterdam feels particularly stark. The tunnel under the River Maas, which links the northern and southern parts of the city, could be made car-free too, but after renovation it's reopened by a woman on stilts and a troupe of actors with learning difficulties. We're allowed to walk through it for one day, to celebrate the fact that we can race through the renovated yellow tubes in our cars again tomorrow.

Here too, though, motor traffic around the tunnel melted away when renovation work began. BNR Radio announced, 'The closure of the Maas tunnel is expected to cause major traffic problems,' the evening before it was shut off.[26] The next day, the local broadcasting organisation RTV Rijnmond reported, 'The first evening rush hour after the closure of the Maas tunnel is no different from usual.'[27]

Some Dutch cities have opted to put people's interests above those of traffic in certain areas. In Utrecht, the canal encircling the city centre that was transformed into an urban highway and parking area in the 1970s has now been restored. In 2019, The Hague inaugurated a school street inspired by examples from Flanders. The Abeelstraat, where cars used to stand at the school gates with their engines running, is now reserved for cyclists and pedestrians from a quarter of an hour before the school bell rings to a quarter of an hour afterwards.[28] To ensure there was enough room for social distancing during the COVID-19 pandemic, the local authority went on to expand the pilot project to include another dozen streets. A year later, it began making these school streets permanent, by means of a traffic by-law.

Groningen is in the process of making 'room for you'. The local authority that made a radical choice in the 1970s — a low-traffic city centre — is set to take further action over the next few years. More cars out, more people in. The guidelines on the use of public space, in which Marco has had a hand, state: 'We no longer take a one-dimensional approach to designing street[s] in which mobility is the sole guiding principle. Instead, mobility will join accessibility, safety, human perception [meaning experience], health, social interaction, ecology, climate adaptation, economy and cultural history in making the street: the ten dimensions of the street.'[29]

Before and after the recent restoration of Central Utrecht's historic canal.
Source: https://www.bouwpututrecht.nl.

But other Dutch initiatives that I'd initially thought radical turn out on closer inspection to be aligned with 'car logic' after all.

An example is the 'cars are guests' sign you see in specially designated 'bike streets', which are increasingly widespread in the Netherlands. At first sight, it's a nice idea.

Cycling Professor @fietsprofessor
So people are guests everywhere else in towns and cities? Why don't they put this sign at the beginning of the built-up area? 'Welcome to our town, where cars are guests'?

Plans to reduce the number of traffic accidents to zero are also less ground-breaking than they sound. Take Vision Zero, the European Commission's plan to reach zero traffic mortalities by 2050, which is also the target the Netherlands has set for itself. The initiative originated in Sweden, homeland of Volvo, the car that built its reputation on safety.

Vision Zero is beginning to come within reach in the Nordic countries. Helsinki announced that there were no traffic deaths in the city in 2019 — for the first time since records began.[30] But it soon became clear that people cycle and walk relatively little in the Finnish capital, especially children.[31]

Oslo, too, nearly managed it in 2019, with just one traffic fatality, in a car accident involving a single victim. However, Norway's Vision Zero policy is now that children are 'permitted to cycle on the pavement'. So Norwegian children have to avoid traffic, not vice versa. Is that the aim of Vision Zero? Zero traffic fatalities because there are no people in the streets any more to be knocked down and killed? Despite these measures, a two-year-old was run over and killed in Oslo in January 2020 when both the traffic lights and the pedestrian lights were on green at the same time.[32]

There are alternatives. The approach taken by the Spanish city of Pontevedra is not to save lives, but to avoid the need to do so. There are no traffic deaths there either, not because Pontevedra has opted for Vision Zero, but because the city's administration has banned speed from its streets.

The medieval heart of the city and the surrounding eighteenth-century neighbourhoods have been made car-free. In addition, the speed limit for other vehicles has been brought down to 30 km/h (almost 20 mph). Traffic lights have been removed. The absence of a metro hasn't prevented the local authority from creating a colourful metro-style map. Instead of stations, it shows the walking distances between the city's main squares, streets and public places of interest.

As an indirect result of this policy, Pontevedra's CO_2 emissions have fallen by 70 per cent, without electric cars playing any part in the reduction.[33] Pontevedra shows that you don't need a CO_2 policy or Vision Zero if the local administration aims to make the city a place that prioritises healthy living and getting about in a relaxed way.[34] It also shows that it may be better not to set one-sided goals. If you cut CO_2 by rolling out electric cars, you still have to implement Vision Zero and take children off the streets to stop them being run over. Pontevedra demonstrates that it's possible to achieve safer streets and reduce carbon emissions by implementing just one solution.

Elsewhere in Spain, too, there are discussions about what exactly public space is for. Urban planner Salvador Rueda calls our current practice 'displacement': we've displaced people and cooped them up in restricted spaces.[35] Pedestrians on the pavement, drivers in the street, cyclists somewhere in between — all separated into different flows, just as advocated by Sustainable Safety.

Rueda is in the process of creating *superilles* ('superblocks') in Barcelona. These are car-free neighbourhoods whose streets are once again places where people can spend time.[36] They are rather like 'cauliflower neighbourhoods', but in line with Catalan tradition and based on Barcelona's nineteenth-century street plan. And with benches for elderly people.

———

Under the leadership of a liberal mayor, the Flemish town of Mechelen has given itself a new name: Kinderstad (Children's Town). Taking a look around one day, I see a place that was clearly given over to cars at one time, and which still has lots of massive four-wheel-drive vehicles parked in the streets. However, there are also 'bicycle streets' in the centre where bikes have priority, and parents on cargo bikes are a common sight. It boasts child-friendly cafés and all kinds of contraptions for children to play on. Further out, there are lots of playgrounds and wooded areas designed for children. Mechelen also has a Children's Council, with a Children's Mayor and a Children's Secretary, which meets almost once a month and advises the town council.

In the park, I ask a mother what she thinks of the town. Eline van Dort, originally from the Netherlands, is just back from Mexico, her husband's country of origin. For her, 'child-friendly cafés' are a bizarre concept. 'Apparently we have to label a restaurant "child-friendly" here, which almost suggests that you wouldn't be welcome to take your kids into other restaurants, or that they wouldn't be allowed to be themselves there,' she says. 'Cafés in Mexico don't have special features to suit kids, but kids are welcome there — they're just part of life in a way they aren't here.'

Van Dort moved here not because she'd heard that Mechelen was a 'children's town', and clearly not because of the cafés, but because street life is better for children here than it is in Brussels. It's quieter.

These initiatives in other countries, which involve giving the streets back to pedestrians, older people, and children, stand in contrast to some of the contemporary innovations the Dutch are seeking to promote internationally. These include our efficient pink 'bicycle streets' (where bikes have priority), which just replicate the problems we're familiar with from cars: for instance, children can't cross without a parent to hold up the traffic, as cyclists now ride fast and in large numbers, like motorists on two wheels.[37]

Thinking about it, even the 'chip cone' is essentially a means to streamline the traffic flow. For one thing, it was essential that this innovation should not interrupt the flow of motor traffic: it's based on the assumption that the street is a thoroughfare, not a place to spend time in.

A bicycle as a means to get from A to B with maximum efficiency — that's a far cry from what it was when people were setting up the ENWB (the First, Only, Real, or Fair Dutch Touring Club) and inventing the 'cauliflower neighbourhood'. Back then, a bike symbolised a different world: a world of independence, balance, playfulness, open communication, and freedom for the individual that didn't come at the cost of others; a world in which John Lennon and Yoko Ono lay in bed with a white bicycle that didn't just symbolise a solution to the traffic congestion problem.

> **Cycling Professor** @fietsprofessor
> Maybe we've got everything so ship-shape here now with our segregated cycle paths that it's become even harder to see how our minds have been colonised by efficiency thinking. On the other hand, this might just give us the space we need to think about the drawbacks of the current approach, of putting a cycle path next to a road.

The Race for COVID-19 Streets

Marco's comment came back to me after the outbreak of the COVID-19 pandemic.

Brussels was one of the first cities to announce measures to make room for social distancing. The 'pentagon' — the city centre — was declared a woonerf or residential area with low speed limits. Although it remained possible to get about by car in the centre, drivers were obliged to give all other road users right of way.

This was a revolutionary policy change: suddenly public space in the heart of Brussels was no longer about cars, but about people — regardless of their vehicle. You could still get about by car, but the focus was no longer on roads as channels for motor vehicles. Traffic lights were turned off.

But under pressure of complaints, the city soon decided to adjust the new plan. Brussels is now focusing on becoming a 30 km/h city, an aim also adopted by cities including Berlin, Cologne, and Amsterdam. This too sounds revolutionary, as 30 km/h is much safer than 50 km/h. But is it really? Once again, Brussels is focusing on the speed of our machines. The woonerf, by contrast, is a way of using public space that puts people first.

And then there were the pop-up cycling lanes. By the end of April 2020, urbanist Mike Lydon had listed the top ten cities with 'COVID-19 streets' by the number of bike lane kilometres promised:[38]

1. Paris (403.8)
2. Lima (187)
3. NYC (100) and Portland (100)
4. Oakland (74)
5. Bogotá (49.7)
6. Quito (38.9)
7. Auckland (37.9)

8. Minneapolis/St Paul (36.8)
9. Burlington (25.8)
10. Milan (22)

Rome followed a few days later, announcing 150 km of new bike lanes,[39] while in Montpellier, France, the mayor had himself filmed spraying yellow signs to mark cycle lanes on the asphalt of his city.[40]

Meanwhile, Sadiq Khan, the Mayor of London, and walking and cycling commissioner Will Norman announced: 'London's road to recovery cannot be clogged with cars. It has to be one Londoners can walk and cycle down as part of a greener, cleaner, healthier future.'[41]

It all sounded great. The idea that we should give public space to cyclists instead of cars was the very idea that had made the Netherlands 'a cyclist's paradise'.

Yet we also have our limitations, I realised, as the Netherlands started to feel more and more like the only country where COVID-19 hadn't sparked any fundamental discussion about what we use public space for. Could that be because we have become even more accustomed to the idea that streets exist for fast-moving traffic — and because we have so successfully accommodated this state of affairs? I started to feel like a spoilsport, crankily reflecting on what others dubbed 'The Great Reclamation'.[42]

But it feels important to share this lesson from the Netherlands: while bicycle lanes can make life in cities better, they can also easily reinforce the idea that streets are designed for fast-moving traffic. If there is no debate on what public space is for, they may simply become part of conventional car logic.

As Robert Pirsig wrote in *Zen and the Art of Motorcycle Maintenance*:

If a factory is torn down but the rationality which
produced it is left standing, then that rationality
will simply produce another factory. If a revolution
destroys a government, but the systematic patterns
of thought that produced that government are left
intact, then those patterns will repeat themselves.[43]

The View Through the Windscreen
and the Wobbly Mirror

It's from Roland Kager that I first learn the full extent to which
car logic has colonised our thinking — but also how you can
play with this. I arrange to meet Kager several times, first in the
course of my 'cycling versus congestion' project, at his office in
Rotterdam's Groot Handelsgebouw (business building) next to
Central Station. Kager is a data analyst and multimodal trans-
port-researcher, meaning he's interested in traffic, but not in
cars. 'Though that in itself reflects car logic,' he explains. 'It's like
saying the Church isn't interested in sex. Not concerning myself
with cars actually means that they're of great concern to me.'

Car logic permeates the language we use, says Kager. 'We say
the IJ tunnel is closed for the Dam to Dam Run from Amsterdam
to Zaandam. Why don't we say it the other way around — it's
open for runners?'

He points out: 'We speak of vulnerable road users, but
they've only been vulnerable since the advent of fast traffic with
big, heavy vehicles. Why don't we call those fast, heavy vehicles
dangerous road users?'

This is an amusing game once you've grasped how it works,
like looking at pictures that can be 'read' in two different ways.
Which do you see, the duck or the rabbit?

Why are roads you can't live next to, cycle on, or walk along called 'main roads'? Why do we speak of 'segregated' or 'separate' cycle paths, when it's actually motorists who've been given a 'separate' space of their own? The language of traffic instils a 'windscreen view' of the world, as Belgian mobility expert Kris Peeters wrote a good 20 years ago.[44] Put on a pair of red-tinted glasses, and after a while you'll no longer notice that they turn everything red; it'll just seem normal.

The language of traffic, however, is more than a view or a pair of glasses. It distorts reality, as if you are looking through a car windscreen, or into a wobbly mirror. A distorting mirror alters the way you behave; you start pulling funny faces. That's how reality changes, and after a while we no longer notice the difference. The radical monopoly.

Kager comes across the wobbly-mirror effect all the time in his work. 'It stops us really seeing what's happening in our streets. Why do we talk about traffic accidents? As if the one cyclist who runs down and kills a pedestrian — which hardly ever happens — were part of the same system that kills people day in, day out, which nearly always involves cars.'

Traffic, a curious word indeed. According to the *Oxford Shorter Dictionary*, it wasn't until the early 19th century that it acquired its current meaning, the passage to and fro of vehicles and the like along a route. One of the older meanings of traffic is interpersonal dealings.

But what does it mean in actual usage now? On the news, you'll hear that dense fog has disrupted 'traffic'. That 'traffic' is at a standstill. That there are 'traffic' delays in the wake of a crash. That 'traffic' is gradually returning to normal after such incidents. What traffic means in these instances is cars. But it sounds as if it means all of us.

'In the Netherlands, we actually get about more often by bike or public transport or on foot than by car,' says Kager.[45] 'Especially over short distances. But it doesn't matter whether you walk into your local town centre or drive 80 km (nearly 50 miles) to an outlet store, you're classed as a traffic participant regardless — even though an 80 km drive has an incomparably greater impact on society than a stroll into town.'

Something peculiar happens the other way round, too, says Kager. 'When crowds of people are left stranded at train stations because of some problem with the points, no one says traffic has come to a standstill. We say "There are no trains running between Utrecht and The Hague", and "travellers" can take an alternative route via Schiphol. So don't motorists count as travellers?'

According to Kager, the way we talk about 'traffic' makes cars far more important in our perception than they really are in the Dutch context: the distorting mirror magnifies them. 'The traffic problem you wanted to solve is a good example. Only 15 per cent of Dutch people are caught up in traffic jams each week, and only 5 five per cent of the population say it's a problem that affects them personally. But because we all want a functional traffic system, 35 per cent say they see this as a social problem anyway. So one in every three people here thinks traffic congestion is a problem that affects other people, even though those "other people" are a tiny minority.'[46]

Spot on. I'd classed road congestion as a national problem because I'd thought it was a nuisance to everyone. And that was because of the language we use. Yet for some people, the short drive home from work couldn't take long enough. The fact that it could mean a brief spell in a cocoon, a half-hour's respite between their nagging boss and their whingeing kids, hadn't even crossed my mind.[47] Because we had a congestion *problem*.

'And then there's no conceptual framework for certain things,' Kager continues. Many of the non-car phenomena he encounters and researches in his work as a multimodal mobility-researcher have no names. No categories. That makes it harder to make them visible in reports and advisory papers for government — which means they get less attention and less funding.

That's why Kager also plays the language game seriously, in his professional life.

By giving things different names, can you make other things more visible, and thereby create a new reality?

The 'Train Cyclist'

'Did you know that nearly half of all the people you see on trains in this country have got to the station by bike or are going to continue their journeys by bike?' asks Kager during our first conversation.

'Now you come to mention it,' I say, 'that applies to about three-quarters of all my train journeys.'

'That doesn't surprise me. I've made up a term for people who do that — I call them "train cyclists",' says Kager. 'How many of all the cyclists you see in towns and cities are train cyclists, do you think?'

I haven't a clue. One in ten?

'One in three. So if half of all train passengers are train cyclists, and a third of all cyclists in city centres are train cyclists, why is it that "train cyclist" isn't an official category in mobility surveys?'

If you're travelling to a town or city in the Netherlands, the combination of bicycle and train is a quick way to reach your destination, and often a competitive alternative to the car. It's simple: you cover most of the distance at maximum speed, and you can cycle the first and last few kilometres using a mode of transport that's ideal for local access.

One reason so many trips are made by bike in the Netherlands, says Kager, is that bikes are so useful for linking up with trains. And Dutch trains are used as intensively as they are because so many people cycle. It makes everything more flexible. 'In the big cities, you often have a choice between several stations if you've got a bike to get there. That's why many people choose to be "train cyclists" — because it's a more enjoyable way to travel, you've got your daily exercise, people-watching, unexpected encounters, and time for reading or social media on the train.'

The texture of our lives, the appearance of our cities and the nature of our mobility are closely interrelated, resulting in the way of life typical of Dutch towns and cities, so different from that in countries such as Belgium or France, where the vast majority of people have to drive to hypermarkets outside their villages. And so different from the United States, where a third of people eat daily in fast food joints, many of which are located at traffic intersections and thus accessible only by car.[48] Many Dutch city-dwellers can do their shopping on the way home from the station — a growing trend.

'What you see in town centres nowadays, as well as on campuses or in Amsterdam's "financial mile",' says Kager, 'is that though there are more homes and jobs there, the number of journeys made by car is actually decreasing. Traffic engineers assume that more homes and jobs will automatically lead to more motor traffic: that's the outcome churned out by their models, after all. But urbanisation is having a far more radical impact. People in urban areas are cycling and walking more and more, and they're increasingly opting to take the train rather than the car to go out of town, despite all the investment there's been in infrastructure for cars.' That, in its turn, accounts for the rise in the number of train cyclists, who become more numerous with each year that passes. And yet the term is new to me.

———

Just as I had regarded traffic jams as a problem because I heard so much about them, I'd completely failed to perceive train cyclists as a group, even though I myself was an active train cyclist. That was how I'd ended up focusing on bike highways as an alternative to cars, rather than on a combination of bikes and rail.

I'm not alone. Dutch Railways and ProRail (responsible for railway infrastructure) are taken aback by the popularity of public transport bikes. These continue to break new rental records each year. Yet the Dutch travel planning website 9292.nl only recently adopted door-to-door itineraries that include bikes, and still with very basic functionality. The Dutch Railways site now allows you to indicate whether you plan to arrive at the station or continue your journey by bike, but you have to tick the appropriate box first.

People from other countries are often inspired by their pleasant experiences of Dutch towns and cities, says Kager, and they see that joined-up rail and bike transport are the reason. 'Dutch people who've lived abroad for a while often notice this for the first time when they return. We like living this way, but we hardly ever really put it into words.'

I had that experience myself on my return from Moscow. It was so much easier to cycle or to take a train in the Netherlands; there were no bicycle parking facilities at Russian stations.

I'm fascinated by Kager's story and write an article with the headline: 'Meet the travellers who've only just been given a name — train cyclists'. And once again I see how new words can change reality.

I get an email from the Flemish MP Dirk de Kort. He's read the piece on train cyclists and wants more information. I put him sharing Dutch and Flemish statistics and experiences, after which De Kort incorporates 'train cyclists' into his political vocabulary. He comes up with another variant they have in Flanders, 'bus cyclists'.

Half a year later, De Kort's assistant sends me a press release containing this sentence: 'In the Flemish Parliament, Dirk de Kort has backed an expansion of the Blue-Bike scheme in Flanders to support train and bus cyclists. Minister Ben Weyts has given a positive response.' Blue-Bike, a Belgian public transport bicycle, has been allocated a further €1 million, a significant sum.

Kager made an invisible group of travellers visible and gave them a name. Now they constitute an official category, and policies taking them into account are being actively developed. Kager continues to play around with new categories. What if you were to divide motorists into four groups: the quarter who drive most often, the quarter who drive least often, and the two groups in between? He's studied this new categorisation in Eindhoven: 'What you see is that the 25 per cent who use cars most are responsible for two-thirds of motor traffic in the city. So now we can have a meaningful discussion: should the local authority be making things easier for them? Or doing more for the other 75 per cent who use cars less often or very little, and taking more account of their wishes in decisions affecting the city?'

Picture a situation where one-quarter of the people living in a street produce two-thirds of all the rubbish in the recycling containers, so the containers are always overflowing. Should the local authority provide more containers? Employ more bin men? Or do something quite different? What kind of town do you want?

Meanwhile, Back in Lego City

The same question arises in the world of toys: what kind of town do you want?

'There are bikes in Lego sets,' says Marcel Steeman, who sits on the North Holland Provincial Council during working hours, and who's also a father and a Lego fan. '"But where are the bike paths?" my young son asked. That made me think. We take being able to cycle around for granted here. Yet at the same time we think it's normal that Lego City doesn't have any cycle paths.'

After posts on this subject had garnered thousands of likes on social media, and people had dug out their old Lego sets and discovered that older models allotted far less space to cars, Steeman decided to send Lego Ideas a design including cycle paths. Within three months, he'd collected 10,000 signatures in support. Once you have this many supporters, your design is eligible to be produced and distributed worldwide by Lego.

Yet it was quite a struggle, Steeman says. His design was rejected several times because Lego claims to refrain from political statements. But isn't the lack of a cycle path in Lego City in itself a political statement?

Another issue was that the design had to correspond to international standards, so that people all over the world could understand it. While Steeman was designing the new set, he discovered just how complicated it all is; there are so many different rules on cycle paths. Is a cycle path segregated or not, is it red (as in the Netherlands), blue (as in Denmark), or green (as in Germany)?

While cycle paths vanished discreetly from Lego sets in the 1980s, it's difficult to reinstate them now that all Lego cars are two studs wider and there are so many different regulations to be taken into account. It's just like the real world. The towns and cities with cycling infrastructure in the Netherlands, Denmark, and Germany are the exception, while those without any cycle paths remain the norm.

The Street as a Place to Hang Out

Priority for Children! was absorbed into Traffic Safety Netherlands after the forced merger and disappeared. Yet its underlying principle, the idea of the street as a place where people can spend time, is still around.

They're back — Janneke Zomervrucht, Jan Torenstra, and another ten or so veterans, including people from the Pedestrians' Association too. They have set up a foundation with the same aim they've always had: to make sure that we continue to see and to design our public spaces as places to spend time in, and our streets as streets for people. That's why their organisation is now called MENSenSTRAAT (HUMANandSTREET or Human Street). 'A street where the focus is on strolling about in a relaxed way and meeting other people. A street that's attractive, safe and inclusive. ... Pleasant streets fit for human beings often fail to materialise ... because there are no ordinary people around the drawing board as stakeholders. That has to change,' writes the daily newspaper *Trouw*.[49]

Just as in the days of Priority for Children!, the foundation focuses its efforts at administrative level on the relevant government department, Zomervrucht explains. MENSenSTRAAT also tries to get a seat at the table in consultations where the traffic engineer is often the only expert present — to make the point that although we say a deer runs across a road, we could equally well say that a road runs through a deer's wood.

'There are professorships in traffic engineering, you can study it as a subject,' says Zomervrucht, and I think of Marcus

Popkema, who told me all about how the profession developed in the 1950s. 'But what we might call urban liveability engineering hasn't yet developed the same fund of professional expertise.'

That's where MENSenSTRAAT is trying to make a difference. The initial results are encouraging. A consultative platform called Ruimte voor Lopen (Room to Walk) was set up in 2019, in cooperation with the ramblers' association Wandelnet, and over 30 government bodies, institutions with relevant expertise, and other social organisations. 'We also urged the Ministry of Infrastructure to appoint someone with responsibility for walking as a mode of transport,' says Zomervrucht. There is someone now — Filip van As, a former member of the Zwolle local executive. He manages the Pedestrians Policy programme and also coordinates Room to Walk from within the ministry.

And MENSenSTRAAT isn't alone. Others are looking at what happens if you assume that streets are there not for traffic, but for people: in Groningen and Amsterdam, the cities that made the biggest changes in the 1970s, but also in Rotterdam. Here, two men in their thirties, Jorn Wemmenhove and Lior Steinberg, have set up a consultancy for urban transformation with another 'human' name — Humankind. Their aim is to create streets that meet a range of human needs, not just those of commuters needing to get to work quickly.

'We want to link the database containing the home addresses of all the primary-school-age children in Rotterdam with a database of the city's primary schools,' Steinberg enthuses, 'and then make sure there's at least one route along a continuous pavement from each home to a school, so children don't have to cross any roads.'

We're on a café terrace in front of Rotterdam's Central Station. 'Sounds radical, doesn't it?' he says. 'But all you'd have to do would be to raise a few zebra crossings to the same level as the pavements they link and install a few street intersection ramps.

It could be done everywhere in Rotterdam within just five years!'
If this came to fruition, my children would be able to reach the
playground on the other side of our street on their own. 'Cool!' I
respond.

But I then discover how hard it is to keep going when
you're trying to put an idea like this into practice. For instance,
speed bumps on roads with a 50 km/h speed limit (over 31 mph)
constantly meet with resistance from the emergency services,
which can't meet the targets we impose on them — reaching
emergency callers within 15 minutes — if they have to contend
with speed bumps.

One year later, Steinberg gives me a progress report on his
idea for streets with linked-up pavements. He and Wemmenhove
have presented their plan for more pavements throughout the
city, with sections of road for motor traffic in between, at a
consultation held by the Rotterdam municipal authority about
the areas around schools. As a result, two Rotterdam schools
have now been given permission to conduct a four-month traffic
safety experiment that involves temporary changes in the layout
of their local area. This is set out in the Mobility Climate Deal, a
document featuring an image of a lorry with an electric plug at
the top of each page.

Steinberg remains optimistic. 'That's how it always goes!
Every great idea gets reduced to a small-scale experiment, and
you have to try to get as much out of it as you can.' Wemmenhove
agrees. 'It's pretty good in Rotterdam, you know. You can get
things done quickly here because they're used to change.'

They are battling to recover the city from the car, metre by
metre. They've just installed a rainbow-coloured 'parklet' — a
temporary bench flanked by tubs of flowers — in front of the
Ferry, a gay bar in Westblaak Street. 'No sooner had we set the
flowers down than a bee alighted on one,' says Wemmenhove.
'Nature's quick to adapt. Now the local authority wants to

remove a whole row of parking spaces and replace them with a new green area.'

I get another opportunity to see how keen Rotterdammers are to do things differently when I start attending the traffic safety meetings held in my neighbourhood. The civil servants involved are eager to trial new ideas, and the local authority has a budget for experimental projects. What's lacking at the moment is a large enough number of citizens who are ready to take the initiative, committed people who want to help shape their local environment. People ready to protest, to take to the streets, to make posters — to fight new roads or developments that spoil the area they live in. The civil servants in my neighbourhood are trying to find 'seeds to plant', and they specifically say they're on the lookout for new language, new imagery.

'When the new green area was first mooted', says Wemmenhove, 'it dawned on the local authority that the Westblaak area doesn't *have* to be a thoroughfare.' Instead, it's set to become an area where people can stroll about at their leisure, just like the banks of the Seine.

Build a city around the car and you'll get motorists. But build a city around people and you'll get pedestrians, cyclists, and children in the streets.[50] There's now an ongoing discussion in Rotterdam about how to reintroduce more green areas so it'll be more agreeable to spend time in the city, less slippery in winter and cooler in summer. There's a move away from smooth traffic flows towards 'sticky places', the street as a place to hang out. And more and more sticky places are emerging.

In Amsterdam's De Pijp neighbourhood, where people live as close to each other as was the norm before the arrival of cars, the wheel seems to have turned full circle. Providing residents with a parking space in a nearby underground garage has enabled the first few streets to be made car-free, with only bicycle parking available at street level. It looks both wonderfully old-fashioned and wonderfully modern at the same time; you can play tag, just like in the old days, or run into the street after a Pokémon. Provided the local cyclists don't ride at an anti-social speed, that is.

Much of the resistance to these changes results from the invisible distorting mirror. The ratio of parking spaces to homes is being slashed in a new Amsterdam neighbourhood, Haven-Stad, to three cars per ten households. The same norm will also apply to the Merwede Canal area of Utrecht, not far from Utrecht Central Station: the plans for a new neighbourhood housing 12,000 people don't include any street-level parking space for cars. New residents will be required to commit to shared mobility, using a local app to reserve a car that is part of a shared fleet. 'Is it really acceptable to impose such requirements in such a desirable area?' a banker writes in response to one of Marco's posts about the new Utrecht plan.

'Good question,' Marco replies, 'but funnily enough, that's something no one ever asks when a new neighbourhood with a 1.7 parking ratio goes up next to an intercity station.'

Is it fair to want to build a Bicycle City where car-dependent people can't live? One genuine concern is that it excludes anyone who is physically dependent on a four-wheeled motor vehicle: those with physical disabilities and elderly people with restricted mobility.

Is it fair to build Car Cities in the rest of the country where anyone without a car — over half the Dutch population, including everyone under 18 — has to make way for cars? When the Dutch make more than half their trips without cars?

Mobility as a Common Good

What if we weren't dependent on companies, and all modes of transport were shared among the general public instead?

There is now a tacit assumption, especially among start-ups aiming to improve accessibility in cities, that people are consumers willing to pay for subscriptions that can meet their transport needs. This is known in transport jargon as 'mobility as a service' (MaaS). Uber, a taxi service you can hail by app, is a perfect example.

On my first Uber ride, in Amsterdam, I noticed the driver had set out a bottle of water on the back seat. It later dawned on me that that's precisely what 'as a service' means — maximum service at minimum cost. Initially, it felt as if I was in a Hollywood movie. But later on it occurred to me that he'd put the water there to get a good rating, without our having to talk to each other. It was unclear who I was doing business with when I paid for my trip via an app — the taxi driver, or Uber staff in the United States? Or someone else? Uber gets some of its funding from a Saudi oil sheikh.[51] And runs up losses amounting to billions of dollars each year.[52]

Swapfiets, a Dutch company that also operates in Belgium, Denmark, France, Germany and Italy, is another good example of mobility as a service. You take out a subscription to a bicycle and if there's some fault, Swapfiets will drop by to exchange it for another one. The conditions stipulate that you have to be able to show you've treated it properly if anything goes wrong. It's not your bike. You're ultimately dependent on the investor, Pon, the company that imports Volkswagen and owns the Gazelle bicycle brand.[53] The oBike and Mobike bicycle systems (based in Singapore and China, respectively), proved less successful, showing what happens when a platform company makes its money by attracting venture capital, rather than by committing to long-term service in the real world. In cities across Europe, the bikes broke down or were dumped in waterways or strung up from lampposts. oBike filed for bankrupcy in 2018, with many users reporting difficulty in retrieving the deposits they made through the oBike app. Mobike stopped providing services in many European cities and has now reappeared as an e-bike rental service under a different brand name.

Are there any alternatives to this model? Anna Nikolaeva, an urban planning lecturer at the University of Amsterdam, is working on the concept of 'mobility as a commons'.[54] While the goal of mobility as a service is to maximise ease and comfort, the aim of mobility as a 'commons' — a good shared by a large number of people — is to enable you to organise the way you get about independently from companies, but in cooperation with others. The white bicycle plan thought up by Amsterdam's Provos in the 1960s is one example, as is the childcare centre at Marco's children's school, which loans cargo bikes to local people.

'Mobility's something we share, like the air we breathe or the language we speak, and it's something we need to give meaning to collectively,' says Nikolaeva. It's more than just getting from A to B as fast and comfortably as possible. How you organise mobility also involves deciding whether to learn to mend your bike inner tube yourself or to get to know and support your local bike repair shop. It's about whether, as a citizen, you get involved in deciding how streets are to be laid out through membership of the national cycling association, or make your views known by filling in a complaint form for the firm whose services you subscribe to.

The concept of mobility as something shared by a large community shows that you don't have to be a consumer of platforms such as Uber which acquire a dominant position by reducing their overheads with each new user and which can sustain billions of dollars of losses until they are the only operator left. Like Uber, Swapfiets runs at a loss.[55]

Is it possible to think of examples of mobility as a common good other than hiring out vehicles? Nikolaeva mentions Ring-Ring, an app that allows you to collect points through cycling which you can spend in local shops and businesses, so the money you spend stays within the community.

She also mentions the citizens' budget established by Niek Mouter and economist Paul Koster, officially known as the Participative Value Evaluation.[56] Mouter is the legal philosopher who explained to me how many traffic deaths the building of a new motorway or an increase in the maximum road speed could cost. For the citizens' budget, Mouter and Koster asked people from Amsterdam to divide the limited budget available for the transport region among various construction projects, just as you might budget for a household.[57]

What they discovered through that experiment was that if you approach people not as consumers but as citizens, as members of the community, they are more inclined to choose projects that are good not just for themselves, but for the community in general. The decisions involved can be difficult and there may be human lives at sake. 'In the context of this experiment, you can also opt to delegate these difficult decisions to experts or other citizens if you don't want to take them yourself,' Koster says.

I discover an example of mobility as a common good — or a step in the right direction, at any rate — in my own neighbourhood. Arriving at Fietslokaal, my local bike repair shop, with a broken gear cable, I see five bicycles, all sprayed black and bearing the word 'Fietslokaal' in a stylish old-fashioned font. The bikes have light-green tyres — a nod to Swapfiets's blue ones.

The bike repair man tells me he's started a kind of local bike-share scheme. 'These are bikes I want to hire out mainly to locals,' he says.

'They can subscribe for €20 a month, and they have to drop by every six weeks so I can check the bikes are OK.' It's an experiment: he thinks it'll be particularly useful for parents with growing children.

This should in theory give him a rather more secure income. By subscribing to his scheme, you help him develop his business, rather like those who back an artist via patreon.com.

'Don't they think it's a bit of a nuisance to have to bring the bike back to you regularly?' I ask. It's cheaper to rent a Swapfiets, and the company sends a van to replace your bike if there's anything the matter with it.

'Then they can just get a Swapfiets bike, can't they?' he says firmly. His scheme has other advantages. It fosters local contacts, there's no need to send vans round, and the money stays in the local community. 'This helps children learn to look after their bikes properly,' he says. So it's not for the *Homo economicus* in us, but for the *Homo faber*, that part of us that enjoys making and mending things together.

Mobility as a common good may be a way of liberating human beings from the machine our mobility system has become. But how do you liberate them from machine logic?

The Double Meaning of 'Traffic'

During my foray into the battlefield behind our mobility system, I found myself feeling increasingly down. I spent some time investigating why it is that people act unthinkingly in cars, given the dangers. Once, when I was hungry and tired, I myself reversed fast without looking behind me. I was irritated at a driver in front of me

who was making a hash of manoeuvring out of a parking space —
and I nearly ran into a woman standing behind me in the car park.

Is it being trapped in the cramped space inside a car, unable
to stand up, that can make you feel so frustrated? Or is it the fact
that you spend so much time looking at people's backs, rather
than their faces? That's what Tom Vanderbilt says in his book
Traffic, describing how driving affects people. It's like trying to
talk to someone walking in front of you, as opposed to someone
you can see face-to-face. Vanderbilt quotes sociologist Jack Katz:
'We're looking at everybody's rear, and that's not how human
beings were set up to maximize their communicative possibility.'
This 'muteness' makes people feel angry.

On top of that, you're stuck in a machine that blunts all the
finer points of your communication and amplifies everything: a
voice is replaced by a honk on the horn, the blink of an eye is
replaced by a blinking light, and if you move your foot a couple of
centimetres, the car moves several metres on the road.

What's more, speed gives most people a thrill, which is addic-
tive.[58] That's why people race cars and enjoy go-karting, and why
I use the battery on my cargo e-bike — I can't help myself. As for
Marco, he's a Formula 1 fan.

> **Thalia Verkade** @tverka
> That feeling of having the wind behind me all the
> time is such an irresistible pleasure. And it's fun
> riding like a racing cyclist, like a hare overtaking the
> tortoises. But the next day I'm back on my ordinary
> bike, riding alongside my little boy, and I find myself
> feeling anxious when we're overtaken by ... an
> electric cargo bike.

Cycling Professor @fietsprofessor
I sometimes have that feeling on my racing bike. That sense of entitlement. The feeling that everyone and everything has to yield before me. It's hard to resist.

Richard Sennett, the man who traced the circulation metaphor for traffic all the way back to 1800, saw not the vehicle but the road itself as the source of growing irritation. An open road, a red asphalt cycle path free of obstruction, or railway tracks to the horizon — all these are invitations to put your foot down, keep going, reach your destination.

When Paris was still a city of narrow, meandering streets, delays were just part and parcel of getting from one place to another. But once the wide boulevards were in place, they automatically gave drivers the feeling that anything getting in their way was an imposition. Sennett thinks we regard the urge to be able to drive without any interruption as a natural inclination, when it's actually something we've learned.

Delays on the railways are also viewed as tantamount to a crisis. A train only has to stop for a moment in the countryside for the driver to announce, 'We've stopped at a red signal,' and to say how long the halt is expected to last. Dutch Railways actively try to reassure commuters in a hurry that they have control over their time, even as it dribbles away: 'Passengers want to be spared nuisances.'[59]

And then there's road rage, when the red mist descends. I watch a bit of a current affairs programme featuring Jan de Vos from Wemeldinge: driving along a dike, he was overtaken by a tailgater who then braked abruptly. 'I was livid,' Jan said afterwards. He put his foot right down and gave chase. Until the wheels on the right-hand side of his car swerved onto the verge and he drove straight through the prongs of a wooden crash barrier.

On TV, you could see the car skewered like a kebab. By good fortune, the skewer had missed the people inside. Jan's wife, seated next to him, got off with a broken knee and broken ribs, while his daughter, who was on the back seat, suffered a broken arm.

The local mayor came to visit the patients and reassured Jan that something would be done about that dangerous crash barrier.

The faster you drive, the less you see of what's around you, and the more of a nuisance you are to your surroundings. For example, I never see my own allotment complex from the Intercity Direct train as we flash past. But I can see and hear the train pass from my allotment.

I receive an email from a reader called Iwan Nyst. While I'm busy writing about the horrors of motor traffic, he starts telling me about a different way of looking at it. It's such a lovely note that I read it three times.

Between 18 and 26 I took all the driving licences there are, for cars, lorries and buses, including trailers in each category. When I was volunteering with the Red Cross in my early thirties, I got the opportunity to train as an ambulance driver. At the time I thought I was a pretty good driver and there wasn't much more I could learn about traffic. It turned out I was wrong about that.

In my first lesson, my instructor, Wim Dekker, asked me if I knew what the word 'traffic' meant, or, to be more precise, if I knew where it came from. He said it had to do with social interactions between people. That set me thinking, because it suggests something far more human.

And that was my instructor's message: as the driver of a vehicle that has right of way, with a siren and a revolving blue light, you've got a huge responsibility towards all the road users around you

—on your left, on your right, and even behind you.
People get a scare, or they spot you just in time, which
can make them do very odd and dangerous things.

It's up to an ambulance driver to take care of
everyone, to accept responsibility for *everyone*, just as if
you had a social relationship with them. That lesson
has always remained with me, and it's made me a
better and even more careful driver.

I sometimes wonder how it would be if more
people learned this lesson in one way or another.
Taking part in traffic, after all, is rather like interacting
socially with all the other people around you.

Best wishes,
Iwan Nyst

I write back to Iwan: 'Thank you, it's so nice to know there's
a driving instructor who teaches people how to treat others with
consideration, not just how to deal with traffic. Do you have Wim
Dekker's contact details, by any chance?'

Lower the Headrests

Wim Dekker picks me up at Woerden train station. He's driving
a grey-blue Ford Mondeo, the kind of inconspicuous but dependable car that's done a reliable job for years, but can put on a turn
of speed if needed. The driving instructor himself gives the same
impression — inconspicuous, solid, dependable, experienced. He
wears chunky glasses, and his slightly nasal voice reveals that he
has a cold. I sit behind the wheel, adjust the mirrors, and off we go.

'You can't go wrong — just pretend I'm not here,' says
Dekker. Soon we're on our way down a narrower street and a
lorry approaches at considerable speed. Will the driver brake? He

comes to an abrupt halt in the nick of time. I edge past gingerly: there's just enough room. Then we come out onto a road with a 50 km/h speed limit (over 30 mph) again.

'All drivers are in a hurry, one way or another,' says Dekker. 'Move into the left-hand lane now.' He starts telling me how drivers behind him honk in the morning rush hour whenever he does 70 km/h (nearly 45 mph) in places where you can drive at 80 km/h (nearly 50 mph).

But then the traffic demands our full attention again: I haven't yet found a space to move over, and we've got to turn off pretty soon. 'You're being too polite now. You could put your blinkers on and see if they'll let you in. Didn't you see that bloke in the van, the one at an angle behind you, trying to work out what exactly you wanted to do? He was even chuckling a bit. Come on, you can do it. Look, he's got a big grin on his face now.'

I look at the van behind me in the inside mirror and feel increasingly unsure. I hadn't even registered the driver's face. All my attention had been focused on the van, the distance between the car I'm in and the front wheels of the van, the lines on the tarmac.

'Do you look at people's faces?' I ask.

'Yes, I look at their body language, their expressions, how they behave.'

Aha. 'I find that really hard,' I say. It dawns on me now why we say things like 'the car rammed into the van'; it's because that's precisely what we see, what we perceive.

While we're driving through Utrecht later on, a car with a foreign number plate accidentally moves into the bus lane at a crossroads in front of us. A bus driver follows the motorist until he's right behind him.

'See that bus driver signalling at the car driver? He's angry, but he's stopping him turning back,' says Dekker. 'It's as if he's saying, "Your problem — you solve it."'

So hard, and sadly so recognisable: if another driver fails to yield when I have right of way, I often do just the same kind of thing. 'We don't cut each other much slack, do we?' I say. 'By the way, do you remember telling Iwan Nyst about the different meanings of "traffic"?'

Dekker nods. He points at the car in front of us. We're now in the right-hand lane of a two-lane highway with a 50 km/h speed limit, behind a car indicating left. 'This is the same kind of thing,' says Dekker. 'He's in the right-hand lane but wants to move over to the left. Lots of people are slipping past on his left while they've got the chance — "Tough — he should have moved left before."' But I haven't seen him look in his mirror, only out of the window to his left. So he's trying to figure out where he is relative to the turn-off. He's not sure if he's there yet, so he's put on his left indicator just in case, to show he might want to turn left at the next intersection, or the next one after that.'

Again, I hadn't seen the driver himself, only the car.

'So what he's doing makes sense to you?' I ask.

'Absolutely!' says Dekker. 'Other drivers need to be able to see that he's trying to find his way. And they ought to put themselves in his shoes. How would you like to be treated if you didn't know exactly where you were? And are you prepared to show other people in that situation a bit of consideration?'

No, I'm not, as it turns out when I tailgate a car in a residential street in Utrecht — though Dekker notices that the driver's just trying to find his way. 'Come on, why don't you leave him a bit more room?'

Good question. Because my driving instructor taught me not to leave gaps in traffic and to go with the flow. Oh dear, this is teaching me quite a lesson — how to focus on the driver, not the car. It's really tricky. I'm amazed that Dekker can see so much through all the reflections from the windows, often tinted, and through all the metal that surrounds them, and the back seat headrests. 'I always lower those,' he says.

'How come you can see people in cars when I can't?' I ask.

'It's my age. Years of experience.' He taps his glasses. 'I'm always scanning, scanning, scanning. And I insist on the best glasses my optician has to offer.'

Dekker teaches his techniques to police officers, who have to drive through cities at high speed and under extremely stressful conditions. 'They can only do a good job if they've got their emotions under control. That means they have to be calm when they arrive. So they need to be able to think things through while they're on the way. That's why we always say, "Calm down, I'm in a hurry."'

But even he sometimes leans on the horn. 'At the end of the week, when it's all got a bit much. I'm only human. But after that I can laugh at myself again and try to take things more easily.'

That's how hard it is to remain considerate to others in traffic. But it does help if the vehicle itself and the design of the road or street lend themselves to that state of mind.

In *Traffic*, Tom Vanderbilt quotes Hans Monderman, the traffic engineer from the northern province of Friesland who came up with the idea of shared space, who was still alive when Vanderbilt was writing his book: 'I always say to people: I don't care if you wear a raincoat or a Volkswagen Golf, you're a human being, and I address you as a human being. I want you to behave as a human being. I don't care what kind of vehicle you drive.'

In Utrecht, Dekker directs me to the central train station. I park his car on the side of a building site, behind another car. There's not much room so I park fairly near the edge. While I'm thanking Dekker for the lesson, a van appears that needs to get by, so I turn the key again and awkwardly manoeuvre the car to and fro to free up more space. The van drives past.

Dekker says, 'See that lad in front of you in the parked car?'

'All I could see was a car,' I sigh.

'He could have moved forward a bit to make it easier for you to get in. But he's looking in his mirror, thinking: why bother, it'll be all right.'

In a Flow

A nearby wood to stroll in. Peace. Fresh air. A home where your children can play in the street without fear. Where you can cycle home after delivering food, without being run down and killed. A road that children can jump onto *out of the blue* when they're playing hide and seek. I'm on another café terrace in Amsterdam with Marco, trying to pull together everything I wasn't able to see when I was still focusing on bike highways and traffic jams.

We catch up with each other. I tell Marco about Wim Dekker and the experience of trying to establish human contact in traffic. Marco tells me he's writing a scientific paper about flow, that blissful feeling people can experience when all their attention is in the moment, often leading to flashes of inspiration. There have been decades of psychological research into the subject. The theory was established by the late Hungarian-American psychologist Mihály Csíkszentmihályi.[60]

Flow is also a traffic-engineering term. What Marco's trying to do is to reclaim the word for human beings. 'We don't really know much about how mental processes like this affect our mobility, the choices we make and our behaviour,' he explains. 'We don't know much about human beings themselves when they're on their way from one place to another: that's because we've increasingly tended to look at them as if they were just moving parts in a system.'

It's not just zoologist Frans de Waal or writer Jelle Brandt Corstius who have great ideas while they're out cycling. Star lawyer Bénédicte Ficq prepares her legal cases against the cigarette industry while she's on a bike: she rides around a park, recording ideas on her smartphone.

The graphic artist M.C. Escher was on his bicycle when he had the idea for his *Curl-up*, depicting an imaginary creature able to draw in its feet, roll up and turn into a wheel. The Nobel Prize–winning chemist Ben Feringa says he had his best moments of inspiration about molecules while cycling to and from work.[61]

'Flow isn't the same thing as having your attention elsewhere,' says Marco. 'It's actually the highest level of concentration, involving another area of the brain. I imagine Wim Dekker is another person who experiences flow, when he has to drive fast, and he probably teaches it to his pupils.'

When do people experience flow? Marco summarises the necessary conditions:

1. There must be plenty of unpredictable stimuli
2. Your body must be directly involved
3. You must have enough time to focus on something without interruption
4. There must be some kind of balance between the challenges you face and your skills
5. You must be clear about what you're doing or where you're going
6. There must be immediate feedback

Cycling provides favourable conditions for flow. 'When you're sitting up straight in the saddle — as you do on a typical Dutch "sit-up-and-beg" bike — your senses are wide open to your surroundings, so you can take in lots of different stimuli,' Marco explains. 'That means stimuli from the environment you're cycling through, the things you see, smell and taste — but also from all the information you're exchanging with all the other people around you, when you're "negotiating" at an intersection, for instance.'

It's a bit like a jazz musician who has to listen acutely to be able to join in a fellow performer's jam session, he says. 'Or like a surfer trying to stay upright on a big wave. You need your whole body and all your senses, but you're still in control. We already know that jazz and surfing lead to a state of flow. But what about moving from one place to another?'

The flow theory also accounts for a pattern that doesn't tally with the expectations of most traffic engineers. Cyclists don't always opt for the shortest or the quickest route — far from it. I learned that from my readers in the course of my 'cycling versus congestion' project. Research that Marco was involved in shows that cyclists perceive routes with more variety as being shorter, even when they take them longer to cycle than routes that are more direct but more monotonous.[62]

That's another thing the flow theory explains: your perception of time changes when you're in a flow. Again and again, people told Csíkszentmihályi how differently they'd perceived time at moments when they were experiencing both challenges and satisfaction. 'I'm sure you feel that yourself now and then when you're engrossed in a hobby, a sport, or playing an instrument: with a bit of luck, you experience it from time to time at work. These moments make us happy because they activate another aspect of who we are as humans — Homo ludens, the part of us that revels in playfulness,' says Marco.

What would happen if we applied the psychological rather than the traffic engineering definition of flow when designing our cities? We could design the streets so as to encourage both individual and collective flow, which might increase the likelihood of strangers offering help or chatting to each other.[63]

'There's no single type of cycle path that's ideal for flow,'

Marco says. 'Flow is so multifaceted that only the town as a whole can provide it, as already happens in many Dutch towns.'

In his scientific research, Marco has demonstrated how the stimuli you need to experience flow are amply present on everyday rides on a Dutch bicycle, thanks to the wide variety of cycle paths and other factors. He and a large team of European scientists submitted the resultant paper on flow in everyday travel to a scientific journal, which rejected it. One peer reviewer commented that while you may well experience flow if the purpose of your trip is to be entertained, extrapolating that conclusion to the daily commute seems far-fetched. Getting to work is meaningful: the more meaningful your work, the more meaningful getting there is. Arriving home is probably meaningful too. But the time you spend in transit? No.

He's got a point, Marco concedes. There are no data to support their point of view yet. 'That's the difficult thing when you want to explore a new language.' So members of the research team began to collect the relevant data themselves. After a second submission, the paper was accepted and published in a scientific journal.[64]

I'm thinking how odd it is that you have to be able to prove that travelling is more than just getting from A to B when, on my way home from Amsterdam, I see a personal ad from Dutch Railways' popular lonely hearts service flash up on the screen in my railway carriage:

> You stepped off the train at Amsterdam Central
> Station, and it was love at first sight.
> You were wearing a stunning summer dress. Our eyes
> met on Amsterdam Central Station, on platform 8a,
> where you got out at 21.09 and I boarded the train to

Den Helder. I'm still in love with you!

Much love, Vinny

The Voice of the Majority

Cycling Professor @fietsprofessor
We've hit 50%!!!!!

Thalia Verkade @tverka
No drop-off zone?

Cycling Professor @fietsprofessor
No drop-off zone.

Assessing the amount of support for an alternative plan was touch and go, Marco tells me. It had been decided that at least 50 per cent of residents in his neighbourhood must vote on whether to experiment with transforming the area in front of the school into a 'healthy school playground', and that 60 per cent of those who voted must back the experiment for it to become a reality.

If not, the drop-off zone that the municipal traffic engineer had extracted from CROW's guidelines would be built. 'I was hearing that numbers were stagnating at around 35 per cent, even after I'd given it all I'd got on social media — "Please use your vote!" And I'd already been round everyone in my own block.'

Then Marco went full Rambo. 'After I'd spent a weekend feeling angry and run up a few kilometres on my racing bike, I thought — oh, to hell with it. I made a detailed map with every-one's addresses on it and urged those who wanted the healthy school playground to go from door to door till we'd covered the whole neighbourhood. Then we discovered that people were enthusiastic — not at all irritated, in fact, they were very positive!

But they thought it would all go ahead anyway, and many of them had already absent-mindedly binned their voting cards in the paper recycling container.'

In the end, 62 per cent of residents voted, and 84 per cent of them supported the proposal for a healthy school playground.

Was Marco a radical? A Rambo? An activist? A minority? An ideologue?

You could count the people who wanted a roundabout on the fingers of one hand, but they were extremely vocal and had the establishment behind them. But four out of five residents backed Marco's initiative, which also takes account of motorists, but no longer revolves around them. Practically no one supported the plan presented by the local authority, in which the only expert to have a say was the local traffic engineer, but it hadn't occurred to anyone that you could actually oppose it.

'I Hope You Succeed'

Are there villains at work? People who wilfully imprison us in this unhealthy system that gobbles up space and human lives? This question keeps running through my mind.

When the Minister for Infrastructure and Water Management decides that some roads previously used as active motorway lanes only when the traffic volume is particularly high are to be permanently designated as such — even though one of the bodies that advise her has just produced an extensive scientific report showing why more tarmac won't help — it's momentarily impossible for me to believe there are no evil forces at work.[65]

Thalia Verkade @tverka
I'd have to tie myself in knots to attribute this to a failure to see what's staring her in the face.

Cycling Professor @fietsprofessor
She's just trying to solve the problem as she sees it. Bottlenecks. Remember that traffic jam problem of yours?

What a lot has happened since then.

But can we really be sure there aren't any villains? I run through my experiences over the last three years.

The decisions to call a new section of motorway a 'missing link' and a 'Green Arc', or, like a new motorway in Ede, a 'Parklaan' (park avenue), were conscious choices. Tackling bottlenecks by laying more tarmac guarantees work for road-builders over the next decade.

Cycling from my allotment, I followed a construction industry protest on its way along the motorway: the protestors deployed huge machines to intimidate Parliament in response to the Council of State's ruling on a draft law designed to limit emissions and deposits of nitrogen compounds. These were people with loud voices who were keen to maintain the status quo.

What I do know is that while Maxime Verhagen was a government minister he helped an automotive manufacturer, lobbied on its behalf, and even had the brass neck to get hired as an advisor on talks with the same firm.[66]

I also know that Camiel Eurlings, from the same political party, boosted the number of flights at Amsterdam's Schiphol Airport by tweaking the noise pollution regulations when he was Minister of Transport, Public Works, and Water Management, and that he later went to work for Schiphol.

These are people with obvious vested interests who've exploited their power.

It's very clear that the RAI Association (which represents the interests of the Dutch automotive industry) and the Royal Dutch Touring Club have established comfortable positions as representatives of the status quo; the RAI Association enjoys the privilege of celebrating its anniversary in the Ridderzaal (the hall of ceremonies used for the annual state opening of Parliament), while the ANWB gets to make announcements about traffic jams at half-hourly intervals on national radio — just as if they were neutral organisations serving the interests of the Dutch people as a whole. I also see how the same organisations put pressure on the Dutch government to provide subsidies for electric cars, including Elon Musk's Teslas.

And I now see that while Elon Musk may genuinely wish to convert the planet to electric vehicles, he also just wants to sell cars, like all car manufacturers. Thanks to the climate crisis, the future of automotive manufacturers actually looks more secure than it did: a new electric car for everyone, subsidised and supported by the public purse.

But you can also view all of these phenomena as being motivated by well-intentioned convictions, by a blind, unconscious, and now almost incontestable belief about the purpose of our streets and the reasons for which we organise mobility.

After all, who's contesting the fact that we devote so much of our public broadcasting time to 'traffic information', aka traffic jam updates? No one.

Why does our government need the Council of State to issue a ruling on emissions of nitrogen compounds in order to lower the speed limit from 130 km/h (80 mph) to 100 km/h (almost 65 mph), when traffic engineers themselves say the results will include not just fewer deaths on the road, less damage to the environment, and less noise pollution, but also less road congestion?[67]

It feels as if it goes without saying that roads and streets exist for the sake of traffic and that their purpose is to enable road users to reach their destination as quickly as possible, and that any objections people might raise to fast-flowing traffic seem unrealistic — even to cycling advocates, whose main demand is safe roads and streets so that everyone can drive or cycle fast.

The fact that all this seems to go without saying may account for the government's fear of the 'angry motorist', who supposedly resents the new 100 km/h speed limit. But how real is this 'angry motorist'? A demonstration against the speed limit reduction was called off because there was too little interest.[68] And there are plenty of people who want things to change. If the vote held in Ede to establish how locals want the area in front of the school to be used is representative — in a neighbourhood where the official home/car ratio is 1.7 — the vast majority of people want something different. Columnists writing in national newspapers that span the whole gamut of political views write angry articles whenever someone is injured or killed in their local area.[69]

We don't actually accept this system at all. We just think we do.

And what about the guidelines laid down by CROW — who are we implementing them for, when it comes down to it? When Marco started his battle against the school drop-off zone, a local traffic engineer said to him in private: 'I hope you succeed.'

Thank You, Grown-ups!

I'm on the train to Ede again. Today is a special day at Marco's children's school. After the public opinion poll in which the vast majority of locals voted for a 'healthy school playground', the green light was given for a two-year 'experiment' that would allow local residents to create an alternative to a drop-off zone. The local authority is keeping an eye on developments. The experiment mustn't cause any traffic congestion. If it does, it'll come to an end and a drop-off zone will be put in place as originally planned.

For once, the usual guidelines can be set aside. As part of the experiment, the pupils — from reception class to 12- and 13-year-olds — are going to design their healthy school playground today. This approach was the brainchild of a project group that includes Marco, an educator whose children attend the school, and a landscape designer whose children haven't yet reached school age but already have their names down.

I walk into the building that once housed the managers' offices when this was still a viscose factory. Micha Stolzenburg from OBB, an engineering consultancy that designs play areas, is acting as facilitator. He's busy explaining what to do to a group of eight- and nine-year-olds. The children are given some ready-made materials to use: a sheet full of dozens of pictograms representing things like a sandpit, a look-out point, long grass, a rock, and a strange-looking tree.[70] They can cut out whatever they want and stick it on a big map of the future school playground.

There's just one rule. 'Do you know what "flexible" means?' Stolzenburg asks them. 'Bendy?' suggests one girl. 'Yes, that's right, but when something's "flexible" it can also mean it's easy to change. What we mean here is that we need to be able to take things away again if necessary.' This rule applies to the part of the area where the drop-off zone was originally planned. They have to retain the option to convert it into parking spaces if necessary, if it turns out there are too few elsewhere. 'So this is what we call a flexible space.'

'Can you think of anything you'd like to have?' Marco asks the children. 'A swimming pool!' someone volunteers. 'A football field!'

'If you can't find what you're looking for among these pictures, just grab a pen and draw it in yourselves,' says Stolzenburg.

Marco and I follow the children as they go outside first to have a look at the site of the school playground. At the moment there's still a heap of sand in front of the old factory canteen building, which will house their new school next year. Headteacher Leo Trommel is walking around too. 'This is a really unusual process,' he says. 'But it's just right for this school. The question of what to do in situations where it seems impossible to change anything is something we often look at with our students.'

Then the children get to work: the older classes in the provisional main building a bit further away, the little ones in the temporary prefabs nearby. A group of nine- and ten-year-olds working on a map in smaller groups of four or five. A girl sticks a 'long grass' pictogram on the map. 'It'll be fun to walk through in summer, with bare legs,' she says.

For many boys, the ultimate dream is the biggest possible football field. One you can sit around, like a sort of arena. A striking number of children want shady trees. The area they play in at the moment is bare, and it got very hot last summer.

Everyone, whatever their age, wants hiding places.

Using felt pens and sheets of white paper, a group of six- and seven-year-olds draw their favourite play spots. They draw stick figures and write words next to them: 'tramplean', 'seasaw', 'hiding place'.

Some interesting combinations emerge. How about creating a 'zoo corner' and making a vegetable garden next to it so the children can grow food for the animals themselves? On a lot of the maps the small subgroups are using, the 'flexible space' remains empty, as it poses tricky questions. A girl runs over to me and asks, 'Is there such a thing as a swing you can move from one place to another?' 'Good question. There probably is,' I reply. She hesitates. Are swings OK or not? Two of the oldest girls think it would be great to put a roundabout where the drop-off zone was originally planned — so you could ride around in a go-kart. That would be easy enough to shift if it had to go, wouldn't it?

The reception class is giving free rein to its collective imagination. 'We've come up with a few things it would be fun to have, now it's up to you to see if they're feasible,' says their teacher, Jorien. The infants start talking about what they'd like, and a little lad squeals, 'A pool, a pool, a pool!' He sticks his fists in the air. More hands follow. 'A pool, a pool, a pool!'

In the afternoon, the teachers have a brief discussion about what they want. They establish one thing, at least; what they *don't* want is the infants playing in front of the oldest pupils' classroom windows.

Timon, who teaches the last year of primary, lives not far behind the school and likes to drive to work, eagerly copies the map, putting in all the relevant measurements in metres. He adds lines and crosses — a football field here, a basketball court there, look, there's room for that too — drawing them on top of the reserve parking spaces. Just look how much room there is now.

The area in front of the school in the original plan was 740 square metres (7,965 square feet), with a car park of over 1,100 square metres (11,840 square feet). Thanks to the experiment, there's now room for a school playground with a surface area of 1,400 square metres (12,271 square feet), at least for the time being.

A few days later Marco sends me the first sketches of the project group's draft. The plans include a colour scheme inspired by the fine viscose fabrics that once left the factory in waggons. There'll be plenty of hiding places. Room for football. Materials for the children to build with. Enough space to have lessons outdoors, shaded by greenery. Vegetable gardens to be maintained in cooperation with local residents. Where the drop-off zone was once planned, there'll be a mobile green wall whose position will vary according to the number of parking spaces needed.

There's no money for a swimming pool. But trampolines are under discussion, as is a mini-roundabout which children can ride around in soapbox carts.

All the children's names will be painted on the asphalt — with thanks to the grown-ups for allowing them to play here.

The area at Marco's school that was destined to become a drop-off zone for car-driving parents, before ...

... and after.

Source: Marco te Brömmelstroet.

Epilogue

What's the Next Step?

Some ideas for action

How easy it had all seemed back then, when I still thought that engineers could resolve all our mobility problems: my only task was to welcome their solutions enthusiastically, with the added benefit of profiling myself as terribly progressive and forward-looking. An early adopter.

If I have learned anything from this journey of exploration, it's that all of this rests on a choice. Everyone is at liberty to prioritise speed and efficiency over fairness and equality in the public domain. But politicians who do so must be held accountable. The status quo is not a given. Nor is it a value-neutral solution. It's a choice. Those who fail to question the perpetuation of the existing traffic model are underwriting the notion that the purpose of public space is to facilitate speed and traffic flow.

The tragic death that Marco witnessed as a nine-year-old left its mark on him. Yet its impact wasn't solely negative. 'It's what drives me,' he says at our last get-together before the book comes out. 'I'm glad I can talk about the issues in terms of ethical principles, even though people often find it irritating. That's the legacy of childhood loss.'

Talking about the tragedy taught him something else. 'You can use a crash — or any kind of road accident — to gain a better understanding of our mobility system. In some cases that can make it easier to talk about it, and it may be less painful than you initially thought. That's been my experience, at any rate.'

There are moments when both Marco and I wish we could unsee all this. The knowledge of what has happened to our streets sometimes feels like a curse. When an interesting discussion on the radio is interrupted because we all have to be informed of a momentary hiatus in the traffic machine, after which a news programme presents a boilerplate solution: more roads, more trains, smarter vehicles, and more bicycles; each time we hear a brief news item about death or injury on the roads; we can't help thinking about the terrible impact on yet another family – or families, if there was more than one party involved.

As for me, I'm learning through trial and error to embrace the discomfort that discussions around this topic arouse. It all demands effort, and progress is slow. Yet it also makes my life more vivid and varied: without friction, no traction. Talking about our streets creates meaningful new connections with all kinds of inspiring people. The blessing is the knowledge that I have the power to influence the design and layout of the area I live in. And so do you.

Below you'll find a list of ideas to help you start taking action yourself. We've divided these ideas up into steps you can take on your own, as an individual; action you can take collectively, together with other people; and tips for engaging with politicians and representatives of the established order.

Activities you can start on straight away, as an individual

Take a notebook with you when you're out and about and write down what you hear, see, feel, and think. What changes do you notice? What do these changes mean to you? How might you change the way you look at your own behaviour as regards getting about from A to B? Which aspects might you value more, and which less? What can you do to adjust your choices accordingly?

Educate yourself on how to create change

- Take one or more of the MOOCs offered by the University of Amsterdam: Unravelling the Cycling City, Alternative Mobility Narratives, and Reclaiming the Street for Liveable Urban Spaces or Getting Smart about Cycling Futures.
- Read Marco's free e-book, which forms the academic basis for *Movement*.
- Read *Metaphors We Live By* (George Lakoff and Mark Johnson), *Thinking in Systems* (Donella H. Meadows), *Fighting Traffic: the dawn of the motor age in the American city* and *Autonorama: the illusory promise of high-tech driving* (Peter Norton), and *New Power: how power works in our hyper-connected world* (Jeremy Heimans and Henry Timms).
- Follow and engage with social media accounts that question the language we use to talk about streets, such as those of Tom Flood, Charles Marohn, Jan Kamensky, and Cycling Professor (Marco).

You'll find links to all of these sources and more at https://thelabofthought.co/movement

- Reflect on and challenge the language you use. Ask yourself how the implicit assumptions underpinning our words facilitate our thinking, and how they limit the conversation. What other kinds of language could we speak? Take discussions about lowering the speed limit as an example. Why might 20 mph be referred to as 'slow'? Is 20 mph really slow from the pedestrian's point of view, or is it six times his or her walking speed? If the latter, whose point of view are we taking if we describe 20 mph as 'slow'? And

why exactly do we talk about streets in terms of the speed limit
for vehicles? Reread 'The View Through the Windscreen and the
Wobbly Mirror' (pp. 203–6). Cognitive flexibility is a skill you can
develop in conversations about every conceivable subject.

- Consider how a personal choice (such as participating in a
  car-share scheme rather than owning your own car) can have
  immediate positive effects (such as freeing up a parking space,
  which could then be used to help create a garden or play area).
- Share information on the website roaddanger.org by adding
  news items on crashes and other traffic accidents that you come
  across in the media. By doing so, you can help raise awareness
  of how people write and talk about such events — often in a
  dehumanised way, despite the long-term, deep, and wide-ranging
  impact they have.

Inspire others

- Go to labofthought.co/movement and let us know what *you* plan
  to do.
- Write a letter to your local newspaper in which you set out your
  ideas for concrete action.
- Read the sections on mobility in political parties' manifestos,
  and write to the parties concerned, your MP, or the local council
  member responsible for mobility issues. What changes would
  you like to see? You can do this together with other people as
  well as on your own, and it may be more effective as a collective
  approach.

How you can work together with others

- Talk to your neighbours about the way you'd like your street to be. Accept that this may lead to some awkwardness (about parking, for instance). Talk about positive aspects that would be in many people's interests, such as room for children to play freely. Bear in mind that there will always be a few opinionated people, but that the silent majority may well agree with you (remember the distorting mirror effect). It may take a considerable effort for people to express views that challenge the status quo – the street as a place for motor traffic. Lend this book to people, pass it on or give it to others if you think it may help.

- What if you don't know your neighbours yet? How about setting up a Facebook page or an app group for your street and inviting your neighbours to join by posting a note in their letterboxes or chatting to them in the street? This could start off as a useful way for neighbours to ask each other questions and borrow things they need. Organise a get-together for the adults or a play event for the children in your street and ask them what other street activities they would like to be able to take part in.

- Try to link up with people like yourself, locally or online. They do exist. There are other people with concerns like yours out there! Starting an online petition is a very easy way to find like-minded people if you've no idea where to go looking for them. This is one of the most accessible ways of making your voice heard, as an individual and together with others. Join local associations working in fields like public space, community building, rambling, or cycling, or set one up. Start a reading group. You'll have a more enjoyable time if you get together with other people, and you'll have more impact than you would as an individual.

- Look out for overlaps with other issues. It's likely that some of your neighbours are fired up by the need for green areas, or by other significant issues relating to how we use our streets. Take a look at the Groningen Guideline for Public Space (available at thelabofthought.co/movement), which refers to nine other dimensions in addition to that of mobility: accessibility, safety, human perception, health, social interaction, ecology, climate adaptation, economy, and cultural history. Learn to identify these various dimensions and to look at them as a whole.

- Think up some inventive and creative actions to open up discussion on the function of the street; these appeal to the public and the local media. See The Monkey Wrench Gang Twitter account for inspiration (twitter.com/m_wrenchgang); get together with others to create something attractive and inspiring, and enjoy your efforts to achieve change, whatever the outcome.

- Accept that you're not running a hundred metre sprint, but a marathon — and that it's easier to keep going as part of a group than on your own. Pick your battles. Though impotent frustration will achieve little, anger is a gift — a source of energy and motivation. Hold on to it. Use your anger constructively and experience it as a source of change. Do this collectively.

Tips on how to get in touch with and talk to politicians

- Raise funds in your town, neighbourhood, or street to give copies of this book to members of your local council, your local MP, and/or other local politicians and civil servants. In a number of Dutch municipalities, the Dutch edition of this book was used to initiate discussions and get the ball rolling. If a group of people give the book as a collective gift, the politician concerned will feel under more pressure to actually read it.

- Make the effort to get to know your political representatives. Make it clear to them that the question of how public space is used is a political issue, not a technical one, which means that it's their job to represent our political views. When talking to politicians, civil servants, and traffic engineers, contest their assumption that streets must be designed to promote traffic flow: streets are public space, and as such they can be put to countless different uses (see the Groningen Guideline on Public Space). Remember, you are going to have to keep making this point again and again.

- Contest all models that focus on traffic flow and motor traffic, and don't let yourself be bamboozled by them. Most such models fail to take account of changing human behaviour (such as the possibility of a decline in the number of motorists and an increase in the number of cyclists), and they rest on the assumption that travelling from A to B is a disutility. Traffic models take no account whatsoever of any of the other functions of public space, such as providing a place to spend time out of doors, nature, a restful environment, or facilitating social encounters or play.

- Don't accept a technocratic response to a political question. Make it clear that you want a response from an elected representative to any issues that affect your street: these are political dilemmas that have no simple solution, calling for difficult choices – not just a matter of maximising efficiency or effectiveness. Keep on reiterating this point, and request (or insist) that any discussions held include experts in the relevant fields (an ecologist, a sociologist, etc.), as well as the usual traffic engineer. Make sure that any discussions you're involved in include experts representing more than just one discipline. When exercising your rights as a citizen, always ask for several different types of approach and expertise to be represented.

- Tell the local civil servant responsible for traffic engineering that they should refer the task they've been assigned back to the political level if they are not in a position to do enough to improve the situation in your street. Don't settle for a technical compromise proposed by a traffic engineer if it's not good enough and helps avoid a political decision. Speed bumps and cycle lanes demarcated only by painted lines are good examples. Do they really help create streets where no one has to feel afraid? Or do they just ameliorate the situation slightly, without producing a really satisfactory outcome, and do they reinforce the idea that the sole purpose of streets is to facilitate the flow of traffic? And, above all, do they help the local authority to avoid having to make an explicit choice between the flow of motor traffic and human streets where children can safely play unsupervised and make their own way to school, or where elderly people unable to walk long distances can feel free to get about independently?

- Are you a traffic engineer, or some other kind of expert in this field? If so, help to make everything above possible — starting today.

Acknowledgements

This book grew out of a three-year journey of discovery for which I, Thalia, was provided with ample time and resources by *De Correspondent*, a Dutch online platform for journalism funded by members whose contribution also includes sharing their knowledge and experience in response to correspondents' articles. Without this journalistic base, and without *De Correspondent*'s own publishing house, which enables journalists to develop their long-term research into books, *Movement* would never have come to fruition. I am deeply grateful for all the support we benefited from in the Netherlands to write this book, and for our supporters' confidence in us.

I, Marco, am tremendously grateful to Amsterdam University, especially the Urban Planning group, for their organisational flexibility in enabling me to work on this book. What's even more important, however, is the role my Amsterdam colleagues have played for many years now in sharing their inspiration and their passion for improving our understanding of what underpins our social reality. I am also hugely grateful to both my own and Dion's family for their generous and open-hearted engagement in the conversations we have had. I am still amazed by how much these conversations have changed my life, and I hope very much that the same is true for all of you.

As regards the English edition, we would like to thank Rebecca Carter for finding a publisher who has made us feel welcome and well understood from the outset. Fiona Graham invested boundless creative energy in translating the book (and coined the word 'frownie'). We are also very grateful to Molly Slight for her lucid guidance and editing in the course of versioning and updating the book.

Endnotes

Prologue

1   https://ec.europa.eu/commission/presscorner/detail/en/IP_21_1767
2   https://assets.publishing.service.gov.uk/government/uploads/system/
uploads/attachment_data/file/922717/reported-road-casualties-annual-
report-2019.pdf
3   https://decorrespondent.nl/9156/het-grootste-taboe-in-het-verkeer-we-
kunnen-elkaar-doodrijden/962726618700-4587f239

Part I

1   https://www.iea.org/reports/electric-vehicles
2   Saskia Kluit et al., 'Rutte III moet de autoforens verleiden de fiets te
pakken', *NRC Handelsblad*, 9 May 2017.
3   In the EU a standard pedelec is limited to 25 km/h; a speed pedelec can go
up to 45 km/h.
4   'Nederlander fietst 133 km/u', *NOS*, 15 September 2013.
5   Bas Blokker, 'Fietsers, die zijn als een zwerm spreeuwen', *NRC Handelsblad*,
4 May 2013.
6   My interview with Marco in the series of articles on cycling versus
congestion: 'Door deze fietsprofessor kijk je voor altijd anders tegen het
fileprobleem aan', *De Correspondent*, 26 July 2017.
7   J.H. Kraay et al., *Handleiding voor de conflictobservatietechniek DOCTOR
[Dutch Objective Conflict Technique for Operation and Research]* (SWOV, 1986),
p. 66.
8   Sanne Stenvert, 'Verkeer: Sint in de bres voor De Elzen', *Brabants Dagblad*,
25 November 2013.
9   Bas Vermeer, 'Cityring moet veiliger: tweede proef volgende maand van
start', *Brabants Dagblad*, 20 March 2019.
10   Bas Vermeer, 'Een "midgetgolfbaan" (à 150.000 euro) op de cityring',
Brabants Dagblad, 20 March 2019.
11   Jesse Frederik, 'De oplossing voor bijna alles: duurder parkeren', *De
Correspondent*, 22 September 2018.
12   These data were reported by Donald Shoup, known as the 'founding
father of parking economics', in *Parking and the City* (Routledge, 2018), p. 11.

Shoup also made this calculation: if US levels of car ownership prevailed worldwide, we'd need space for 4.7 billion vehicles on Earth—a car park the size of France (https://parkade.com/post/donald-shoup-the-high-cost-of-free-parking-summarized). A fun fact: in SimCity there are no parking lots: all cars are parked underground—the game world would be too boring otherwise (https://www.theverge.com/2013/5/9/4316222/simcity-lead-designer-stone-librande-talks-about-building-game).

13 2020 values: https://thomapost.amsterdam/dit-zijn-de-huizenprijzen-per-m2-in-amsterdam/#:~:text=De%20vierkante%20meterprijs%20in%20 Amsterdam,de%20top%2025%20duurste%20gemeenten.

14 Peter Walker, 'Why parking your car is too cheap', *The Guardian* on YouTube, 30 October 2018. https://www.youtube.com/watch?v=V1hg20SngXo.

15 That was the cost of a parking space in Rotterdam in 2019. The local authority raised the rate considerably in 2020, to €115.20.

16 The drop-off zone for the school in Marco's neighbourhood is based on CROW's old IT tool 'Verkeersgeneratie en Parkeren' ('Traffic generation and parking'). A new tool is being developed which seems likely to allow greater flexibility.

17 'Beleidsregeling Parkeernormen auto en fiets gemeente Rotterdam 2018' (Municipality of Rotterdam, 1 February 2018).

18 'Nota parkeernormen auto en fiets, 3e herziening, slimmer en beter' (Municipality of Soest, 26 March 2018).

19 'Comfortabel parkeren door NEN 2443' (Stichting Koninklijk Nederlands Normalisatie Instituut, 24 February 2014).

20 'Infographic: My, How Big Our Cars Have Gotten!', slideshare.net, 13 August 2014.

21 Arie Bleijenberg, *Nieuwe Mobiliteit. Na het autotijdperk* (Eburon Academic Publishers, 2015), pp. 22–23.

22 'Ontwikkeling totaal aantal kilometers snelwegen in Nederland per jaar', wegenwiki.nl, 1 December 2019.

23 Edwin van der Aa, 'Miljarden schade door groeiende files', *Algemeen Dagblad*, 23 October 2017.

24 Onno Blom, 'Omringd door snelwegen schiep Jan Wolkers zijn paradijs', *De Volkskrant*, 20 August 2018.

25 'Gemeenteraad Rotterdam stemt in met maatregelenpakket inpassing A13/ A16' (Municipality of Rotterdam, 9 October 2015).

26 *Nota onderbouwing A13/A16. Onderbouwing van de keuze voor de Rijksweg 13/16 Rotterdam* (Goudappel Coffeng, n.d.).

27 Gert Onnink, 'Nieuwe A16 Rotterdam moet files rond Rotterdam oplossen', *Algemeen Dagblad*, 3 November 2018.

28 *Informatieboekje gebiedstafels A13/A16* (Rijkswaterstaat, 2013).

29 Source: A. Szalai (ed.), *The Use of Time. Daily Activities of Urban and Suburban Populations in Twelve Countries* (Mouton, 1972).

30 Source: Geurt Hupkes, *Gasgeven of afremmen. Toekomstscenario's voor ons vervoerssysteem* (Kluwer, 1977), p. 262.

31 Peter Peters et al., *Een constante in beweging? Reistijd, virtuele mobiliteit en de Brever-wet: eindrapport* (Ministry of Transport and Water Management, 2001).

32 Annie Ridout, 'Super-commuters: a London salary with lower living costs ... and a beach', *The Guardian*, 11 August 2018.

33 Pierre Kemp, 'Excuse', *Verzameld werk. Deel 1*, (Van Oorschot, 1976). Translation by Fiona Graham.

34 N.C. Henkens and G.W. Tamminga, *Capaciteitswaarden Infrastructuur Autosnelwegen. Handboek, versie 4* (Ministry of Infrastructure and the Environment, 2015).

35 H. Schuurman, *Capaciteitswaarden Infrastructuur Autosnelwegen. Handboek, versie 2* (Ministry of Transport and Water Management, 2002).

36 *Nota Mobiliteit: Naar een betrouwbare en voorspelbare bereikbaarheid* (Ministry of Transport and Water Management, 2004), p. 33.

37 'Personenauto's: Aantal personenauto's neemt verder toe' (Statistics Netherlands, 2019).

38 Sources: UK, https://www.gov.uk/government/statistical-data-sets/veho2-licensed-cars#licensed-vehicles; USA, https://www.bts.gov/content/automobile-profile; Australia, https://www.abs.gov.au/statistics/industry/tourism-and-transport/survey-motor-vehicle-use-australia/latest-release; China, https://www.statista.com/statistics/278423/amount-of-passenger-cars-in-china/#:~:text=In%202019%2C%20approximately%20224.74%20million%20passenger%20cars%20were%20registered%20in%20China; world total, https://www.carsguide.com.au/car-advice/how-many-cars-are-there-in-the-world-70629.

39 'Nederland telt 1 miljoen lease-auto's' (Vereniging van Nederlandse Autoleasemaatschappijen (VNA, association of Dutch vehicle leasing companies), 15 February 2019).

40 Hans Baaij, 'De dodelijke asobak', *Follow the Money*, 4 December 2019.

41 Arie Bleijenberg, 'Vijf taboes over mobiliteit', *Verkeerskunde*, 2 October 2019.

42 'Studio Plaats — Bibliotheek referentiebuurten' (Studio Bereikbaar, 2020).

43 On housing density: Lloyd Alter, 'Cities need Goldilocks housing density — not too high or low, but just right', *The Guardian*, 16 April 2014, https://www.theguardian.com/lifeandstyle/2014/apr/16/cities-need-goldilocks-housing-density-not-too-high-low-just-right

44 Tweet from Cycling Professor @fietsprofessor (2 May 2018).

45 The standard work used in the urban and regional planning department of the University of Amsterdam is L. Bertolini, *Planning the Mobile Metropolis. Transport for People, Places and the Planet* (Palgrave, 2017).

46 Bert van Wee, Piet Rietveld and Henk Meurs, 'Is average daily travel time expenditure constant? In search of explanations for an increase in average travel time', *Journal of Transport Geography*, vol. 1, no. 2 (2006), pp. 109–122.

47 'Minister Van Nieuwenhuizen geeft startsein voor aanleg A16 Rotterdam' (Rijkswaterstaat, 18 March 2019).

48 Tim Verlaan, 'Mobilization of the masses: Dutch planners, local politics, and the threat of the motor age 1960–1980', *Journal of Urban History* (2019), p. 12. https://doi.org/10.1177/0096144219872767

49 Tim Verlaan, *De ruimtemakers. Projectontwikkelaars en de Nederlandse binnenstad 1950–1980* (Uitgeverij Vantilt, 2016), p. 55.

50 'Verkeerspolitie doet aanval op Amstel, Singel en Rokin', *De Volkskrant*, 22 October 1954.

51 Eva Wolf and Wouter Van Dooren show how the metaphor of motorways as scars is used in Flanders: 'How policies become contested: a spiral of imagination and evidence in a large infrastructure project', *Policy Sciences*, vol. 50, no. 3 (2017), pp. 449–468.

52 The comparison between road congestion and an obesity sufferer is based on a comment by Lewis Mumford in *The New Yorker*, 15 October 1955, p. 166.

53 'Microplastics door slijtage van banden is nauwelijks tegen te gaan' (Plastic Soup Foundation, 4 July 2018), and Paola Tamma, 'Tires tread on the environment', *Politico*, 14 May 2018.

Part II

1   Pete Jordan, *De fietsrepubliek. Een geschiedenis van fietsend Amsterdam* (Uitgeverij Podium, 2014), chap. 2.

2   See more street intersection ramps (referred to in the film as 'continuous sidewalks') and how they work in this video by Jason Slaughter on the YouTube channel 'Not Just Bikes': https://youtu.be/9OfBpQgLXUc

3   'Peter van der Knaap: "Verkeersveiligheid moet een nationale prioriteit worden"', *NM Magazine*, no. 2 (2017).

4   'Factsheet. 30 km/uur-gebieden' (SWOV, 31 May 2018).

5   The municipality of Amsterdam, for example, refers to *stadstraten* (city streets), *stroomstraten* ('flow streets') and *verkeersaders* (arterial roads) in *Amsterdam Aantrekkelijk Bereikbaar. Mobiliteitsaanpak Amsterdam 2030* (Municipality of Amsterdam, 2013), p. 60.

6   Tara Lewis, 'Rotterdam wil het stadsverkeer hufterproof maken', *NRC Handelsblad*, 28 January 2020.

7   Tjitte de Vries, '"Meneer Correct" is verbaasd over zijn eigen succes', *Het Vrije Volk*, 13 February 1988.

8   'Automobilisme', *Algemeen Handelsblad*, 15 December 1908.

9   Ford produced 250,000 Model Ts in 1920, and 900,000 just three years later (https://www.mtfca.com/encyclo/fdprod.htm).

10 Diana T. Kurylko, 'Model T had many shades; black dried fastest', *Automotive News*, 16 June 1988.

11 Frederick S. Crum researched the proportion of car accidents to those involving horse-drawn vehicles. His conclusion was that the number of accidents shot up with the advent of the car. 'Street traffic accidents', *Publications of the American Statistical Association*, vol. 13, no. 103 (1913), pp. 473–528.

12 Shanthi Ameratunga et al., 'Death and injury on roads', *BMJ* 333 (2006) no. 53. https://www.bmj.com/content/333/7558/53

13 Roger Roots, 'The dangers of automobile travel: a reconsideration', *American Journal of Economics and Sociology*, vol. 66, no. 5 (2007), pp. 959–976.

14 Frederick S. Crum, 'Street traffic accidents', *Publications of the American Statistical Association*, vol. 13, no. 103 (1913), pp. 473–528.

15 You can read more about Norton's and Prytherch's books in the e-book Marco wrote as an accompaniment to *Movement*, which you can download at corr.es/snelste.

16 Marcus Popkema, *Tussen techniek en planning. De opkomst van het vak verkeerskunde in Nederland 1950–1975* (Amsterdam University Press, 2015).

17 Stan Huygens, 'De strijd om twéé plaatsen voor één Haags station. Revolutionair idee van een Amerikaanse ingenieur', *De Telegraaf*, 26 May 1962.

18 One of my most enthusiastic pieces about Tesla and Elon Musk was 'Hoe Tesla in Amerika aan een mijn bouwt waar auto's uit komen', *De Correspondent*, 27 January 2017.

19 *De Telegraaf*'s motoring editor, 'Jokinen's verkeersplan is opmerkelijk: minder kostbaar, en reëler dan bestaande plannen', *De Telegraaf*, 7 December 1967.

20 'Amerikaanse "Doorbraak" in Nederland. In Amsterdam 6 citywegen. Plan tot behoud stadskernen. Prof. Jokinen: invalswegen oorzaak verkeersnood', *De Volkskrant*, 8 December 1967.

21 'Amsterdam is een deltaplan waard (2). Cityvorming tast de binnenstad aan', *NRC Handelsblad*, 10 June 1971.

22 Footage from 1972 of children in De Pijp neighbourhood demanding a street without cars: https://www.youtube.com/watch?v=YY6PQAI4TZE&t=14s

23 Andere Tijden, 'De slag om de stad', VPRO 2015: https://www.youtube.com/watch?v=et476ZnT9js

24 Reinier van den Hout (director), 'De Slag om Amelisweerd', *Andere Tijden*, 6 January 2013.

25 '"I think therefore I cycle": 50 years of Dutch anti-car posters — in pictures', *The Guardian*, 25 June 2019.

26 *Tussen techniek en planning* (2015), p. 69.

27 'Robert Jasper Grootveld over het wittefietsenplan (1966)', *YouTube* (9 January 2009), https://www.youtube.com/watch?v=gbKX7cDVLiI.

28 The photo of John Lennon and Yoko Ono in bed with a white bike accompanies an article in *De Groene Amsterdammer*: Beatriz Colomina, 'Liggen is en werkwoord. Het 24/7-bed', *De Groene Amsterdammer*, 31 October 2018. This photo, taken on 27 March 1969, can be found in the Dutch National Archives, in the Spaarnestad collection.

29 'Fietsdemonstratie op het Museumplein in Amsterdam (8000 deelnemers), op 5 juni 1977: Fietsers willen "vrij baan" en herdenken liggend of zittend naast hun fiets verkeersslachtoffers' (Dutch National Archives, Spaarnestad collection, 5 June 1977).

30 Fred Feddes in collaboration with Marjolein de Lange, *Bike City Amsterdam: How Amsterdam Became the Cycling Capital of the World* (Uitgeverij Bas Lubberhuizen, 2019), p. 63.

31 Patrick Barkham, '"We're doomed": Mayer Hillman on the climate reality no one else will dare mention', *The Guardian*, 26 April 2018.

32 Alexa Delbosc et al., 'Dehumanization of cyclists predicts self-reported aggressive behaviour toward them: a pilot study', *Transportation Research Part F: Traffic Psychology and Behaviour*, vol. 62 (2019), pp. 681–689.

33 Lance Dixon, 'Fort Lauderdale asks Las Olas pedestrians to wave safety flags at drivers', *Miami Herald*, 7 September 2014.

34 Lucas Harms and Maarten Kansen, 'Fietsfeiten Kennisinstituut voor Mobiliteitsbeleid | KiM' (Ministry of Infrastructure and Water Management, March 2018), p. 3.

35 Maaike Kempes and Jasper Bunskoek, 'Verkeer bij scholen onveilig: 10.000 ongelukken in 3 jaar', *RTL Nieuws*, 7 September 2018.

36 The Provos' declaration about the White Bicycle Plan can be found (in Dutch) at https://hart.amsterdam/nl/page/49069/witte-fietsenplan.

37 The historian Ruth Oldenziel writes about the history of cycling in cities worldwide (outside the Netherlands) in her series of books *Cycling Cities*. A graph produced by Oldenziel which shows how cycling dwindled with the arrival of cars in various major international cities can be found in the Fietscommunity blog: 'DCA — Make America Cycle Again', *Fietscommunity* (7 February 2017). https://www.fietscommunity.nl/blogs/make-america-cycle-again/

38 'Mobilisation of the Masses' (2019), p. 4.

39 Quoted from 'De eerste auto in Schagen', *Het geheugen van Schagen*, 17 August 2005.

40 'Kameroverzicht. Tweede Kamer. Vergadering 8 mei', *De Maasbode*, 9 May 1924.

41 'Van het Binnenhof: Eerste Kamer', *Voorwaarts*, 30 October 1924.

42 'Van het Binnenhof: Tweede Kamer', *Voorwaarts*, 30 October 1924.

43 'Tweede Kamer', *Nieuwsblad van het Noorden*, 22 May 1924.

44 'De nieuwe motor- en rijwielwet', *De Noord-Ooster*, 20 December 1924.

45 One of the advocates of these extensions of liability was Auke R. Bloembergen, a professor at the University of Leiden, and later himself a member of the Supreme Court.

46 See section 185 of the Dutch Road Traffic Act (Wegenverkeerswet), for the situation in 2020.

47 'Frankrijk: de tien geboden voor den voetganger', *Algemeen Handelsblad*, 16 December 1924.

48 Jacob van den Berg, *De Bromfiets 1948-2015. Een geschiedenis van de verschoppeling van de weg* (Target Press, 2015), p. 5.

49 'Meer dan 200 maal zo veel personenauto's als in 1927' (Statistics Netherlands, 28 January 2020).

50 A reader of the Dutch book found the clipping about my father's accident in the online newspaper archive, after the newspaper had been digitised. In the text, no mention is made of a moped,

only of a cyclist and indeed a nine-year-old boy crossing the street 'out of the blue': https://www.delpher.nl/nl/kranten/view?coll=ddd&identifier=MMKB19:000301092:mpeg21:p00007.

51 '1920: Het verkeer in Amsterdam, een verkeersfilm van de ANWB — oude filmbeelden', YouTube (7 December 2017). https://www.youtube.com/watch?v=uLVpN5ibe_k

52 '"Straatganzen" maakten allerlei rare verkeersfouten. Publiek was even achteloos als zij', *Arnhemse Courant*, 7 September 1951.

53 Traffic Safety Netherlands (Veilig Verkeer Nederland) has a framed example of Maarten Toonder's Traffic Safety Game on the office wall.

54 For example: http://www.roadsafetyeducation.vic.gov.au/teaching-resources/primary-school/introducing-stop,-look,-listen,-think-to-cross-the-road-safely (Australia); https://www.think.gov.uk/news/new-think-road-safety-campaign-launched-to-help-cut-child-deaths/ (UK).

55 *Stop Killing our Children* (Environmental Transport Association, 2019). The documentary can be found online: 'Stop Killing Our Children', Vimeo (20 September 2019). https://vimeo.com/361286029

56 'Ouders primair verantwoordelijk. "Veilig Verkeer" valt actiegroepen fel aan', *De Volkskrant*, 25 January 1973.

57 'Prins Claus steunt "Stop Kindermoord"', *Trouw*, 15 January 1973.

58 'Mentink: wie wil hobbel in straat?', *Het Vrije Volk*, 8 February 1975.

Part III

1 Gerard van Westerloo, *De pont van kwart over zeven. De beste journalistieke verhalen* (e-book, 2015), loc. 194.

2 Fleur van der Bij, *De Nijl in mij. Een ontdekkingsreis naar het hart van de waanzin* (Atlas Contact, 2018), and Fleur van der Bij, *Verkeersslachtoffer 22/10. Op zoek naar de man die mijn zusje doodreed* (Querido Fosfor, 2019).

3 The article about the 12-year-old girl whose father ran into and killed another 12-year-old girl appeared anonymously. It later emerged that the victim was in fact 13. 'Zo dreunt een onverwerkt verkeerstrauma door bij de volgende generatie', *De Correspondent*, 2 May 2019.

4 https://ec.europa.eu/eurostat/statistics-explained/index.php?title=Road_accident_fatalities_-_statistics_by_type_of_vehicle.

5 https://www.washingtonpost.com/local/trafficandcommuting/more-people-died-in-car-crashes-this-century-than-in-both-world-wars/2019/07/21/0ecc0006-3f54-11e9-9361-301ffb5bd5e6_story.html.

6 https://www.who.int/data/gho/data/themes/topics/topic-details/GHO/road-traffic-mortality.

7 http://ghdx.healthdata.org/gbd-results-tool; http://www.popten.net/2010/05/top-ten-most-evil-dictators-of-all-time-in-order-of-kill-count/.

8 This organisation ceased its activities on 1 March 2020.

9 Werner Herzog, *From One Second to the Next — Texting While Driving*, Saville Productions (8 August 2013). https://www.youtube.com/watch?v=9qf85X3extY.

10 Ivan Illich, *Tools for Conviviality* (Harper & Row, 1973), p. 52.

11   Carlton Reid, 'Volvo's "World First" Bicycle-Helmet-Versus-Car Test Flags Helmet Safety Flaws', *Forbes*, 3 June 2019.

12   Tweet from @marktraa (18 December 2018).

13   'Busje op zijn kant bij ongeval afrit Hoograven', *RTV Utrecht*, 11 January 2019.

14   We've written several articles about our findings. One of them is '"Busje ramt auto", "file na ongeluk". En de mensen dan?', *De Correspondent*, 14 March 2019.

15   'Flink wat oponthoud door aangereden voetganger', edestad.nl, 14 December 2019.

16   Peter Koop, 'Maaltijdbezorger overleden na aanrijding op Amsterdamsestraatweg', *Algemeen Dagblad*, 10 January 2019.

17   '"Verkeersles" voor bezorgers maaltijden in strijd tegen ongelukken"', *NOS*, 19 February 2020.

18   Marleen de Rooy, 'Inspectie wil verbod op 15-jarige maaltijdbezorgers', *NOS*, 19 February 2020.

19   Michiel van Beers, 'FNV vindt maaltijden bezorgen te gevaarlijk voor kinderen', *NOS*, 11 January 2019.

20   Tim de Hullu, 'Ontwapenende Ruiz (15) wilde dolfijnen bestuderen, maar stierf op de Straatweg', *Algemeen Dagblad*, 1 August 2019.

21   Marco Gerling, 'Automobilist (21) had niet gedronken bij dodelijk ongeval met maaltijdbezorger (15) op fiets', *Algemeen Dagblad*, 30 June 2019.

22   Dutch 'coffeeshops' are cafés authorised to sell small quantities of cannabis for personal consumption.

23   Marco Gerling, 'Drie maanden cel voor man die maaltijdbezorger Ruiz (15) doodreed', *Algemeen Dagblad*, 15 August 2019.

24   'Inspectie wil verbod op 15-jarige maaltijdbezorgers', *NOS*, 19 February 2020.

25   Roland de Jong, 'Veertig maanden cel voor fataal ongeluk Goes', HVzeeland.nl, 28 June 2019.

26   Albert and Mireille Meijer, 'Toespraken ouders Ruiz', memorial site for Ruiz Meijer (1 August 2019).

27   'Vragen en antwoorden over roekeloos rijgedrag' (Council for the Judiciary, 23 January 2017).

28   Siebrand Vos, 'Werkstraf voor scheppen voetganger in Wijnandsrade', *De Limburger*, 7 May 2019.

29   'Geen celstraf voor doodrijdster die epilepsie verzweeg', *Algemeen Dagblad*, 15 August 2019.

30   For example, 'If You Want To Get Away With Murder Buy A Car' is the subtitle of *Crash Course* (Street Noise Books, 2020), a book in graphic novel format by Woodrow Phoenix.

31   Ch. Goldenbeld et al., 'Relatie tussen verkeersovertredingen en verkeersongevallen. Verkennend onderzoek op basis van CJIB-gegevens' (SWOV, 2011).

32   https://www.theguardian.com/lifeandstyle/2017/sep/18/cyclist-charlie-alliston-jailed-for-18-months-over-death-of-pedestrian

33   https://twitter.com/ormondroyd/status/910244326567006211. The Alliston
     case involved a rare event: a cyclist killed a mother of two by riding
     recklessly (the cyclist was sentenced to 18 months in prison).

34   Pim Warffemius, *De maatschappelijke waarde van kortere en betrouwbaardare
     reistijden* (Ministry of Infrastructure and the Environment, 2013).

35   *Onderzoek invoering verhoging maximumsnelheid naar 130 km/h. Samenvattende
     analyse experiment en uitwerking voorstel landelijke snelheidsverhoging*
     (Rijkswaterstaat, 2011).

36   Kim Visbeen, 'Brandon (5) werd voor zijn deur doodgereden: "Zijn droom
     was om voor Feyenoord te spelen"', *Algemeen Dagblad*, 25 October 2019.

37   *Berekening risicotoename bij overschrijding va de snelheidslimiet* (SWOV, 2016),
     p. 8.

38   Bruce Corben et al., *Development of the Visionary Research Model —
     Application to the Car/Pedestrian Conflict* (Monash University Accident
     Research Centre, 2004), p. 26.

Part IV

1   According to the Dutch environmental organisation Milieudefensie,
     cars take up 55 per cent of space in towns. See: *Van wie is de stad?*
     (Milieudefensie, 2017), p. 5. There's a sketch on YouTube (in German)
     about what would happen if someone were to invent the car now: 'Die
     Erfindung des Autos/extra 3/NDR', YouTube (5 September 2019). https://
     www.youtube.com/watch?v=ZRtOdeq7Td4.

2   https://www.independent.co.uk/news/world/americas/why-does-nothing-
     get-done-about-gun-control-the-reasons-obama-cannot-change-us-
     infatuation-with-firearms-a6676876.html.

3   Firearm injuries are a serious US public health problem. In 2019, there
     were 39,707 firearm-related deaths in the United States — 14,414 of which
     were homicides (https://www.cdc.gov/violenceprevention/firearms/
     fastfact.html and https://www.cdc.gov/nchs/fastats/homicide.htm).
     In 2018, 458 people died from firearm-related accidents (https://www.
     aftermath.com/content/accidental-shooting-deaths-statistics/).

4   https://www.cdc.gov/nchs/fastats/accidental-injury.htm.

5   Tineke Netelenbos, speech (Ministry of Transport and Water
     Management, 29 May 1999).

6   *Statuten Veilig Verkeer Nederland* (Traffic Safety Netherlands, 2011).

7   'Guidelines for speed bumps, speed tables and exits', €56 excluding VAT.

8   'Basic characteristics of intersections and roundabouts', €76, excluding
     VAT.

9   Tool for Traffic Generation and Parking (€69, excluding VAT).

10   Research project, *Op weg naar een veilige schoolomgeving. Exploratief onderzoek
     naar drijfveren en barrières bij haal- en brenggedrag van ouders van schoolkinderen*
     (PubLab, 2019), p. 2.

11   Yvonne Hofs, 'Helft subsidies elektrisch rijden in 2018 naar "rijke" Tesla-
     en Jaguar-rijders', *De Volkskrant*, 30 January 2019.

12   https://evbox.com/uk-en/learn/faq/incentives-buying-electriccar

13   'Ja, de e-fiets is echt goed voor het milieu', *Fietsberaad*, 19 February 2020.

14   *Bruzz*, 19 June 2019: https://www.bruzz.be/analyse/elektrische-step-vervangt-vooral-voetgangers-en-amper-autos-2019-06-19

15   Laura Bliss, 'Another Study Blames Uber and Lyft for Public Transit's Decline', *CityLab*, 24 January 2019; and Andrew J. Hawkins, 'Uber and Lyft finally admit they're making traffic congestion worse in cities', *The Verge*, 6 August 2019.

16   'De leasefiets als geheim wapen tegen de files', *NOS*, 6 December 2019.

17   Mariëtte Pol and Bas Hendriksen, *Evaluatie nieuwe wegmarkering op snelfietsroutes: Het effect op beleving en gedrag van weggebruikers* (Van Rens Mobiliteit, 2018).

18   Mark Healy, 'Captcha if you can. Every time you prove you're human to Captcha, are you helping Google's bots to build a smarter self-driving car?', *Ceros Originals*, 31 May 2018.

19   'Zo ziet Mercedes de zelfrijdende auto', auto55.be, 22 November 2014.

20   Angelique Rondhuis, 'Steeds meer wild doodgereden: schade in miljoenen met meer dan tienduizend aanrijdingen per jaar', *De Stentor*, 20 August 2019.

21   *De fietsrepubliek* (e-book, 2014), loc. 2741.

22   https://www.youtube.com/watch?v=fcs9qr4KSgE.

23   David Shepardson and Heather Somerville, 'Uber not criminally liable in fatal 2018 Arizona self-driving crash: prosecutors', *Reuters*, 5 March 2019.

24   Carlton Reid, 'Bicyclists could prevent Netherlands becoming #1 nation for driverless cars, says KPMG report', *Forbes*, 13 February 2019.

Part V

1   Tijs van den Boomen, 'Woonerf klassiek of nieuwe stijl', tijsvandenboomen.nl, 1 July 2001.

2   John Schoorl, 'Wat is er over van de idylle van het woonerf?', *De Volkskrant*, 26 September 2015.

3   Bernard Hulsman, 'Dwarse bedenker van de bloemkoolwijk', *NRC Handelsblad*, 27 February 2016.

4   The Functional City was a concept originating from CIAM, Congrès Internationaux d'Architecture Moderne (International Congresses of Modern Architecture), in the 1930s. Richard Sennett provides a detailed history in *Building and Dwelling: Ethics for the City* (Allen Lane, 2018) chap. 3.

5   'De eerste lag er in 1949', nrc.nl, 26 February 2014.

6   *99% Invisible* made an excellent podcast (produced by Katie Mingle) about the modernist philosophy underlying the Bijlmer: 'Bijlmer: City of the Future' (20 February 2018).

7   https://nacto.org/docs/usdg/woonerf_concept_collarte.pdf.

8   Carl Honoré, *In Praise of Slow. How a Worldwide Movement is Challenging the Cult of Speed* (Orion, 2016), p. 96.

9   'Nieuwbouw scholen' (Delft local authority).

10   It's clear from an official record of driving speeds which Marco sends me that drivers in his neighbourhood regularly drive at 39 km/h.

11   From W.A.M. Weijermars et al., 'Duurzaam Veilig, ook voor ernstig verkeersgewonden' (SWOV, 2013), part 3, annex 1.1. The 'Zone 30' model

was rolled out in 1984. Evaluation based on models showed that this could lead to a reduction in the number of accidents.

12 'Woonerf klassiek of nieuwe stijl', tijsvandenboomen.nl, 1 July 2001.

13 In 2013, 'at a walking pace' was replaced by '15 kilometres per hour' in Article 45 of the Dutch Highway Code. 'Reglement verkeersregels en verkeerstekens 1990 (RVV 1990)'; wetten.overheid.nl.

14 Joske van Lith, 'Verkeerswereld geeft te weinig aandacht aan woonerf', *Verkeerskunde*, 27 December 2019.

15 'Woonerf klassiek of nieuwe stijl', tijsvandenboomen.nl, 1 July 2001.

16 'Guidelines for speed bumps, speed tables and exits', €56 excluding VAT.

17 Nicolette de Boer, 'Er komt niet zomaar een drempel op het Van Barneveld-erf', *De Gelderlander*, 17 May 2019.

18 Aleksandar Erceg et al., 'Franchising in transport law — bike sharing as business model of urban transport development', 7th International Scientific Symposium. Economy of Eastern Croatia — Vision and Growth (May 2018).

19 Louise Nordstrom, 'Vélibgate: the rise and fall of Paris's bike-sharing program', france24.com, 5 April 2018.

20 Sally Cairns, Stephen Atkins, and Phil Goodwin, 'Disappearing traffic? The story so far.' *Proceedings of the Institution of Civil Engineers: Municipal Engineer*, vol. 151, no. 1 (March 2002), pp. 13–12.

21 Feargus O'Sullivan, 'Court says Paris's car ban is illegal', *CityLab*, 22 February 2018; and Jila Varoquier and Benoît Hasse, 'Paris: mais si, le trafic autour des voies sur berge s'améliore!', *Le Parisien*, 18 February 2018.

22 Feargus O'Sullivan, 'Can the Paris Metro make room for more riders?', *CityLab*, 13 November 2019.

23 Feargus O'Sullivan, 'Paris gets to keep its car ban', *CityLab*, 25 October 2018.

24 Kim Willsher, 'Paris mayor unveils "15-minute city" plan in re-election campaign', *The Guardian*, 5 February 2019.

25 Carlos Moreno, a professor at the Sorbonne, is the person who came up with the idea of the 15-minute city. See his TED talk, 'The 15-minute city' (October 2020). https://www.ted.com/talks/carlos_moreno_the_15_minute_city?language=en.

26 Kay Rutten, 'Flinke problemen verwacht door sluiting Maastunnel', *BNR*, 3 July 2017.

27 'Eerste avondspits bij dichte Maastunnel niet anders dan anders', *RTV Rijnmond*, 3 July 2017.

28 'Nominatie Schoolstraat NVVC Verkeersveiligheidprijs' (Dutch National Traffic Safety Congress (NVVC), 2020).

29 Michiel Van Driessche et al., 'Leidraad Openbare Ruimte Groningen', Felixx. nl, 30 June 2021.

30 Aleksi Teivainen, 'No pedestrians died in traffic accidents in Helsinki in 2019, writes Helsingin Sanomat', *Helsinki Times*, 24 January 2020.

31 'Hoe veilig zijn onze steden voor fietsers en voetgangers?', *RTL Nieuws*, 12 February 2020.

32 Hanne Brønmo, 'Barn omkom i trafikulykke i fotgjengerfelt på Holmen i Oslo', *Aftenposten*, 13 January 2020); Silje Løvstad Thjømøe, 'Mor ble vitne til att sønnen (2) ble påkjørt og døde: — Plutselig forsvant han under bilen', *Avisa Oslo*, 28 January 2021.

33 Stephen Burgen, '"For me, this is paradise": life in the Spanish city that banned cars', *The Guardian*, 18 September 2018.

34 How to design a happy city so that it quite naturally becomes clean and safe is the subject of an inspiring book, *Happy City*, by the Canadian author Charles Montgomery (Penguin, 2015).

35 *Multiple Uses of Public Space. Superblock Pilot in Poblenou* (2016–2018) (BCN-ecología, 2018).

36 David Roberts, 'Barcelona's radical plan to take back streets from cars: introducing "superblocks"', *Vox*, 26 May 2019.

37 Ard Schouten and Indra Jager, 'Ouders nemen heft in handen: klaar-overs bij onveilige zebrapaden Oog in Al', *Algemeen Dagblad*, 23 January 2020.

38 https://twitter.com/MikeLydon/status/1255487675215347726

39 https://twitter.com/BrentToderian/status/1256594334062796803

40 https://twitter.com/fietsprofessor/status/1255952332627599360

41 https://twitter.com/SadiqKhan/status/1256527221516382208

42 https://twitter.com/brettpetzer/status/1255479872849358850

43 Robert Pirsig, *Zen and the Art of Motorcycle Maintenance. An Inquiry into Values* [1974] (William Morrow, 2008), p. 87.

44 Kris Peeters, *Het voorruitperspectief. Wegen van het impliciete autodenken* (Garant Uitgevers, 2000).

45 Forty-seven per cent of trips in the Netherlands are made by car, accounting for 71 per cent of the total number of kilometres travelled within the country. 'Onderzoek Verplaatsingen in Nederland (OViN) 2017: Plausibiliteitsrapportage' (Statistics Netherlands, July 2018), pp. 7 and 9.

46 Peter Jorritsma, Marije Hamersma, and Jaco Berveling, *Blik op de file: De file door de ogen van de Nederlandse burger* (Ministry of Infrastructure and Water Management, 2020). The percentages cited by Kager come from tables 2.3 and 3.3.

47 Karin Bijsterveld, 'Acoustic cocooning: how the car became a place to unwind', *The Senses and Society*, vol. 5, no. 2 (July 2010), pp. 189–211.

48 https://www.cdc.gov/nchs/products/databriefs/db322.htm

49 Janneke Zomervrucht and Walther Ploos van Amstel, 'Laat de straat een plek voor mensen zijn', *Trouw*, 7 September 2019.

50 Inspired by William H. Whyte: 'If you plan for cars and traffic, you get cars and traffic. If you plan for people and places, you get people and places' (*The Social Life of Small Urban Spaces*, Conservation Foundation, 1980).

51 The Dutch TV programme *Zondag met Lubach* made a very instructive programme about venture capitalism, Uber and the money behind it: 'Kapitalisme', *Zondag met Lubach* (S11)', YouTube (16 February 2020). https://www.youtube.com/watch?v=VIc5crNUBBU

52 *Zondag met Lubach* gave a detailed account of how Uber can make losses amounting to billions of dollars in 'Kapitalisme', 16 February 2020.

53 Tim Fraanje, 'Om het jaar goed te beginnen heb ik mijn Swapfiets opgezegd', *Vice*, 10 January 2020.

54 Anna Nikolaeva et al., 'Commoning mobility: towards a new politics of mobility transitions', *Transactions of the Institute of British Geographers*, vol. 44, no. 2 (February 2019), pp. 346–360.

55 Jeroen Molenaar, 'Gierende verliezen op blauwe bandjes bij Swapfiets', *Quote*, 8 January 2020.

56 The Participative Value Evaluation has a website: www.tudelft.nl/pwe.

57 Paul Koster and Niek Mouter's website enabling citizens to divide up the budget of the Amsterdam transport region can be found at: www.burger-begroting.nl.

58 Dag Balkmar and Tanja Joelsson, 'Feeling the speed — the social and emotional investments in dangerous road practices', in *Gender and Change. Power, Politics and Everyday Practices* (Karlstad University Press, 2012), pp. 37–52.

59 '"Gedoe is taboe tijdens reizen"' (Goudappel Coffeng, 11 December 2018).

60 Mihaly Csikszentmihalyi, *Flow: The Psychology of Optimal Experience* (Harper Perennial Modern Classics, 2008).

61 For an account of some of the ideas dreamed up on Dutch bicycles, see: 'Ideeën die zijn ontstaan op de fiets', *De Correspondent*, 27 August 2018.

62 Marie-José Olde Kalter, Mark van Hagen, and Laura Groenendijk, *Reistijdbeleving als beleidsinstrument: Over wat we kunnen leren van de reistijdbeleving van fietsers en de invloed hiervan op het verplaatsingsgedrag* (Goudappel Coffeng, 2017).

63 This is the piece we wrote about flow back then: 'Geniale inzichten krijg je op de fiets. Zo kom je in de fietsflow', *De Correspondent*, 24 August 2018.

64 The article has since been published: Marco te Brömmelstroet et al., 'Have a good trip! Expanding our concepts of the quality of everyday travelling with flow theory', *Applied Mobilities* (April 2021). https://doi.org/10.1080/238 00127.2021.1912947

65 Bard van de Weijer, 'Minder rode kruizen bij drukte op de weg: minister offert spitsstrook in strijd tegen files', *De Volkskrant*, 12 December 2018; and *Van B naar Anders. Investeren in mobiliteit voor de toekomst* (Dutch Council for the Environment and Infrastructure (Rli), May 2018).

66 Joep Dohmen, 'Limburg ontslaat "klussende" oud-politici', *NRC Handelsblad*, 13 February 2020.

67 Martha Uenk, 'De 130 km/u-maatregel gewikt en gewogen: meer of minder fileleed?', *Verkeerskunde*, 14 February 2019.

68 Yamilla van Dijk, 'Protest tegen maximumsnelheid van de baan': "Te weinig animo onder boze automobilisten"', *Algemeen Dagblad*, 19 November 2019.

69 Articles by angry columnists: Rosanne Hertzberger, 'Een dode in het verkeer: gekmakend en onsexy', *NRC Handelsblad*, 17 August 2019; Arjen van Veelen, 'Rotterdam moet niet langer doorrijden na een ongeluk', *Vers Beton*, 16 August 2019; Roos Schlikker, 'Er lag een jongetje op het zebrapad',

Het Parool, 16 June 2018; Marieke Dubbelman, 'Ik ben helemaal klaar met die onoverzichtelike, schuine kutkruising', *Algemeen Dagblad*, 25 February 2018; Suzanne Mensen, '"Beste scooteraar, kom je even 'sorry' op het been van mijn dochter schrijven?"', *De Telegraaf*, 23 November 2017.

70 The pictograms used by the schoolchildren in Ede to develop public space and play areas were from the Belgian 'Picto-play' method.

Glossary

Bike/bicycle highway — Also known in the UK as 'cycle superhighways', bike highways are cycle routes segregated from the road, often with fewer traffic lights, smooth surfaces, and less intersections with motorised traffic, designed to accommodate fast-moving cyclists.

Bike/cycle path — A marked route that is specifically for cyclists, sometimes on the edge of the road, sometimes segregated from the road entirely.

Bike-friendly speed bumps — Speed bumps that aren't an obstacle for bicycles so as to maintain safety for bike riders.

Bike traffic lights — Traffic lights specifically for cyclists, sometimes incorporating rain sensors to help to reduce cyclists' waiting times in wet weather.

Cauliflower neighbourhoods — A cluster of *woonerfs* (see *woonerfs*) that together look like a cauliflower.

Cargo bike — A bike that has been built to carry heavy cargo or several children.

Chicane — A road with curves added in for design rather than because of geography.

Conflict — In traffic engineering, a conflict is a disagreement or clash of interests. The DOCTOR (Dutch Objective Conflict Technique of Operation and Research) model definition is a situation in which someone takes longer that is necessary to do something in order to avoid a potential collision.

Conflict observation technique — A traffic engineering method used to assess road design and measure the risk of collisions to see whether changes need to be made.

Congestion — When an area is crowded with an excess of vehicles moving at slow speeds or stopped completely.

Cul de sac — A road that is closed at one end.

Electric/e-bike — A bike with an electric motor that doesn't have to be used all the time but can be turned on to help with pedalling.

E-mobility — Electric mobility. Electric street-vehicles that are powered by an electric motor, rather than a petrol- or diesel-fuelled engine.

Exit construction — See *street-intersection ramp.*

Flow street — Traffic-engineering language for a road in the Netherlands that has a speed limit of 50km/h.

Hyperloop/vacuum train — A futuristic train that would use vacuum tubes as a means of transportation and be able to travel at very high speeds.

I/C ratio — Traffic-engineering language referring to the ratio of intensity (the expected pressure on the road) and capacity (how many cars can drive through in an hour). If the ratio is unbalanced, if the capacity is too low and the intensity too high, then there is a higher chance of gridlock.

Marchetti's constant/the travel time budget — The average time a person spends travelling each day (about 1–1.5 hours).

Mobility — The ability to move or be moved.

Mobility as a service — A service that improves accessibility and mobility, for example a taxi service app, like Uber.

Motorbus — An old-fashioned word used to describe a bus powered by a motor.

Parking standards — Guidelines about parking set by the local authority, for example, in an area you might only be able to have one parking spot per apartment.

Peer-to-peer car sharing — Car owners can list their vehicles on a site or platform which allows them to share their car with others.

Recumbent bike — A bike designed so riders can cycle in a more comfortable reclined position, leaning against a backrest, rather than sitting upright.

Self-driving car — Technology under development that will enable a car to be moved and navigated autonomously by a computer without the need of a driver.

Sleeping policemen — See *speed bump*.

Social cost-benefit analysis — A method governments use to assess whether a policy should be put into place. It weighs financial benefits and risks compared to social benefits and risks, to calculate monetary gain vs societal loss.

Speed bump — A raised hump installed into a road that forces vehicles to slow down.

Speed pedelec — A bike with an electric motor that helps riders travel longer distances at higher speeds. They are legally classed as mopeds in the UK.

Street furniture — Objects and equipment put in the street for public use, for example road signs, benches, bus stops, and bins.

Street intersection ramp — A section of the street that is raised to match the level of the pavement, linking the pavements on either side. Also known as exit construction.

Superilles — Also known as superblocks, they are car-free neighbourhoods that are being built in Barcelona.

Tailback — A queue of stopped or slow-moving traffic.

The fundamental law of road congestion — Traffic increases proportionally to an increase in the number and length of roads in an area.

Traffic control systems (TCSs) — Traffic-engineering language meaning traffic lights. A system of traffic management wherein a computer is programmed to ensure road safety by controlling timed traffic lights.

Train cyclist — A commuter that travels partly by bike, and partly by train.

Traffic engineering/engineer — A branch of engineering that deals with transportation, and designing and building infrastructure. A traffic engineer designs the layout of new-build areas.

Travel friction — Trying to travel faster, more cheaply, and more comfortably over ever-increasing distances, but in the same amount of time.

Traffic island — A raised or painted area between opposing traffic lanes that moving vehicles are not allowed to enter to help passengers to get across a road.

Traffic model — A model of the traffic that passes through an area to help analyse, plan, and fix issues with road traffic infrastructure.

Traffic planning/planner — A traffic planner works for the local authority to ensure road safety, assessing whether changes need to be made in an area to minimise the danger of collisions.

Trolleybus — A bus powered by electricity that it gets from overhead wires.

Underlying road network —Traffic engineering language meaning all streets and roads in a country except for motorways.

Urban planner — Someone who is commissioned to help designs a new urban area, or redevelop/make an existing area better.

Vehicle detection loops — They detect when vehicles pass by using magnetic fields. Sometimes connected to traffic lights, they can send a signal to prompt the light to turn green.

Vehicle hour lost — Traffic engineering logic. When a vehicle is stuck in a traffic jam for an hour, or when 60 vehicles are stuck in a tailback for a minute each.

Vehicular space — An area that is assigned to vehicles over pedestrians; that puts the needs of vehicles over that of people. For example, an intersection.

Wethouder — Members of the Dutch local executive, elected by the local council.

Woonerf — Literally translated to 'residential plots', these are Dutch neighbourhoods designed around people instead of vehicles. They have no pavements, restricted parking, railway sleepers, planters that double as barricades, or other road furniture.

Index